D1508757

SPORTS STARS

SPORTS STARS
VOLUME 2

L - Z

Michael A. Paré

U·X·L

An Imprint of Gale Research

SPORTS STARS

Michael A. Paré

Staff

Kathleen L. Witman, *U•X•L Assistant Developmental Editor*
Carol DeKane Nagel, *U•X•L Developmental Editor*
Thomas L. Romig, *U•X•L Publisher*

Keith Reed, *Permissions Associate (Pictures)*
Margaret A. Chamberlain, *Permissions Supervisor (Pictures)*

Shanna P. Heilveil, *Production Assistant*
Evi Seoud, *Assistant Production Manager*
Mary Beth Trimper, *Production Director*

Mark Howell, *Page and Cover Designer*
Cynthia Baldwin, *Art Director*

The Graphix Group, *Typesetting*

Paré, Michael A.
    Sports stars / Michael A. Paré.
        p.   cm.
    Includes bibliographical references and index.
    ISBN 0-8103-9859-1 (set : alk. paper) : $38.00 —ISBN
0-8103-9860-5 (v. 1 : alk. paper). — ISBN 0-8103-9861-3 (v. 2 : alk. paper)
        1. Athletes—Biography—Juvenile literature.   [1. Athletes.]
I. Title.
GV697.A1P32   1994
796' .092' 2—dc20
[B]

94-21835
CIP
AC

Cover photographs (from left to bottom right): Jim Abbott, Kristi Yamaguchi, and Shaquille O'Neal, all AP/Wide World Photos.

∞™ This book is printed on acid-free paper that meets the minimum requirements of American National Standard for Information Sciences—Permanence Paper for Printed Library Materials, ANSI Z39.48-1984.

Printed in the United States of America

10 9 8 7 6 5 4 3

Contents

Athletes by Sport...ix

Reader's Guide xiii

Photo Credits xv

Biographical Listings
VOLUME 1: A-K

Jim Abbott 1

Andre Agassi 8

Troy Aikman...15

Roberto Alomar 23

Arthur Ashe 30

Oksana Baiul..37

Charles Barkley 43

Larry Bird 50

Bonnie Blair...58

Tyrone "Muggsy" Bogues 65

Brian Boitano...72

Barry Bonds 78

Riddick Bowe 83

Michael Chang...89

Roger Clemens...96

Jim Courier 103
Clyde Drexler 109
Lenny Dykstra 115
John Elway 121
Janet Evans 127
Patrick Ewing 133
Nick Faldo 141
Cecil Fielder 148
Emerson Fittipaldi 154
George Foreman 162
Juan Gonzalez 169
Steffi Graf 175
Wayne Gretzky 183
Ken Griffey, Jr. 191
Florence Griffith Joyner 197
Evander Holyfield 204
Brett Hull 212
Miguel Induráin 218
Bo Jackson 223
Dan Jansen 231
Earvin "Magic" Johnson 238
Larry Johnson 247
Michael Jordan 253
Jackie Joyner-Kersee 262
Jim Kelly 268
Julie Krone 275

Further Reading

    By Athlete 281
    By Sport 299
Index 301

Biographical Listings

VOLUME 2: L-Z

Mario Lemieux 317
Carl Lewis 325
Eric Lindros 332
Nancy Lopez 338
Greg Maddux 346
Karl Malone 353

Diego Maradona 360
Dan Marino..367
Mark Messier 375
Shannon Miller 381
Tommy Moe 388
Joe Montana 395
Warren Moon 404
Martina Navratilova..411
Hakeem Olajuwon 419
Shaquille O'Neal 426
Scottie Pippen 433
Kirby Puckett 440
Jerry Rice..446
Cal Ripken, Jr...453
David Robinson 460
Nolan Ryan 467
Pete Sampras...474
Arantxa Sanchez Vicario 480
Ryne Sandberg 487
Barry Sanders..494
Deion Sanders 500
Monica Seles...507
Emmitt Smith..514
Lyn St. James..522
Frank Thomas 527
Isiah Thomas...534
Thurman Thomas...542
Alberto Tomba 549
Reggie White 556
Dave Winfield...562
Katarina Witt...569
Kristi Yamaguchi 575
Steve Young..581

Further Reading

  By Athlete...587
  By Sport..605

Index..607

Athletes by Sport

AUTO RACING

Emerson Fittipaldi 154
Lyn St. James 522

BASEBALL

Jim Abbott 1
Roberto Alomar 23
Barry Bonds 78
Roger Clemens 96
Lenny Dykstra 115
Cecil Fielder 148
Juan Gonzalez 169
Ken Griffey, Jr. 191
Bo Jackson 223
Greg Maddux 346
Kirby Puckett 440
Cal Ripken, Jr. 453
Nolan Ryan 467
Ryne Sandberg 487
Deion Sanders 500
Frank Thomas 527
Dave Winfield 562

BASKETBALL

Charles Barkley 43
Larry Bird 50
Tyrone "Muggsy" Bogues 65
Clyde Drexler... 109
Patrick Ewing... 133
Earvin "Magic" Johnson 238
Larry Johnson 247
Michael Jordan... 253
Karl Malone 353
Shaquille O'Neal 426
Hakeem Olajuwon 419
Scottie Pippen 433
David Robinson 460
Isiah Thomas.. 534

BICYCLE RACING

Miguel Induráin 218

BOXING

Riddick Bowe 83
George Foreman 162
Evander Holyfield.. 204

FIGURE SKATING

Oksana Baiul.. 37
Brian Boitano... 72
Katarina Witt.. 569
Kristi Yamaguchi 575

FOOTBALL

Troy Aikman.. 15
John Elway.. 121
Bo Jackson... 223
Jim Kelly.. 268
Dan Marino... 367
Joe Montana... 395
Warren Moon 404
Jerry Rice... 446

Barry Sanders...494
Deion Sanders...500
Emmitt Smith...514
Thurman Thomas...542
Reggie White 556
Steve Young 581

GOLF

Nick Faldo 141
Nancy Lopez...338

GYMNASTICS

Shannon Miller 381

HOCKEY

Wayne Gretzky 183
Brett Hull 212
Mario Lemieux 317
Eric Lindros 332
Mark Messier 375

HORSE RACING

Julie Krone...275

SKIING

Tommy Moe...388
Alberto Tomba 549

SOCCER

Diego Maradona 360

SPEED SKATING

Bonnie Blair...58
Dan Jansen...231

SWIMMING

Janet Evans 127

TENNIS

Andre Agassi 8
Arthur Ashe 30
Michael Chang..89
Jim Courier 103
Steffi Graf 175
Martina Navratilova...411
Pete Sampras...474
Monica Seles..507
Arantxa Sanchez Vicario 480

TRACK AND FIELD

Florence Griffith Joyner 197
Jackie Joyner-Kersee 262
Carl Lewis..325

Reader's Guide

The many outstanding athletes participating in amateur and professional sports today cannot all be profiled in one two-volume work. Those whose stories are told in *Sports Stars* meet one or more of the following criteria. The individuals are:

- Currently active in or recently retired from amateur or professional sports

- Considered top performers in their fields. Most athletes profiled in *Sports Stars* will be well known to the reader

- Role models who have overcome physical obstacles or societal constraints to reach the top of their professions.

Format

The 80 entries in *Sports Stars* are arranged alphabetically in two volumes. Each biography begins with a section titled "Growing Up," focusing on the athlete's early life and motivations, followed by a section called "Superstar," highlighting the career of each profiled athlete. Each entry also contains a "Scoreboard" box that lists the athlete's top awards and other statistics for quick reference, sidebar boxes with information of high interest to the reader, and one or more photographs. Readers can write to their favorite athlete by referring to the "Where to Write" section at the end of most entries.

Additional Features

Sports Stars includes a list of athletes by sport and a comprehensive subject index to allow easy access to people and events mentioned throughout the two volumes. Cross references are made in the entries, directing readers to other athletes in the set who are connected in some way to the person whose life is being described. Sources are provided for each entry, as well as a list for further reading by sport.

Acknowledgments

The editor would like to thank the U•X•L staff for their patient guidance in the completion of this work. Most of all, the editor would like to express his gratitude to his wife, Ellen, without whose hard work and support *Sports Stars* could never have become a reality.

Comments and Suggestions

We welcome your comments on this work as well as your suggestions for individuals to be featured in future editions of *Sports Stars*. Please write: Editor, *Sports Stars*, U•X•L, 835 Penobscot Bldg., Detroit, Michigan 48226-4094; call toll-free: 1-800-877-4253; or fax: 313-961-6348.

Photo Credits

Permission to reproduce photographs appearing in *Sports Stars* was received from the following sources:

AP/Wide World Photos: pp. 3, 11, 18, 26, 28, 32, 39, 45, 52, 61, 63, 74, 77, 80, 85, 91, 98, 105, 111, 123, 130, 135, 150, 156, 158, 164, 186, 193, 199, 201, 215, 220, 226, 228, 234, 240, 249, 258, 264, 271, 277, 280, 320, 334, 343, 355, 369, 390, 397, 407, 413, 416, 421, 429, 435, 442, 448, 449, 456, 462, 471, 477, 489, 497, 503, 505, 510, 518, 524, 529, 537, 551, 558, 564, 571, 578, 584; UPI/Bettmann: pp. 35, 117, 210, 340, 469, 490; Reuters/ Bettmann: pp. 67, 94, 143, 172, 207, 233, 256, 327, 348, 378, 384, 386, 392, 483, 509, 516, 544, 553; Reuters/Bettmann Newsphotos: p. 71; UPI/Bettmann Newsphotos: p. 177; Allsport: p. 363.

MARIO LEMIEUX

1965—

In French the name Lemieux means "the best." Since he joined the National Hockey League in 1984, Mario Lemieux has become one of, if not the, "best" players in the league. Twice he's won the Hart Memorial Trophy as the NHL's Most Valuable Player (MVP), has led the league in scoring four times, and was the captain of two Stanley Cup championship teams with the Pittsburgh Penguins. Some experts think Lemieux is a better player than **Wayne Gretzky** (see entry), considered by many to be the best player of all-time. Lemieux has risen to the top despite a serious back injury and a life-threatening disease. His fans call him "Super Mario."

GROWING UP

Mario Lemieux was born October 5, 1965, in Montreal, Quebec, Canada. He grew up in the suburb of Ville Emard, only ten minutes from the Forum—home of the fabled Montreal Canadiens. In Quebec most of the people speak French as their primary language, and Mario grew up speaking only French. He began playing hockey when he was young and was a star by the age of nine. He started skating on a rink his father built by packing snow wall-to-wall in the front hallway of their house.

"I have no sympathy for goalies. No sympathy at all."— Mario Lemieux

SCOREBOARD

TWO-TIME HART MEMORIAL TROPHY WINNER AS NHL'S MOST VALUABLE PLAYER (1987-88 AND 1992-93).

FOUR-TIME NHL SCORING CHAMPION (1987-88, 1988-89, 1990-91, AND 1992-93).

LED NHL IN GOALS TWICE (1987-88 AND 1988-89) AND ASSISTS ONCE (1988-89).

CAPTAIN OF TWO PITTSBURGH PENGUINS STANLEY CUP CHAMPIONSHIP TEAMS (1990-91 AND 1991-92).

A GREAT PLAYER WHO HAS OVERCOME CAREER- AND LIFE-THREATENING INJURIES.

A tough competitor, Lemieux often threw tantrums when he lost games, but his dad says he was a good kid, overall.

Like Gretzky, Lemieux could not avoid publicity as a child. "Almost from the time he began playing organized hockey ... Lemieux has attracted scouts and journalists," reported the *Montreal Gazette*. "His bedroom is filled with trophies, newspaper reports of his heroics, and other hockey memorabilia [souvenirs]." Lemieux began playing junior hockey for the Laval [Montreal] Voisins when he was fifteen, then dropped out of school the next year to play hockey full-time. "My father tried to talk me out of it [quitting school] when I told him during the summer I was not going back to school. Finally he agreed with me that I should concentrate on hockey because I was only two years away from the [NHL] draft."

NUMBER 66. Though Gretzky is only five years older than Lemieux, "The Great One" was Lemieux's idol when he was growing up. Out of respect for Gretzky, Lemieux now wears number 66—Gretzky's number 99 upside down. Lemieux broke all junior records in Canada during the 1982-83 season. His totals—133 goals and 149 assists for 282 points—set league records for goals and points and helped lead the Voisins to the Quebec Major Junior Hockey League championship. He also broke a league record by scoring a goal in 44 straight games. Lemieux had a goal or assist in 61 straight contests.

NHL scouts were calling him "the closest thing to Gretzky" while Lemieux was still playing junior hockey. The Pittsburgh Penguins had the first draft pick in the 1984 NHL draft. Minnesota North Stars general manager Lou Nanne offered the Penguins any twelve players from his team for the first pick, but Pittsburgh general manager, knowing how good Lemieux was, just laughed. Both the Quebec Nordiques and the hometown Montreal Canadiens tried to trade for Lemieux, but Pittsburgh said no.

Pittsburgh drafted Lemieux, but had a hard time signing him to a contract. Asked at the draft if he thought he was as good as Gretzky, Lemieux said he didn't think so, "but I want to get paid what I'm worth," he told the *Detroit Free Press*. Finally, Lemieux accepted a contract that made him the highest paid first draft pick in NHL history. The contract battle turned off many fans in Pittsburgh and put a lot of pressure on Lemieux to prove he was worth the salary. When Lemieux scored in a preseason scrimmage game, four hundred fans screamed, "Our savior has arrived!"

JOINS PENGUINS. Lemieux scored on his first shot in the NHL, then went into a slump, going 12 games without a goal, and the fans began to boo their high-priced rookie. Lemieux handled the taunting well, telling reporters that the team was more important than his personal statistics. But his slump didn't last long, and Lemieux was named to the All-Star Game where he scored two goals, including the game winner, and added an assist in a 6-4 win. Lemieux was voted the game's Most Valuable Player.

In the end Lemieux could not save the Penguins. They finished with 53 points, 20th out of 21 NHL teams, but Lemieux was a bright spot, scoring 43 goals with 57 assists, making him only the third rookie in NHL history to score 100 points. He was voted the winner of the Calder Trophy as Rookie-of-the-Year and was a unanimous selection to the league's all-rookie team. Penguins's attendance rose by 100,000, with most of the new fans coming to see Lemieux.

In his second season, 1985-86, Lemieux became a star. He finished second to Gretzky in the NHL's scoring race (141 points, 48 goals and 93 assists) and in the MVP vote. The Penguins again missed the playoffs, but improved to 76 points. Lemieux missed 17 days with an injured knee at the beginning

Mario Lemieux

of the 1986-87 season while the Penguins struggled without him. "He means at least a point and a half or two points a game for us," said Pittsburgh General Manager Eddie Johnston. "When he's out there, he upgrades the skills of everybody else." Lemieux finished the 1986-87 season with 107 points (54 goals and 53 assists), but the Penguins still missed the playoffs, dropping to 72 points.

MVP. In the pre-season Canada Cup tournament in September 1987, Lemieux was the star of the Canadian team that won the championship, leading the tournament in scoring with 11 goals—including two game winners against the Soviet Union. He also learned from teammate Gretzky, whose hard work inspired Lemieux. At the NHL All-Star game in February 1988, Lemieux set a record by earning six points, including the game-winning goal in overtime, and won his second All-Star MVP award. He then scored 50 goals in less than 50 games, joining Gretzky as the only other player to accomplish this feat.

For the first time in eight years Gretzky did not lead the NHL in scoring. Lemieux took the title, scoring 70 goals (first in the NHL) and 98 assists (second in the NHL) for 168 points. When Lemieux was voted winner of the Hart Memorial Trophy as the NHL's MVP, he broke an eight-year Gretzky streak. Gretzky won the Stanley Cup however, while Lemieux and the Penguins once again missed the playoffs. "It hurts a lot," Lemieux told the *Sporting News*. "I'd give up all the personal achievements to be in the playoffs."

PLAYOFF BOUND. In the 1988-89 season the Penguins finally made the playoffs, finishing second in the Patrick division with 87 points. Lemieux had a monster season, leading the NHL in goals (85), assists (114), and points (199). His point total is still the highest ever by a player other than Gretzky. In the playoffs for the first time, Lemieux made a splash. After sweeping the Rangers for the Penguins's first playoff series victory since 1979, Lemieux tied an NHL playoff scoring record with eight points (five goals and three assists) in Game Five of their second series against the Philadelphia Flyers. Eventually the Penguins lost that series in seven games, but the playoffs were a learning experience.

Great players are often measured by their ability to lead their teams to championships. Lemieux could bring people out of their seats, but couldn't seem to bring out the best in his teammates. His frustration increased during the 1989-90 season when he missed 31 games with a back injury that has bothered him ever since. He still scored 45 goals (a record 13 of them when his team was shorthanded because of a penalty), 78 assists, and 123 points. Lemieux also scored points in 45 straight games, five short of Gretzky's NHL record. The Penguins, however, missed their star and once again missed the playoffs.

SUPERSTAR

STANLEY CUP. Things did not go well for the Penguins when Lemieux had back surgery in July 1990. Lying flat on his back in the hospital, he fought off the fear that he would never play again. Through determination and hard work Lemieux returned near the end of the 1990-91 season, playing in 26 games. In his absence Lemieux's teammates, forwards Mark Recchi (113 points) and Kevin Stevens, defenseman Paul Coffey, and goalie Tom Barraso improved their games and led the Penguins to 88 points and the Patrick division title.

In the playoffs, the Penguins did things the hard way, losing the first game of every series they played. In the Stanley Cup finals, the Penguins played another surprise team, the Minnesota North Stars, and after losing the first game, the Penguins won four of the next five to win the series and the Stanley Cup. The Conn Smythe Trophy, given to the MVP of the playoffs, went to Lemieux, who had 16 goals and 44 points in the championship run.

GRETZKY VS. LEMIEUX

During his career Lemieux has most often been compared to Wayne Gretzky, possibly the best player in NHL history. Which one is better? It's hard to say. Lemieux is bigger, the two players are equally fast, and both can handle the puck, pass, and score with the all-time best players. Lemieux's career statistics have been held down by injuries and he has been unable to put together as many consistently great seasons as Gretzky. Gretzky has won four Stanley Cup titles and Lemieux two, but Gretzky probably played on better teams. When it comes down to deciding which one is best, the right answer is probably that it doesn't matter: they are both great.

CHALLENGES. During the 1991-92 season Lemieux and the Penguins were faced with new challenges. Before the season started, Pittsburgh coach Bob Johnson found out he had brain cancer. (He died in November.) Johnson was replaced by Scotty Bowman, (the all-time winningest coach in NHL history) who had guided the Canadiens to five Stanley Cup championships. Lemieux fought through injuries, which caused him to miss 16 games, to lead the NHL in scoring for the third time (44 goals, 87 assists, and 131 points).

The Penguins dropped to third place in their division, and disaster struck in the playoffs against the New York Rangers. The Penguins lost Lemieux when Adam Graves of the Rangers hit him with his stick and broke his hand. The Penguins were not to be stopped, however. They beat the Rangers in six games without Lemieux and swept the Boston Bruins (with Lemieux) and advanced to their second straight Stanley Cup finals appearance. In the finals, the Penguins swept the Black Hawks to win the championship and in the process tied an NHL record with 11 straight playoff wins. Lemieux won his second straight Conn Smythe Trophy as playoff MVP after earning 34 points—16 of them goals—and tying the NHL record with five game-winning goals in 15 playoff games.

Because he is so big and so talented, Lemieux is always the target of the opposing teams toughest players. The hits he has taken over the years have forced him to miss many games due to injuries. The hardest hit he ever took, however, came from nature and not another player. After scoring 104 points in his first 40 games of the 1992-93 season (he was on target to break Gretzky's single-season point record of 215), Lemieux was told he had Hodgkin's Disease, a form of cancer that threatened his life. He cried when he first heard the news, but as he had always done, Lemieux fought back, missing only

23 games and playing just 12 hours after undergoing his last radiation treatment.

Not only did Lemieux come back, he won his fourth scoring title with 160 points (69 goals and 91 assists), was given his second Hart Memorial Trophy as league MVP, and was awarded the Masterton Trophy, given to the player who shows the most determination. The Penguins broke the NHL record of 16 straight victories and finished the season with the NHL's best record (119 points). They were prevented from winning a third straight Stanley Cup when they were upset in the playoffs in seven games by the New York Islanders, the last game being decided in overtime.

Lemieux's struggles continued during the 1993-94 season. He played only 22 games because of his back problem and earned career lows in goals (17) and assists (20). The Penguins were eliminated in the first round of the playoffs by the Washington Capitols.

WHY SO GOOD? A big player at six-feet-five inches and 210 pounds, Lemieux uses his long arms to reach around defenders to pass or shoot the puck and steal opposing players' passes. Once only a offensive player, Lemieux worked early in his career to improve his defensive play. A fast skater for his size, he also has the strength to outmuscle defenders for the puck. And Lemieux can score goals. "I have no sympathy for goalies," Lemieux told *Sports Illustrated*. "No sympathy at all. My job is to go out there and score goals, and their job is to try and stop me."

OFF THE ICE. Lemieux lives with his wife, Nathalie, and their daughter, Lauren, in Sewickley, Pennsylvania. When not playing hockey, Lemieux is an excellent golfer who may someday play professionally. Once addicted to cigarettes, Lemieux has broken the habit. He collects vintage wines and has been a spokesperson for hockey equipment makers and Snickers candy bars. Though his is learning to speak English, Lemieux still has a French accent, making him shy when talking to reporters. His brother Alain played in the NHL for parts of six seasons, including one game with his brother. Lemieux had back surgery in July 1993 which forced him to miss the beginning of the 1993-94 season and he remains in constant pain. While he no longer has any signs of cancer, it is possible the disease could come back. As he has shown in his career, however, injuries will not stop Super Mario. "I'm a very positive person," he told *Sports Illustrated for Kids*. "The cancer and everything were just something I had to go through and then forget about. The future looks pretty good for me right now."

WHERE TO WRITE

C/O PITTSBURGH PENGUINS, CIVIC ARENA,
PITTSBURGH, PA 15219.

CARL LEWIS
1961—

For most of the 1980s, no one could outrun or outjump Carl Lewis. He was the number-one-ranked 100- and 200- meter sprinter and long jumper in the world. As world record holder in the 100-meter dash, Lewis earned the title, "the world's fastest man." Lewis has won eight Olympic gold medals, with his greatest moment occurring during the 1984 Olympic Games in Los Angeles, California, when he won four gold medals (the 100- and 200-meter sprints, the 4 x 100-meter relay, and the long jump). This feat matched the accomplishment of the legendary Jesse Owens, the only other athlete to win four gold medals in track and field during a single Olympics (1936 in Berlin). His success on the track has made Lewis rich; numerous commercial endorsements, personal appearances, and prizes from meets have made him a millionaire.

"The best track and field athlete ever."—Mike Powell, track and field athlete

GROWING UP

Lewis was born on July 1, 1961, in Birmingham, Alabama. Athletics were in his genes since his father, Bill, ran track and played football, and his mother, Evelyn, represented the United States as a hurdler in the 1951 Pan-American Games. The

Lewises moved to the middle-class Philadelphia, Pennsylvania, suburb of Willingboro, New Jersey, where they became teachers and eventually established the Willingboro Track Club. Lewis started running for his parents' track club when he was eight, but was not a standout. His parents told the *Philadelphia Daily News* that Lewis was "the third-best athlete in a family of four," and that they encouraged him to pursue music lessons instead.

LEWIS HAD OTHER IDEAS. He went out in his back yard and measured off 29 feet, 2-½ inches, the world record long jump distance at the time. Even though the best athletes in the world were unable to jump that far, Lewis was determined that someday he would do it. "He was a serious kid," Bill Lewis told the *Philadelphia Daily News*. "Some kids want to be a fireman one day, a movie star the next. Carl set his mind on track and that was it. He said he wanted to be the best, period."

Lewis was skinny and short when he entered high school, and he lost more track events than he won. At age 12, Lewis won the long jump at a Jesse Owens Youth Program meet in Philadelphia with a leap of 17 feet 6 inches. Owens told the other participants to "take a lesson" from "this spunky little guy."

Shortly before his junior year at Willingboro High School, Lewis had a growth spurt and his skills greatly improved. "I didn't mature until high school," he recalled in *Inside Sports*, "while others began maturing in the seventh, eighth grades. There was talent there all the time, but it was only when I got older that I really blossomed."

NUMBER ONE. While at the 1978 national junior championships in Memphis, Tennessee, Lewis ran the 100-yard dash in 9.3 seconds and set a national high school record with a long jump of 25 feet 9 inches. As a high school senior, he was an All-American in the 200-meter sprint and the long jump. By the time he finished high school he was the number-one-ranked high school track athlete in the country. The years of patience and hard work had paid off.

COLLEGE. In 1979 Lewis accepted an athletic scholarship to the University of Houston. There he met Tom Tellez, an expert on how the body and its muscles work. Tellez immediately noticed several problems in Lewis's long-jump style. Lewis had a hard time with his approach to the jumping point because his last four strides were too long. This problem kept him from jumping as far as he could and put stress on his knee, causing it to swell. Tellez told him to increase the distance he ran before he jumped.

Carl Lewis

Lewis was set to participate in the 1980 Olympics when the United States led a boycott against the games, in response to the Soviet Union's invasion of Afghanistan. Instead of feeling sorry for himself, Lewis worked to improve. In 1981, Lewis participated in the National Collegiate Athletic Association (NCAA) indoor championships. He finished first in the 100-meter dash with a time of 9.99 seconds (just .04 seconds behind Jim Hines's world record) and first in the long jump with a leap of 27 feet, 3/4 inches. This was the first time in the 17-year history of the meet that an individual had ever won two track and field events. Lewis repeated his performance at the U.S. outdoor track and field championships in Sacramento, California. Later that year he was presented with the Sullivan Award from the Amateur Athletic Union as the best amateur athlete in the United States.

Lewis was disqualified from collegiate competition for academic reasons during the 1981-82 season and began to compete for the Santa Monica (California) Track Club. Coach Tellez followed him west and continued to work closely with him. In 1982 Lewis achieved his third major double (winning two track and field events) at the national outdoor championships in Knoxville, Tennessee. The following year, he had made his most impressive outing to date at The Athletics Congress (TAC) outdoor championships in Indianapolis, Indiana. In that meet, Lewis jumped 28 feet, 10 1/4 inches to win the long jump, won the 100-meters in 10.27 seconds, and won the 200-meters in 19.75 seconds.

SUPERSTAR

OLYMPIC CHAMPION. At the world championships in Helsinki, Finland, in August 1983, Lewis won three gold medals (100-meters, long jump, and 4 x 100-meter relay). Having won world-class competitions in four different events (100- and 200-meter dashes, 4 x 100-meter relay, and the long jump), Lewis announced that he would participate in all four events at the upcoming 1984 Olympics in Los Angeles, California. Not only would he participate, he predicted he would win each event. Some people thought that Lewis was conceited and that he was more interested in making money than in representing the United States. The pressure was on Lewis to back up his boasts.

Lewis went to the 1984 Olympics under intense media scrutiny, and he fulfilled his astounding predictions. He won a gold medal in the 100-meter sprint with a time of 9.99 seconds. In the long jump, his first leap of 28 feet, 1/4 inch was good enough to win. For his third gold medal, Lewis set an Olympic record with a 19.8-second run in the 200-meter race. Last, but not least, the athlete ran the last 100 meters of the U.S. 4 x 100-meter relay team that set a new Olympic record of 37.83 seconds. Despite his accomplishments, many said Lewis's performance was not as great as it seemed since the Soviet Union and most of its allies did not compete in the games in retaliation for the U.S. boycott of the 1980 Moscow Olympics.

OLYMPIC REPEAT. After the Olympics, Lewis continued to compete in events across Europe and North America. Because of his great speed and athletic ability, Lewis was drafted by the Dallas Cowboys in the twelfth round of the 1984 National Football League draft and the Chicago Bulls obtained his National Basketball Association rights. But Lewis was not interested in either sport. Instead, he set his sights on the 1988 Olympics in Seoul, South Korea. Lewis's dominance in the 100-meter dash was being severely challenged by Ben Johnson, a Canadian sprinter, who began to defeat him regularly. Lewis entered the Olympics as an underdog. In Seoul, Lewis defended his long-jump title with a leap of 28 feet, 7-½ inches, but he lost the 200-meter dash to his training partner, Joe DeLoach. The U.S. 4 x 100-meter relay team failed to qualify for the finals when they dropped the baton during the last exchange.

In the 100-meter dash, Lewis finished second to Johnson, who broke the world record in victory. Lewis was disappointed, but soon after the event he was awarded the gold medal when Johnson was discovered to have used illegal steroids. Despite being eventually recognized as the winner, Lewis once again felt that his victory was tarnished and that he didn't receive the credit he deserved.

DISAPPOINTMENT AND TRIUMPH. Lewis continued training for the 1992 Olympics. Despite breaking the world record in the 100-meters, overall the quality of his performances began to go down. For a decade he had worked to break the outdoor long-jump world record of 29 feet 2-½ inches, set by Bob Beamon in the high-altitude atmosphere of Mexico City, Mexico, during the 1968 Olympics. (At high altitudes, such as in the mountains, the air is thinner, allowing athletes to jump farther than they can at lower altitudes.) At the 1991 world track and field championships in Tokyo, Japan, Lewis not only lost his first long-jump competition since February 1981, but watched as teammate Mike Powell shattered the world record by jumping 29 feet, 4-½

JESSE OWENS

In August 1936 Jesse Owens was one of ten African Americans selected to the 66-member U.S. Olympic team. The Olympics were held that year in Berlin, Germany. Germany's chancellor, Adolf Hitler, called the black athletes subhuman and said they could easily be defeated by his superior German athletes. Nevertheless, Owens won four events, the 100- and 200-meter sprints, the 4 x 100-meter relay, and the long jump. Hitler was reportedly so angry that a black athlete had defeated the Germans that he refused to congratulate Owens. This story was not true, but the apparent snub made Owens's success a symbol of triumph over Hitler and his Nazi government.

inches. "Probably the biggest reason I jumped as far as I did was we are both competitors and we didn't want to lose," Powell told the *Washington Post*. "I wasn't thinking so much about breaking the record as about beating him [Lewis]."

Suffering from a sinus infection, Lewis failed to qualify for the 100- and 200-meter sprints and the 4 x 100-meter relay team at the 1992 U.S. Olympic trials. He did qualify for the long jump, after finishing second to Powell, but, more importantly, at the lowest point in his career Lewis finally gained appreciation from the American public. "I'm only 30 years old and I've had to deal with more than most people in an entire lifetime," he told the *New York Times Magazine*. "I went through the Olympics and people tried to put me down and tear me down and force me to retire. And for some silly reason I kept on running and ignored them, and now I've made it and I'm reaping the benefits of that perseverance [determination]. I'm publicly bigger than I've ever been, and it's a great thing to go through a career and be at this stage and everybody loves you the most."

Lewis entered the 1992 Olympics in Barcelona, Spain, in an unfamiliar position—as an underdog in the long jump. Facing a serious challenge in the long jump for the first time in Olympic competition, Lewis found the strength to jump 28 feet, 5-½ inches, good enough to win his third Olympic gold medal in the event. When sprinter Mark Witherspoon injured his Achilles tendon, Lewis was placed on the U.S. 4 x 100-meter relay team. Running the last 100 meters, Lewis won his eighth Olympic gold medal as the U.S. team won the event.

THE FUTURE. As of 1994, Lewis plans to compete through the 1996 Olympics in Atlanta, Georgia. As Lewis's athletic career winds down, he is casting his sights toward a political career. He has even gone so far as to meet with local political consultants and fund raisers to explore a campaign for office and has expressed an interest in running for mayor of Houston. "I am extremely interested in the political scene of today and what's going on," Lewis told the *New York Times Magazine*.

Seven of Lewis's Olympic gold medals are still in his possession. The eighth—his first, for the 100-meter sprint at the 1984 Olympics—was buried with his father, Bill, after his death in May 1988. "My father was most proud of the 100," Lewis recalled in the *Philadelphia Daily News*. "More than anything, he wanted me to win that medal.... Now he has it and he'll always have it."

WHERE TO WRITE

C/O UNITED STATES OLYMPIC COMMITTEE,

ONE OLYMPIC PLAZA, COLORADO SPRINGS, CO 80909

ERIC LINDROS

1973—

"I have seen the future, and it wears number 88"—Wayne Gretzky, describing Eric Lindros

Before Eric Lindros ever played a game in the National Hockey League (NHL), he was being called hockey's next superstar, following in the footsteps of **Wayne Gretzky** (see entry) of the Los Angeles Kings and **Mario Lemieux** (see entry) of the Pittsburgh Penguins. It took Lindros several years to reach the NHL, but in the 1992-93 season he arrived, after a blockbuster trade between the Quebec Nordiques and the Philadelphia Flyers. A rare combination of speed, size, and toughness, Lindros figures to be a superstar for many years to come.

GROWING UP

Eric Bryan Lindros was born February 28, 1973, in London, Ontario, Canada. He was able to ride a two-wheel bicycle before he was three, and by the age of five was such a nasty competitor in neighborhood hockey games that he had a hard time making friends. He joined his first hockey team at age seven and a year later scored 132 goals. At the age of nine, Lindros was playing with older kids and dominating the league. "He wasn't bigger and stronger than most of the other kids at that age," his mom, Bonnie, told *Sports Illustrated.* "He was just better. One night the realization hit me that I had a special child on my hands."

Lindros's father, Carl, had played minor-league hockey with the Chicago Blackhawks organization, and at first tried to discourage his son from playing the game. As a player, Carl Lindros didn't like the violence of hockey. "We wanted him to play basketball or football," the senior Lindros told the *San Francisco Examiner.* "We let him play hockey in a non-competitive church league. We paid $2 for a pair of skates ... we didn't exactly purchase the best of everything for him. We had no intentions of his playing hockey."

GROWTH SPURT. But the young Lindros had different ideas. His family moved from London to Toronto, Ontario, Canada, when he was 12 and he talked his parents into making the new backyard swimming pool into an ice rink for himself and younger brother, Brett. During this time Lindros was dominating every league in which he played and began to grow at a fast rate. "It was awful," he told the *St. Paul Pioneer Press.* "I think I grew eight or nine inches in one year when I was 14. I used to fall down the stairs at school. I'd say, 'Hi, I'm Eric Lindros' and—boom—down I'd go. And I was always injured. The ligaments [muscles] could not keep everything intact [together]." Eventually, Lindros grew to be six-feet-five inches and 225 pounds.

Playing for his prep school team, the St. Michael's Buzzers, Lindros scored 25 goals and made 43 assists in just 33 games. Next he moved up to junior hockey, the minor leagues for the NHL. The Sault Sainte Marie [Michigan] Greyhounds made Lindros the number-one pick of the 1989 Ontario Hockey League junior draft, but his parents wanted him to play for a team closer to home (Sault Sainte Marie is 400 miles from Toronto), so that he could stay in school and lead a semi-normal teenage life. When the Greyhounds refused to trade Lindros, his parents sent him to Bloomfield

Eric Lindros

Hills, Michigan, to live with friends, finish high school, and play for an amateur [unpaid] team there.

YOUNG STAR. Lindros played for the Detroit-based Compuware team of the North American Junior Hockey League. He led the club to a 17-0 record, scored a team-leading 23 goals and 29 assists, and gained a reputation as a tough guy. "He's a man playing against boys," *Sports Illustrated* wrote at the time. "He can take the puck to the net anytime he desires, but for the sake of variety, of sharpening his playmaking and of keeping his teammates happy, he often passes it off. He goes from backhand to forehand with ease, flicks sharp diagonal passes to cutting teammates and zings hard, accurate wrist shots with an impressively quick release. He's too big to make dazzling pivots [spins], but he starts well, reaches a long stride [picks up speed] quickly and finishes plays [scores] with the power of the superstar he almost certainly will become."

HIT FOR HIT. In January 1990 Lindros signed with the Oshawa Generals of the Ontario Hockey League, who played only 20 miles from his parents' Toronto home. As a 17-year-old rookie, he averaged close to two points per game and led Oshawa to the league championship. The next season, 1990-91, Lindros led the league with 71 goals and 149 points in just 57 games. "What impresses me about Eric, even more than all of his skills, is his intelligence and the physical nature of his play," Generals coach Rick Cornacchia told the *Philadelphia Inquirer.* "Every night teams try to pound the heck out of him and every night he answers them hit for hit." Lindros was the top scorer and Most Valuable Player in the 1991 World Junior Championships.

When Lindros was a teenager, Red Berenson, coach of the University of Michigan hockey team, told the *Philadelphia Inquirer:* "He's [Lindros] the best 16-year-old player I've ever seen. Anywhere. He has no shortcoming: He's one of those rare kids that comes along once in a lifetime—if ever." Lindros was becoming a star. When he turned 18 he would be old enough to play in the NHL. Asked if he was nervous about playing with men ten years older than himself, Lindros told the *Boston Globe:* "A pond is a pond. The next pond for me is a little bigger, that's all. We're all the same fish. Except in the NHL, the fish are a little bigger, quicker and hungrier."

FIRST PICK. In the NHL the worst teams get the best draft picks. There was no question that the team with the first selection in the draft would choose Lindros. In fact, the NHL was afraid that teams might try to lose on purpose in order to draft him. As the *Detroit Free Press* wrote in 1991: "The mere mention of Eric Lindros causes owners, general managers and coaches to salivate [drool], visions of Stanley Cups dancing in their heads."

From the start, Lindros said he preferred to play in the United States. At the end of the 1990-91 season, however, the last-place team was the Quebec Nordiques. Lindros made it clear that he did not want to play for the Nordiques, but on June 22, 1991, they chose him anyway. "You can't pass up a guy like that," Quebec associate coach Jacques Martin told the *Chicago Tribune.* "Gretzky now is passing the baton to Mario [Lemieux], and this kid will get the baton from Mario in due time."

SAYS NO TO QUEBEC. Quebec offered Lindros a record salary for a rookie—over $1 million per season. Lindros said he didn't want to play in a small city and didn't want to play in Quebec, where French is the official language (see box). Beyond these reasons, Lindros said he didn't think the NHL draft was fair and that he should be able to play for any team he chose. The people in Quebec became angry with Lindros, and accused him of being anti-French. His refusal to play in Quebec became a political issue, and Canadian Prime Minister Brian Mulroney tried to talk Lindros into signing with the Canadian team.

In response to people talking against him, Lindros told the *Detroit Free Press* that he planned to return to junior hockey and wait until the next year's draft: "The Nordiques keep saying they won't deal [trade] me, but I've made it as clear as possible: I won't play in Quebec. If a trade isn't made, I'll be in Oshawa for the year and I don't have a problem with that at all."

SUPERSTAR

OLYMPIC HERO. If there was any doubt about Lindros's ability to star in the NHL, it was wiped out a month before the 1991-92 season started. Lindros was named to the Canadian national team, along with professional stars, and was a standout in the five-game Canada Cup series against international competition, scoring three goals and assisting on two others. Wayne Gretzky, who played on the same line with Lindros during the series, told the *Toronto Globe and Mail,* "I have seen the future, and it wears number 88 [Lindros's jersey number]."

Refusing to trade Lindros, the Nordiques opened the 1991-92 season with their number-one draft pick playing junior hockey. In February 1992, Lindros starred on the Canadian Olympic hockey team, leading them to the finals, where they lost to the Unified Team (the former Soviet Union team), 3-1. The silver medal was Canada's first medal in hockey since 1968.

BIG TRADE. Following the 1991-92 NHL season, Lindros was finally traded—to two teams. Both the Philadelphia Flyers and the New York Rangers claimed to have traded for Lindros. It was eventually decided that Lindros would play for the Flyers, who traded goalie Ron Hextall, centers Mike Ricci and Peter Forsberg, defensemen Steve Duchesne and Kerry Huffman, and winger Chris Simon to Quebec. Philadelphia also agreed to give the Nordiques first-round draft picks in 1993 and 1994 and $15 million. The trade was one of the biggest in NHL history, and Lindros was faced with the job of proving he was worth what Philadelphia gave up to get him.

ENTERS NHL. Lindros entered the NHL with high expectations, but there was little he could do alone to make the Flyers winners during the 1992-93 season. He had a solid first season, scoring 41 goals and 75 points, but missed 23 games with a knee injury. (Lindros was scoring at a pace that would have given him 56 goals and 103 points if he had played the entire 84 game schedule.) Philadelphia missed the playoffs, finishing fifth in their division with 83 points. Many experts said that Lindros's physical (some said reckless) play led to his being injured so much of the season. Answering his critics, Lindros told the *Sporting News:* "Just because I've injured both my knees, I'm not going to change my game. If somebody's on the tracks, they'll get hit by a train if they're in my way."

Lindros was still bothered by injuries in his second season (1993-94). He scored 44 goals and had 53 assists, but played only 65 games. The Flyers again failed to make the playoffs.

OFF THE ICE. To become as great as he can be, Lindros, now in his early twenties, must become more mature, avoiding off-ice problems that hurt him in his first season. (Lindros was involved in several fights outside of hockey.) If he can control his temper, his potential seems endless. He is still trying to adjust to being a superstar. "Sometimes I have to make sure I do things that just keep me in touch with reality," Lindros told the *Buffalo News.* "I do things like other kids. I hang out, I eat hamburgers, I have a social life. You have to do those things to keep some sort of reality. Hockey is a game and it's also a business. I know both those things. I know I have to deal with both those things, but I try to keep touch with my life too. I have to be something besides hockey or I'd go crazy. Anyone would."

WHERE TO WRITE

C/O PHILADELPHIA FLYERS,

THE SPECTRUM, PHILADELPHIA, PA 19148.

NANCY LOPEZ

1957—

In 1978 Nancy Lopez became an instant celebrity when she won eight tournaments—a record five in a row—in her rookie season on the Ladies' Professional Golf Association (LPGA) tour. Since then she has consistently been one of the finest golfers on the women's tour and has earned a place in the LPGA Hall of Fame. In addition to her busy schedule on the course, Lopez is a wife and mother. Her accomplishments both in golf and in life make her a true champion.

GROWING UP

Nancy Lopez was born January 6, 1957, in Torrence, California. Her father, Domingo, was an auto repair shop owner, and her mother, Marina, was a housewife. Lopez, who has an older sister named Delma, is of Mexican-American descent. Her family moved to Rosewell, Texas, soon after Nancy was born. She began playing golf at the age of eight when her parents took up the game as exercise for her mother. Her father shortened the shaft of a golf club so his daughter could swing it.

At the age of nine Lopez won her first pee-wee golf tournament by 110 strokes over her nearest opponent. By the age of eleven she was a better golfer than either of her parents. Her father, who was once an excellent baseball player, gave her lessons and became convinced that Lopez was talented. The family passed up buying a new house and washing machine to save money to help finance Lopez's golfing. There were some chores, like washing dishes, that Lopez didn't have to do as a child because they might injure her hands.

ALL-AROUND ATHLETE. Lopez was active in swimming, basketball, track, gymnastics, Girl Scouts, and a sorority called "Chums" in high school. She played on the otherwise all-boy golf team, and was ranked number one and led the team to the state championship. Her best friend in school was Mexican-American, but most of the people she knew were Anglo Americans. Though Lopez got along well with everyone, she did suffer at times from discrimination. "I dated a guy whose parents didn't like me because I was Mexican-American," she recalled in the *New York Times*. Many citizens of her small community supported her golf career by bringing their auto repair business to her father's garage.

By her early teens, Lopez was winning major tournaments. She won the New Mexico Women's Amateur when she was 12, and won the United States Golf Association (USGA) Junior Girls Championship twice—in 1972 and 1974. In 1975, when she was a senior in high school, Lopez entered the U.S. Women's Open and finished second against the best golfers in the world. After graduating from high school in 1976, Lopez accepted a scholarship to play golf at the University of Tulsa.

TURNS PRO. During her freshman year at Tulsa, Lopez won the Association of Intercollegiate Athletics for Women (AIAW) golf championship. That same year she was an All-American and was Tulsa University's Female Athlete of the Year. After her sophomore year, Lopez turned professional. "I felt that there was no other place to go," she admitted to the *New York Times*.

SCOREBOARD

WON A RECORD FIVE CONSECUTIVE LPGA TOUR TOURNAMENTS IN 1978.

THREE-TIME WINNER OF THE LPGA CHAMPIONSHIP, ONE OF THE FOUR MAJOR TOURNAMENTS OF WOMEN'S GOLF.

FOUR-TIME LPGA PLAYER OF THE YEAR.

ONE OF THE GREATEST WOMEN GOLFERS OF ALL TIME.

Nancy Lopez

"I needed to go forward and set other goals, reach the highest point of my whole career."

SUPERSTAR

RUNAWAY ROOKIE. Lopez joined the LPGA tour in 1978. She won eight tournaments that first year, including a record five in a row, becoming an instant sensation. She began the year by winning the Bent Tree Classic in Sarasota, Florida—her first tournament victory. She dedicated the win to her mother, who had died in the summer of 1977 after an appendix operation.

Lopez's record-breaking winning streak began with a victory at the Greater Baltimore Classic. With a win at the LPGA Championship, one of the major tournaments of women's golf—the others being the Nabisco Dinah Shore, the U.S. Women's Open, and the du Maurier Classic in Canada—her streak reached four. She won her record-setting fifth consecutive tournament, coming from behind in the final round to win the Bankers Trust Classic. Her streak was broken the next week when she finished 13th in the Lady Keystone Open. By the end of the year Lopez had won $200,000 and was also the spokesperson for several golf products. She was named LPGA Rookie of the Year and Player of the Year, and also won the Vare Trophy, given to the player with the best scoring average for the season.

Because of her golfing talent and her warm personality, Lopez was a favorite of golf fans. "I was walking down the street with my manager and people were yelling from cars!" she said in the *New York Times,* recalling an incident that occurred after her fourth consecutive win. "One walked across the street and said, 'I hope you make it five.'" Lopez was mobbed during tournaments by a group of fans, known as "Nancy's Navy." (The idea for the group's name came from "Arnie's Army," a group of fans that followed the legendary golfer Arnold Palmer.)

SECOND-YEAR SENSATION. Lopez was married before the 1979 season, but matrimony didn't slow her down. She won nine of 19 tournaments that year—an amazing record. Bruce Newman, in *Sports Illustrated,* called Lopez's 1979 season "one of the most dominating sports performances in half a century." For the second straight year Lopez was named LPGA Player of the Year and won the Vare Trophy. Rarely has an athlete dominated a sport in their first two seasons like Lopez did in women's golf during 1978 and 1979.

PERSONAL PROBLEMS. Lopez had great seasons in 1980 and 1981, but they couldn't compare to her first two. She was also having personal problems and was unhappy in her marriage. Her husband objected to the amount of time she spent playing golf. Though she didn't want to give up the sport, Lopez agreed to stay home to make him happy. She began to overeat which led to a weight gain, and Lopez became more and more unhappy.

WHAT MAKES HER SO GOOD?

Golf experts have said that Lopez does not have a good golf swing, but it seems to work for her. At five-feet-seven inches and 135 pounds, Lopez is not one of the women's tour's bigger players, but is able to hit the ball as far as anyone. She is an excellent putter, a talent she attributes to hours of practice. Lopez plays well under pressure, especially in close tournaments. "When I get really psyched up ... I can do anything," she told the *New York Times.* More importantly, she tries not to forget that golf is a game to be enjoyed. "I'm very confident in myself and I love what I'm doing," Lopez observed in *Newsday.* "I'm very relaxed when I'm playing because it's not a job. It's a game."

During this time Lopez became friends with Ray Knight, a major league baseball player who knew her husband. "Tim [her husband] would always say such nice things about Ray, but we weren't really friends yet," Lopez recalled in *Sports Illustrated.* "We just kind of admired each other." One day Lopez told Knight she was leaving her husband. "He was really my only friend during that period when I was struggling the most," she explained to the same magazine.

STARTS OVER. After she divorced her husband, Lopez came to realize that she was in love with Knight. "It was really a friendship that turned into a romance," Knight observed in *Sports Illustrated.* In March 1982 they were married. Since Knight was also an athlete, he understood how important golf was to Lopez. "After I married Ray, I felt that golf was sec-

RAY KNIGHT

Ray Knight made headlines when he married Nancy Lopez, but he was also a pretty good third baseman. He played 13 seasons in the major leagues and spent time with five different teams. He has a lifetime batting average of .271, and hit 84 home runs during his career. Knight was hired as a commentator for the ESPN television network after he retired from baseball in 1989 and is now the hitting coach for the Cincinnati Reds.

ond," Lopez continued. "He made me happier than golf did. But he never pressured me not to go anywhere to play golf, and I had often felt that pressure from Tim." Knight added: "Nancy is known the world over because she has such great talent, and I don't want her to waste it. It never entered my mind as a problem that she needed to play golf, as long as she loves me."

BIRDIES AND BABY. Lopez won two tournaments in 1983, but her biggest thrill came in November when she gave birth to her first child, Ashley Marie. Within four weeks she was back out practicing. She won two tournaments in 1984 and ranked seventh on the LPGA tour, a good year but not up to her high standards. That changed in 1985, as Lopez won the Player of the Year award and Vare Trophy for the third time. Her season scoring average set an LPGA all-time record (since broken by Beth Daniel in 1989). During the year she won five tournaments, including her second LPGA Championship. Lopez finished in the top ten in 21 of the 25 tournaments she played in, and at the Henredon Classic she finished 20-under-par—a record that still stands. She had 25 birdies during that tournament.

Lopez missed most of the 1986 season after giving birth to her second daughter, Erinn Shea, in May, and played only four tournaments near the end of the season. It was a big year, however, for her husband, as Knight won the Most Valuable Player award in the World Series when his New York Mets defeated the Boston Red Sox in seven games. The year before Knight had considered retiring from baseball after a bad season but Lopez talked him out of it. "I didn't feel like Ray was a quitter," she told *Sports Illustrated,* "and I was pretty sure he would be a miserable person to live with if he just dropped out."

HALL OF FAMER. Lopez returned to the tour in 1987 hoping to regain her spot as the number-one player. "I'm so happy with my life, that now when I play, there is no pressure," she com-

Nancy Lopez blasts out of a sand trap.

mented in *Sports Illustrated*. "It's just all fun, and when it's fun, you perform better." When Lopez won the Sarasota Classic, she earned her 35th LPGA career victory. With that win she qualified for the LPGA Hall of Fame and was inducted in July as the Hall's 11th member. She was also named women's "Golfer of the Decade" by *Golf* magazine for the years 1978-87.

RETURN TO TOP. In 1988 Lopez was named player of the year for the fourth time. She won three tournaments and passed the $2 million mark in earnings. In 1989 she won three tournaments, including the LPGA Championship. Tied with Ayako Okamoto mid-way through the final round, Lopez missed a short putt to bogey and Okamoto birdied, putting Lopez two shots behind. "Those are the kinds of putts I hate to miss," she confessed to *Sports Illustrated*. "They have kept me from winning all year. On the other hand, it was very good because it really made me mad." When Lopez was mad, she was unbeatable. She took charge of the tournament, earning five birdies in the last eight holes to win the tournament by three strokes. The win was her third in the important LPGA Championship. "Nancy is Number One under the skies," Okamoto told *Sports Illustrated*. "Thanks. That's how I'd like to be remembered when I leave," Lopez replied in the same magazine.

BALANCING CLUBS AND KIDS. Lopez gave birth to her third child, Torri Heather, in October 1991, and announced that she was cutting back on her golf schedule. Today she rarely leaves home for more than two weeks at a time and has never been separated from her children for more than 10 days. "Being home is a time you can really enjoy sharing things," Lopez told *Golf* magazine. "I'm fortunate enough to say that I could stop [playing golf] right now—I have all the money I'll ever need and enjoy what I have." Before her first child started school, Lopez took her kids along with her on tour. But with three children it became more difficult to do and Lopez stayed home more often.

Lopez also wanted to spend more time with her husband, who she didn't see very often since they were both on the road much of the time. "Probably the single most important thing we do as a family is spend quality time together," Knight told *Golf* magazine. "And any time we're home is quality time. Our careers have spread us so much that when we do get together, it's almost an event. I relish my time at home. It's almost sacred to me."

QUITE A CAREER. Lopez has won at least one tournament every year since 1978, except in 1986 when she played a limited schedule due to her pregnancy. During her career she has won 47 tournaments and earned close to $4 million. Her talent and outgoing personality have helped Lopez make women's golf almost as popular as the men's tour. Golf fans will miss her when she decides to hang up the clubs.

OFF THE COURSE. Lopez lives in Albany, Georgia, with her husband and three children. She is a playing editor for *Golf* magazine and enjoys cooking, listening to Top 40 music, riding four-wheel all-terrain bikes, and hunting and fishing. "Just being out in the woods, seeing the morning open up and the animals come out," she told *Golf* magazine, explaining what she liked best about hunting. Her favorite breakfast foods are eggs, grits, and biscuits. One of Lopez's favorite keepsakes is a baseball glove autographed by **Nolan Ryan** (see entry), who was Knight's teammate on the Houston Astros.

Lopez loves to play golf, but at all times her family comes first. "All the glamour, fame, signing autographs and admiration doesn't mean anything if you don't have anything at home," she told *Golf* magazine. "We have a lot of love in our family."

WHERE TO WRITE

LADIES' PROFESSIONAL GOLF ASSOCIATION,

2570 VOUSIA ST., SUITE B, DAYTONA, FL 32114.

GREG MADDUX

1966—

Greg Maddux was recognized as the best pitcher in the National League when he won the Cy Young Award in 1992 playing for the Chicago Cubs. He proved he was the best again in 1993 with his second Cy Young Award, this time with the Atlanta Braves. He became the first pitcher in major league history to win consecutive Cy Young Awards with different teams. Maddux knew it was a gamble to leave Chicago for Atlanta, but he was used to gambling. He grew up in Las Vegas.

GROWING UP

Gregory Alan Maddux was born April 14, 1966, in San Angelo, Texas. His father, Dave, was in the air force and his family moved from Texas to Indiana, and then to North Dakota, California, and Madrid, Spain, before finally settling in Las Vegas, Nevada. "I think growing up the way we did helped prepare us for what we do now," Maddux's older brother, Mike, a major league pitcher with the New York Mets, observed in *Sports Illustrated.*

VIVA LAS VEGAS. Las Vegas is best known for its casinos, gambling, and bright flashing lights. Maddux says that's not all there is to his home town. "Las Vegas is just like any other place," he explained in *Sports Illustrated*. "It has churches and parks and Little League and movie theaters. The only difference is that when you go to the grocery store ... there are a couple of slot machines outside. And the weather is usually nice." His dad, now retired from the air force, works as a poker dealer in a casino.

TURNS PRO. Maddux was named to the All-State team in his junior and senior seasons at Valley High School in Las Vegas, Nevada. He was chosen in the second round of the June 1984 major league draft by the Chicago Cubs and began his professional career after graduating from high school. In his first minor league season with the Cubs (1984), Maddux went 6-3 with a 2.63 earned run average (ERA). He made the Midwest League All-Star team in his second year (1985) with a 13-9 record and 3.19 ERA.

In 1986 Maddux was promoted to Triple-A, the highest level of minor league baseball. He won ten games and lost one with an ERA of 3.02 for the Iowa Cubs of the American Association. *Baseball America* magazine named him to its Triple-A All-Star team. Maddux made his major league debut for the Chicago Cubs in September 1986. He was the youngest Cub (20) to ever play when he pitched against the Houston Astros on September 2. He made his first major league start on September 7 and beat the Cincinnati Reds, 11-3. On September 29 Maddux defeated his brother Mike, also a rookie, in the first-ever major league pitching match-up of two rookie brothers. Maddux finished the 1986 season with a 2-4 record and 5.52 ERA.

BIG LEAGUE STARTER. In 1987 Maddux became a regular in the Cubs's starting rotation. He won 6, lost 14 and had an unimpressive ERA of 5.61. The Cubs finished last in the National League East, 18½ games behind the division-winning St. Louis Cardinals. Maddux showed dramatic improvement

---

SCOREBOARD

TWO-TIME NATIONAL LEAGUE CY YOUNG AWARD WINNER— 1992 AND 1993.

FIRST PITCHER IN MAJOR LEAGUE HISTORY TO WIN CONSECUTIVE CY YOUNG AWARDS WITH DIFFERENT TEAMS—THE CHICAGO CUBS AND ATLANTA BRAVES.

THE BEST PITCHER IN THE NATIONAL LEAGUE FOR TWO CONSECUTIVE YEARS.

Greg Maddux

in 1988. He won 18 (fifth in the National League), lost only 8, pitched 249 innings (fifth in the National League), and had an ERA of 3.18. In July he was named to his first All-Star team but did not pitch.

DIVISION CHAMPS. Maddux and second baseman **Ryne Sandberg** (see entry) led the Cubs to an East division title in 1989. Maddux finished second in victories in the National League with 19 wins—he lost 12—pitched 238 innings, and for the first time had an ERA under 3.00 (2.95). He finished third in the voting for the National League Cy Young Award—given annually to the league's best pitcher—behind winner Mark Davis of the San Diego Padres. The Cubs won 93 games and finished six games ahead of the defending world champion New York Mets.

Maddux pitched the opening game of the National League Championship Series against the West division champion San Francisco Giants. The Giants, led by first baseman Will Clark, pounded Maddux and the Cubs, 11-3. Clark hit two home runs—one a grand slam— off of Maddux. The Cubs split the next two games and Maddux pitched again in Game Four. He lasted only three innings and gave up four runs. Chicago lost the game and fell behind three games to one. San Francisco won Game Five and the series.

Maddux had another strong season in 1990 but the Cubs fell to sixth place. He won 15 and lost 15, pitched 237 innings (second in the National League), and had an ERA of 3.46. Maddux also finished fourth in the National League in complete games (with eight), and won his first Gold Glove Award for fielding excellence. (He would also win the award the next three seasons.) In 1991 Maddux won 15 and lost 11, pitched a league-leading 263 innings, and had an ERA of 3.35. He struck out 198 batters (second in the National League) and had seven complete games (fourth in the National League). The

Cubs continued to struggle, however, finishing 20 games behind the Pittsburgh Pirates.

SUPERSTAR

CY YOUNG I. In 1990 Maddux became the best pitcher in the National League. He won 20 games (tied for first in the National League) for the first time. He finished with a 20-11 record, had an ERA of 2.18 (third in the National League), and pitched a major league leading 268 innings. He struck out 199 (third in the National League) and threw four shutouts (second in the National League). His nine complete games were the third-highest in the National League. The Cubs failed to score in seven of Maddux's eleven losses. He was the first Cubs pitcher to win 20 games since Rick Reuschel in 1977.

On November 12 it was announced that Maddux had won the 1992 National League Cy Young Award. He finished ahead of 1991's winner, Tom Glavine of the Atlanta Braves. Maddux became the first pitcher from a losing team to win the Cy Young Award since Randy Jones of the San Diego Padres in 1976. The Cubs finished fourth in their division, 18 games behind the Pirates.

FREE AGENT. Since Opening Day of 1988 no pitcher had won more games or pitched more innings in the National League than Maddux. He became a free agent after the 1992 season and could sign with any team. Maddux accepted a five-year, $28 million contract to play with the Atlanta Braves, but he was sad to leave the Cubs. "I was in a place where I was happy," he confessed to *Sport*. "A place where I wanted to play, a place that I knew. I was willing to take less [money to stay in Chicago]."

WHAT MAKES HIM SO GOOD

Maddux is not big for a major league pitcher—six-feet tall and 175 pounds. "It's an attitude; size never seemed to bother him," catcher Damon Berryhill, who caught for Maddux with the Braves and the Cubs, explained to *Baseball Digest*. "You know when you throw him out there you're going to be in the game. He even wins when he doesn't have his best stuff." Maddux is a fierce competitor who hates to lose. "Winning is what it's all about," he told the *Atlanta Journal*. "That's why you play the game, to win." Maddux has been accused of trying to knock down batters. "I don't try to knock guys down," he told *Sport*. "But at times, you need [to pitch inside]. You can't pitch scared." He also studies hitters, trying to gain any advantage he can. "You always try to watch the hitters," he explained to *Sport*, "the whole game's about getting an edge.... I might pick two hitters out of the lineup and watch what they do ... I usually make a little mental note." Maddux hits well for a pitcher, and is considered by many to be the best-fielding pitcher in baseball.

But you never know what your worth is until you go through the [free-agency] process." Maddux turned down more money from the New York Yankees because he didn't want to play in the pressure-packed atmosphere of New York.

The main reason Maddux gave for signing with the Braves was that he thought they had the best chance to win the World Series. The Braves had played in two consecutive World Series and Maddux joined what was already the best pitching staff in baseball. "With this pitching staff, the Braves have the ability to win for the entire five years that I'm here," he told *Sport*.

BEST TEAM. The Braves were the best team in baseball during the regular season of 1993. Atlanta's top-four starting pitchers won a combined 75 games—Glavine (22), Maddux (20), Smoltz (15), and Avery (18). The pitching staff was so good that three of its members—Avery, Glavine, and Smoltz—were named to the All-Star team. Maddux finished fourth in the National League in wins and led the league with a 2.36 ERA, 267 innings pitched, and eight complete games. He gave up only 226 hits in 267 innings and finished third in the National League with 197 strikeouts. "You change teams and you want to make a good first impression," Maddux confided to the *New York Times*. "I feel like I've done that. I didn't really change anything in the way I pitched. I pretty much tried to do the same things that have always worked in the past."

But even with their great pitching, the Braves trailed the San Francisco Giants most of the season. The team started its comeback after making a big trade to acquire first baseman Fred McGriff from the San Diego Padres. Maddux was strong in the second half of the season with a 12-2 record and a 1.79 ERA. The Braves overcame the Giants's lead and entered the last game of the season tied with San Francisco. On the final day of the regular season Atlanta beat the expansion Colorado Rockies and the Giants lost 12-1 to longtime rivals, the Los Angeles Dodgers. This combination gave the Braves their third straight West division title. Atlanta finished the season with 104 wins—the most in the major leagues.

PLAYOFF WOES. Atlanta lost Game One of the National League Championship Series against the East division champion

Philadelphia Phillies. Maddux started Game Two of the series and won 14-3. The Braves scored six runs in the third inning and four more in the eighth. When the Braves also routed the Phillies in Game Three it appeared Atlanta would easily win the series. But the Phillies won Games Four and Five to set up a do-or-die situation for Atlanta.

Maddux, now the hottest pitcher in baseball, was on the mound for Atlanta in Game Six. He had won 14 of his last 16 starts and had not given up more than two earned runs (runs not caused by an error) in his previous 14 starts. But disaster struck in the first inning when he was hit by a line drive off the bat of Philadelphia second baseman Mickey Morandini. Maddux continued to pitch though he was obviously in pain. He allowed six runs, two more than he had given up in any game all season. The Phillies won the game, 6-3, and the series, four games to two. Maddux did not use his injury as an excuse. "I'm not going to sit there and feel I was cheated, because I wasn't cheated," he commented in the *Detroit Free Press*. "If anything, I cheated the team."

REPEAT CY YOUNGS

Only five pitchers in major league history have repeated as Cy Young Award winners. The chart below lists these pitchers, their team(s), and the years in which they accomplished this feat.

Pitcher/ Years	Team(s)
Sandy Koufax 1965-66	Los Angeles Dodgers
Denny McLain 1968-69	Detroit Tigers
Jim Palmer 1975-76	Baltimore Orioles
Roger Clemens 1986-87	Boston Red Sox
Greg Maddux 1992-93	Chicago Cubs, Atlanta Braves

CY YOUNG II. When the voting for the 1993 National League Cy Young Award was announced, Maddux won by a wide margin over Bill Swift of the San Francisco Giants and his Atlanta teammate Glavine. He became the first player to win consecutive Cy Young Awards with different teams. (Gaylord Perry is the only other pitcher to win the Cy Young Award with two different teams—with Cleveland in 1972 and San Diego in 1978.) But the playoff disappointment left Maddux unsatisfied with his season. "I didn't pitch this year to win the Cy Young," he told the *Atlanta Journal*. "I pitched to get to the World Series."

OFF THE FIELD. Maddux lives in Las Vegas during the off-season with his wife Kathy and their daughter, Amanda Page. He enjoys playing golf and video games and taking care of his dogs. Maddux led all major league pitchers in wins (107), games started (212), innings pitched (1,522), and complete games (48) during the years 1988-93. *Baseball Digest* quoted Philadelphia Phillies manager Jim Fregosi as saying of Maddux: "He is the best pitcher in the [National] league. Maybe in all of baseball."

WHERE TO WRITE

C/O ATLANTA BRAVES, P.O. BOX 4064, ATLANTA, GA 30302.

KARL MALONE

1963—

Karl "The Mailman" Malone has been delivering for eight seasons for the Utah Jazz. At six-feet-nine-inches tall and 250 pounds, Malone is one of the most physically powerful players in the National Basketball Association (NBA). Able to battle under the boards for rebounds, Malone also has the speed to run the court on the fast break. As all-star Los Angeles Lakers forward James Worthy said, he is "probably the most dominant player at his position. His strength is just phenomenal [outstanding]. Speed. Quickness. Every play you have to play him your hardest."

Malone frustrates his opponents in numerous ways—he plays a physical game, he refuses to back down when other players try to push him around, and he hates to sit on the bench. "I want to play all 48 [minutes]." Malone told *Sports Illustrated*. "I don't want ... [anybody] coming in for Karl Malone." This wasn't always the case, however; Malone had to learn how important hard work was to being a successful NBA player. Today no one outworks, and only a few outplay, The Mailman, come rain, sleet, or dark of night.

"When you play The Mailman, be ready to bang, be ready to run, be ready to go all night."—Larry Smith, former NBA player

GROWING UP

Karl Malone was born July 24, 1963, in Summerfield, Louisiana. He grew up in Mount Sinai, a small town close to the Arkansas border. His father left his family when Malone was four years old, and his mother, Shirley Malone, refused welfare and worked three jobs in order to support her eight children. She worked days in Louisiana sawmills, ran machinery, and then spent a nightly shift cutting chickens into parts. His mother's hard work made an impression on Malone, and the two of them often went hunting and fishing together. "I saw my mother wear cardboard in her shoes, just so each of us could have a good pair," he told *Sports Illustrated*. "I saw what the water did to that cardboard. I can never repay her."

TEENAGER. When Malone was a child, his mom told *Sports Illustrated for Kids*, he hated spinach (but liked collard greens and bannana pudding) and loved to collect frogs and lizards. As a teenager, although he never drank alcohol or used drugs, Malone got into his share of trouble. He and his brother, Terry, got whipped for such pranks as shooting out windows with BB guns, smashing melons, chasing cows, and crashing cars. Playing basketball helped keep Malone off the streets, and he led Summerfield High School to three straight state championships. Soon many colleges were interested in him attending their schools. Malone averaged 30 points and 20 rebounds per game in high school, and at six-feet-nine-inches tall and 230 pounds he was considered an impressive college prospect.

COUNTRY BOY. Malone's mother convinced him to attend Louisiana Tech, which was only 40 miles from home, instead of the faraway University of Arkansas. "I wanted to stay near home because, deep down, I'm a small-town guy who wants to be near friends and relatives," Malone told the *Sporting News*. "The bright lights of the big city are really not for me. I like it when you can walk down a street and say hello to everybody."

When Malone arrived at Louisiana Tech, however, his high school grades were not good enough for him to qualify for a scholarship or to play basketball. Though hard at the time, Malone told *Sports Illustrated* "that was the best thing that ever happened to me. My last years of high school, I was starting to think I was better than other people, that I was special and things would just come to me." Malone had to borrow money to pay for college, and he managed to earn good enough grades by his sophomore year at Louisiana Tech to be able to play basketball. He majored in elementary education.

When Malone entered Louisiana Tech, the school was better known for its women's basketball team. Malone helped change that. In the three years that he played there, Tech went 19-9, 26-7, and 29-3. The school received its first invitation to the National Collegiate Athletic Association (NCAA) tournament Malone's second year. The next year (1984-85) Tech was nationally ranked, defeated powerful teams from the University of Pittsburgh and Ohio State University, and won the Southland Conference championship.

Karl Malone

EARNS NICKNAME. It was during the 1984-85 season that "The Mailman" earned his nickname, because he always delivered points, rebounds, and blocked shots in the clutch. During his career Malone smashed so many backboards that Louisiana Tech began mailing pieces of the broken glass to its fans. Malone played a physical game, often finding himself in early foul trouble. He averaged 15.6 points and almost nine rebounds per game during his college career. Feeling he was ready for the NBA, Malone decided to give up his last year of college eligibility and enter the 1985 draft.

DRAFT DISAPPOINTMENT. Malone expected to be drafted by the Dallas Mavericks. He was so sure that he bought a house in Dallas. Surprising him, the Mavericks passed him by. He was chosen thirteenth, by the Utah Jazz. As the fans of his new team listened via telephone, the stunned Malone told the Jazz coach, "I'm looking forward to playing in the town of Utah." When Malone arrived in Utah, he soon became friends with Adrian Dantley, a veteran player who gave Malone valuable information on how to be successful in the NBA, but who also had a reputation for being more concerned about his own statistics than about the success of his team.

CHANGE IN ATTITUDE. Not much was expected of the Jazz in Malone's rookie season, and they earned a 42-40 record and lost to the Dallas Mavericks in the first round of the playoffs. Malone averaged 14.9 points and 8.9 rebounds per game and earned a spot on the NBA's All-Rookie team. His biggest problem seemed to be his attitude. Jazz coach Frank Layden thought that Malone needed to push himself to excel if he wanted to be a great player. According to Layden, Malone's friendship with Dantley was a problem, since Dantley told Malone to take it easy during games because the Jazz were a bad team and would lose anyway. In order to remove what he saw as a bad influence, Layden traded Dantley to the Detroit Pistons at the end of the 1985-86 season. The change helped Malone grow up. "I wanted to be an athlete just to make money," Malone told *Inside Sports*. "Then coach Layden traded Adrian Dantley, and all of a sudden not just a little responsibility was on me, but now a great deal. It's a situation where [I asked myself], 'What do you really want in life? Do you want to just please Karl Malone, or do you want to touch other lives?'"

Malone decided to become the leader of the 1986-87 Utah Jazz. Helped by the arrival of playmaking point guard John Stockton, Malone averaged 21.7 points and grabbed 10.4 rebounds per game. He improved those statistics the next season, 1987-88, averaging 27.7 points (fifth in the league) and 12 rebounds (fourth in the league) per game. The Jazz became a powerful team, winning 47 games and advancing to the Western Conference finals against Earvin "Magic" Johnson (see entry) and the defending NBA champion Los Angeles Lakers. Malone averaged 29 points and 12 rebounds in the series, but the Lakers eventually won four games to three.

SUPERSTAR

ALL-STAR MVP. Malone became a superstar in 1988-89, finishing second in the NBA—behind Chicago Bull's **Michael Jordan** (see entry) in scoring, averaging 29.1 points, and fifth in rebounding at with 10.7 per game. He was also the leading vote-getter for forwards for the All-Star team. During the All-Star game, Malone scored 29 points and grabbed nine rebounds. He also grabbed the game's Most Valuable Player award. After the game, he answered questions with his mom at his side. "I brought my mother to sit up here for a reason," Malone told the gathered reporters. "When I was growing up, she worked two jobs at one point and still found the time to come out in the backyard and serve as a basket for me by joining her arms in front of her chest. A lot of people would pass by and say, 'What is she doing? He's never going to amount to anything.' Well, I guess they were wrong. I may be from the country, but for one day I'm king of the city."

At the end of the season Malone was also picked for the All-NBA first team (the first of five straight selections). The Jazz won 51 games and the Midwest division title, but were upset in the first round of the playoffs by the Golden State Warriors. In 1989-90 Malone again increased his scoring (31 points per game, second in the league to Jordan) and rebounding (11.1 per game, fourth in the league) averages, and scored 61 points in one game. The Jazz won 55 games during the regular season, but suffered another painful playoff loss in the first round.

CONSISTENTLY AWESOME. Malone, remaining amazingly consistent, averaging 29 points and pulled down a career best 11.8 rebounds per game in 1990-91. The Jazz, however, con-

BARKLEY VS. MALONE

The player most often compared to Malone is **Charles Barkley** (see entry) of the Phoenix Suns. Here is how the two players have matched up in scoring (SC) and rebounding (RB) throughout their careers:

Year	Malone		Barkley	
	SC	RB	SC	RB
1984-85	–	–	14.0	8.6
1985-86	14.9	8.9	20.0	12.8
1986-87	21.7	10.4	23.0	14.6
1987-88	27.7	12.0	28.3	11.9
1988-89	29.1	10.7	25.8	12.5
1989-90	31.0	11.1	25.2	11.5
1990-91	29.0	11.8	27.6	10.1
1991-92	28.0	11.2	23.1	11.1
1992-93	27.0	11.2	25.6	12.2
1993-94	25.2	11.5	21.6	11.2
Average	25.9	11.0	23.3	11.6

tinued to disappoint their fans in the playoffs, losing in the second round to the Portland Trail Blazers. Although Malone had the highest playoff scoring average among active players (27.3 points per game), the Jazz were looked upon as a team that could not win the big games in the playoffs. Behind Malone—who averaged 28 points and 11.2 rebounds per game—the Jazz tried to change that image in 1991-92. They won the Midwest division with a 55-27 mark and advanced through the playoffs to the Western Conference finals. After losing the first two games to the Portland's Trail Blazers, Utah came back to tie the series at two games apiece, only to lose a heartbreaking fifth game, 127-121, in overtime. They then lost the series by losing game six, 105-97.

DREAM TEAM. Malone had tried out for the 1984 U.S. Olympic team while at Louisiana Tech, but he was not chosen. He made up for that disappointment when he was named to the 1992 U.S. Olympic "Dream Team," which dominated the competition in Barcelona, Spain. But, the extra strain of playing during the summer showed during the 1992-93 NBA season, as the Jazz won only 47 games and lost in the first round of the playoffs to the Seattle Supersonics. Malone scored 25.2 points and pulled down 11.5 rebounds per game during the 1993-94 season, and the Jazz once again qualified for the playoffs. Utah reached the Western Conference finals but lost in five games to **Hakeem Olajuwon** and the Houston Rockets.

HARD WORK PAYS OFF. Malone has become one of the hardest working players in the NBA. During the season, he not only plays more minutes than almost any other NBA starter, he also runs wind sprints and lifts weights every morning. In the off-season he continues to workout to stay in shape, running long distances and playing in pick-up basketball games. This training program gives Malone an edge over other players, who often have to foul him when they can't guard him.

(Malone is always among the league leaders in attempted free throws.) He still feels strong when his opponent becomes tired and, in the Jazz's running style of play, Malone also has developed the speed to beat the man guarding him down court. Malone's competitiveness does get Malone in trouble, as he is always one of the league leaders in technical fouls for bad behavior on the court.

THE FUTURE. Malone owns Malone Enterprises, a trucking company he wants to work in when he retires from basketball. "Basketball is my job," Malone told *Sports Illustrated*, "but this is my love." Malone lives in Salt Lake City, Utah, with his wife and two daughters. He built his mother a new house and calls her before many games. At age 30, Malone should be able to play basketball for some time, something that does not make the rest of the NBA very happy. "When you play the Mailman," opposing forward Larry Smith said, "be ready to bang, be ready to run, be ready to go all night."

WHERE TO WRITE

C/O UTAH JAZZ, FIVE TRIAD CENTER, SUITE 500, SALT LAKE CITY, UT 84180.

DIEGO MARADONA

1961—

Soccer is the most popular sport in the world, and the most popular soccer player in the world is Diego Maradona, star of the national team of Argentina and a professional who has led his team to championships in Argentina, Italy, and Spain. In the 1986 World Cup tournament, won by Argentina, Maradona gave what was perhaps the greatest performance in World Cup history. A national hero in Argentina, Maradona has also earned a reputation for being outspoken and controversial. In what is probably his last international competition, Maradona will lead Argentina into the 1994 World Cup tournament in the United States.

GROWING UP

Diego Armando Maradona was born October 30, 1960, in Lanus, Argentina, a suburb of the Argentine capital of Buenos Aires. He was one of eight children and raised in the poor area of Villa Fiorito, one of the roughest neighborhoods in Buenos Aires. His father, also named Diego, was a factory worker and his mom, Dalma Franco, was a housewife. Though the family was poor, there was always food on the table. His father encouraged him to play soccer, giving him a ball at the age of three. Young Diego practiced all day and slept with the ball at night.

WONDER BOY. Maradona was soon playing for Argentina's best youth team, Los Cebollitos (the Little Onions). His team won 140 straight games and Maradona was given number 10, the same number worn by the great Brazilian star Pele. When he was 10 Maradona put on a spectacular exhibition during the halftime of a professional game. "He walked onto the field and proceeded to juggle his soccer ball for the entire intermission—keeping it in the air by bouncing it off his feet, knees, chest, ankles, head, and shoulders as if it were a balloon and his body a spring breeze. When the two teams returned to the field to resume play, the crowd began chanting to the wonder boy, 'Stay! Stay!'"

TURNS PRO. When he was 15 Maradona signed his first professional contract with the Argentinos Juniors for $400 a month. Two years later he became the youngest-ever member of the Argentine national team, which at the time was preparing to host the 1978 World Cup—the international soccer tournament featuring national teams from countries all over the world. Just before the tournament, coach Cesar Luis Menotti made Maradona the last cut from the team, which went on to win the title. Maradona was so upset that he did not speak to Menotti for six months, but later admitted the coach was correct. "The manager was right," Maradona told the *New York Times Magazine.* "I was too young and inexperienced to cope with the pressures of the World Cup."

Maradona gained more experience in 1979 when he led the Argentine national team to the Junior World Cup title and was named South American Player of the Year. Quickly becoming a national hero, Maradona led his professional team, now the Boca Juniors, to the Argentine national championship

---

SCOREBOARD

MOST VALUABLE PLAYER OF THE 1986 WORLD CUP SOCCER TOURNAMENT, LEADING ARGENTINA TO TITLE.

PLAYED IN 1982 AND 1990 WORLD CUP TOURNAMENTS OR ARGENTINA.

ONE OF HIGHEST PAID PROFESSIONAL PLAYERS OF ALL TIME, HAS LED TEAMS IN ARGENTINA, ITALY, AND SPAIN TO CHAMPIONSHIPS.

THE MOST POPULAR SOCCER PLAYER IN THE WORLD, HE RANKS WITH THE LEGENDARY BRAZILIAN PLAYER PELE AS ONE OF THE GREATEST OF ALL TIME.

during the 1980-81 season. Then, in 1980, Maradona signed a six-year, $12 million contract to play for Barcelona of the Spanish League. This made his fans in Argentina angry because now they wouldn't be able to see him play. The Argentine Football Association made a deal with Maradona, allowing him to play on the 1982 Argentine World Cup team if he agreed not to leave Argentina until after the tournament.

WORLD CUP DISAPPOINTMENT. The 1982 World Cup—held in Spain—was a disaster for Maradona and the Argentine team. Not only was Argentina eliminated by arch-rival Brazil, 3-1, but Maradona was ejected from the game for a rough foul on a Brazilian player. The fans in Spain remembered his bad sportsmanship when he began to play there professionally. He had a hard time winning over Spanish fans, even though he scored twenty-two goals in thirty-six games and led the Barcelona team to the 1983 Spanish Cup. In 1984 Barcelona sold Maradona's contract to Naples of the Italian League for $10.8 million. Maradona was soon the best player in the top-flight Italian League, raising his team from 12th place to eighth to third in just two seasons and finally winning the loyalty of Naples fans.

SUPERSTAR

MVP. Maradona returned to the Argentine national team to play in the 1986 World Cup tournament. It was during this tournament—held in Mexico—that he became an international superstar. In helping Argentina reclaim the Cup it had lost to Italy four years earlier, Maradona scored five goals in a six-game effort to wipe out the memory of his poor play in the 1982 tournament and turned in what some experts call the best performance in World Cup history. He had three assists in a 3-1 win over South Korea, scored his team's only goal in a 1-1 tie with Italy, and then scored both of Argentina's goals in a 2-1 victory over England. "He changed gears like a fantastic sports car," soccer observer Julio Mazei told the *New York Times,* describing Maradona's second goal against England. "It was unbelievable. The ball looked like it was glued to his feet."

In the semifinal game, Maradona scored both of Argentina's goals in a 2-0 victory over Belgium. The stage was set for a dramatic final showdown between Argentina and West Germany for the Cup title. West Germany, aware of what Maradona had already done in the tournament, guarded him closely, which opened up opportunities for his teammates. After a German player fouled Maradona, Jose Luis Brown scored on a free kick, giving Argentina a 1-0 lead. Maradona set up his teammate, Hector Enrique, with a perfect pass and the resulting goal made the score 2-0.

Diego Maradona

West Germany would not quit, however, and soon tied the score at two. Just when it seemed like the title was slipping away, Maradona made a play that will live in history: Guarded closely by Karlheinz Foerster, Maradona somehow threaded the needle with a pass through four German defenders, hitting his teammate Jorge Burruchaga on the dead run. Burruchaga scored and Argentina won its second World Cup in its last three tries. When it came time to give out the tournament's Most Valuable Player award, there was no doubt that it could go to only one player, Diego Maradona.

After the World Cup victory Maradona returned to Naples, leading his club to its first Italian League championship in 1987, and its first European title two years later. But Maradona was slowed down by several injuries. His coach and Naples fans became unhappy, claiming he was faking his injuries. When fans at one game threw things at his wife and manager, Maradona asked to be traded. Naples, realizing that

WORLD CUP

The World Cup is the international championship of soccer. Held every four years since 1930 (except during World War II), the tournament unites the national teams of countries throughout the world. Only six countries have ever won the World Cup—Argentina, Brazil, England, Italy, Uruguay, and West Germany. Brazil, Italy, and West Germany each have won the World Cup three times.

he was the best player in the world, refused, and in the 1989-90 season Maradona led his team to its second Italian League title in four years.

WORLD CUP III. Maradona returned to the Argentine national team for the 1990 World Cup in Italy. Bothered by a painful ingrown toenail, he had a difficult time trying to match his 1986 performance. Teams did everything to stop Maradona, including fouling him repeatedly. Argentina lost its first game, 1-0, to Cameroon, in one of the biggest upsets of all time. Despite the loss, Argentina was able to advance to the tournament's second round, where they faced arch-rival Brazil. The Brazilians outplayed Argentina, but another beautiful pass by Maradona led to the only goal of a 1-0 Argentine victory. Argentina then defeated Yugoslavia, 3-2, to set up a semifinal showdown with host country Italy.

Although the game against Italy was difficult emotionally for Maradona (because he had played on their team) that didn't stop him from doing his best. With Italy leading the game 1-0, Maradona once again worked his magic, setting up teammate Claudio Caniggia, who headed the ball past the Italian goalie. The game remained tied throughout regulation time and a 30-minute overtime period. In the World Cup soccer tournament the rules say games still tied in this situation will be settled in this way: Each team takes five penalty shots and the team that scores most, wins. (During a penalty shot, the goalie is alone in defending his team's goal. He must try to stop one player, who can take one shot from the top of the penalty box. The player shooting may not move the ball and the goalie cannot move until the ball is kicked.) Argentina scored on four of its kicks (the last by Maradona) against only three by Italy, and were awarded the win in one of the most exciting games in World Cup history. Maradona ran out of magic in the finals against West Germany, a team that used a tight defense to keep him off the scoreboard, and defeated Argentina, 1-0.

ALL-AROUND PLAYER. Maradona has become a star because of his great all-around game. A consistent scorer, he is known for his ability to dribble the ball, fake out opponents, and then find a teammate with a beautiful pass, or drill the ball past the goalie himself. A small man at five-feet-five inches and 165 pounds, Maradona uses his size to his advantage, with quick bursts of speed to avoid defenders. He is most often compared to **Wayne Gretzky** and **Magic Johnson** (see entries).

Throughout his career Maradona has been very outspoken and made many mistakes. In April 1991 he tested positive for cocaine after an Italian League game and was suspended for 15 months. One month later he was arrested while trying to buy cocaine. "I [messed] up," he told the *Washington Post.* Maradona has always been controversial, but says he won't change. "They can say what they want about me," he told *People.* "[But] I won't change. Remember, it's the players who bring 90,000 people to the stadium. I am Maradona, who makes goals, who makes mistakes. I can take it all, I have shoulders big enough for everybody."

COMEBACK. In the summer of 1993, Maradona, showing only flashes of his former brilliant play, announced his retirement from soccer. The Argentine national team barely missed their star, winning 33 straight games and two South American championships following the World Cup. But when the team lost to Columbia 5-0 in Buenos Aires, the Argentine team faced elimination from competing in the 1994 World Cup. "I cried a lot that day—a lot," Maradona, who had watched the game from the stands, told the *Washington Post.* "It was like they were touching my flag. My dad came into my bedroom, my wife, my daughters, and couldn't make me stop crying. I tried to explain to my girls that their father had given blood, ankle, knee, guts, everything to that jersey that had lost 5-0 that day, and that I needed to come back."

Maradona lost 30 pounds, got in shape, and began playing again in the Argentine soccer leagues. Argentina defeated Australia in a two-game series in order to qualify for the World Cup, and Maradona seemed to inspire his teammates. He will play for Argentina in the 1994 World Cup, to be held in the

United States. "I think we will be the big surprise in the next World Cup," Maradona told the *Washington Post*. "God willing, we will win. We have the most powerful offense of any team." Later, he told the *Washington Post:* "I'll probably retire after the World Cup—if my heart lets me."

OFF THE FIELD. In 1989 Maradona married his high school sweetheart, Claudia Villafane, in what was called the social event of the year in Argentina. The wedding was so big that Maradona rented a boxing arena to hold the reception. He and his wife have two daughters and live in Buenos Aires. Maradona is the spokesperson for many products in Italy and Argentina and is known as the "Michael Jordan of Soccer." When he retires from the game, Maradona hopes to coach the Argentine national team. He also wants to teach soccer to children, in an effort to give something back to the sport that has given him so much. "Soccer gave me everything," Maradona told the *Washington Post*. "It gave me the chance to do what I like, have fun, get paid a lot and make happy the people I love. Every morning that I get up, I should light a candle to the soccer ball."

WHERE TO WRITE

C/O INTERNATIONAL FEDERATION OF ASSOCIATION FOOTBALL (FIFA), HITZIGWEG, POSTFACH 85, CH-8030, ZURICH, SWITZERLAND

DAN MARINO

1961—

Dan Marino, blessed with a strong arm and the ability to throw the ball accurately in a split-second, has shattered numerous National Football League (NFL) records and is threatening to break many more. Marino has passed for more yards (5,084) and touchdowns (48) in a single season than any quarterback in history and may soon hold the career records in these categories. A remarkably sturdy quarterback, Marino started 145 straight games before an injury sidelined him in 1993. A career that started with playing catch with his dad has now led Marino to a place with the all-time greats.

Dan Marino "plays the position [quarterback] as well as anybody this league has ever seen."

GROWING UP

Daniel Constantine Marino, Jr., was born September 15, 1961, in Pittsburgh, Pennsylvania. The oldest of three children, and the only son, of Dan Marino, Sr., and Veronica Marino, he grew up in an area of the United States famous for producing great quarterbacks. Hall-of-Famers Johnny Unitas and Joe Namath grew up nearby, as did **Jim Kelly** (see entry) of the Buffalo Bills. Marino was raised in Pittsburgh's South Oakland area, known for its strong Italian and Irish cultural roots, and credits his strong arm to his dad, who came home from his newspaper delivery job to play catch with his son. "The biggest thing in my early development is that my dad had a job where he could be home in the afternoon, waiting for me to get out of school," Marino told *Inside Sports*. "Then we would throw to each other the rest of the day ... he's the best coach I ever had."

His dad was Marino's official coach at St. Regis, a Catholic school right across the street from his house. Marino became the school's quarterback, but was almost kicked off the team because his grades were so bad. "Danny could recall everything from a bubble-gum card, but couldn't remember when the Civil War started," his father told *Sports Illustrated.* After his dad told him he wouldn't be allowed to play football unless he studied harder, Marino hit the books. He brought his grades up just enough to be accepted to Central High School, one of the best schools for athletics in the city.

DOUBLE THREAT. Marino was a multi-sport star in high school, playing both baseball and football. A pitcher in baseball, he earned a 25-1 record during his career and threw the ball 92 miles-an-hour. He also batted .550 in his senior year. It was on the football field, however, that Marino received the most attention, playing quarterback as well as punting and placekicking. Several colleges wanted Marino to play football for them when he graduated from high school (where he carried a B average). He was also drafted by the Kansas City Royals major-league baseball team in 1979, and considered playing both sports. He finally decided to accept a scholarship to play with the University of Pittsburgh, four blocks from his home. "I have strong personal and family ties to the city of Pittsburgh," Marino told the press conference announcing his decision to attend Pittsburgh.

PANTHER PASSER. Marino became the Panthers starting quarterback midway through his freshman season (1979) when

Dan Marino

starter, Rick Trocano, was injured. In his first season Marino completed 130 of 222 passes for 1,680 yards and ten touchdowns. The team finished 11-1 and defeated the Arizona Wildcats 16-10 in the Fiesta Bowl. Marino suffered a knee injury during the season, missing three games, and was forced to have surgery in the off-season. He would have knee surgery five more times during his career, although he rarely missed any games because of the injury.

Continuing to improve in his second season (1980), Marino led the team once again to an 11-1 record and a Gator Bowl victory. He became a star in his junior year, passing for 2,876 yards and 37 touchdowns. He earned All-American honors and finished fourth in the voting for the Heisman Trophy, awarded annually to the best college football player in the United States. The Panthers finished 11-1 and Marino finished off a great season by winning the Most Valuable Player award in the Sugar Bowl, throwing for 261 yards and three touchdowns—one the game-winner, with 35 seconds left, in a 24-20 victory over the University of Georgia.

SENIOR SLUMP. Entering his senior season (1982), Marino was the favorite to win the Heisman Trophy and Pittsburgh was considered the best team in the country. But Marino and the team could not live up to the hype. They finished 9-3 and lost the Cotton Bowl to Southern Methodist University, 7-3. Marino's statistics were also down as he passed for 2,432 yards but only 17 touchdowns and was booed by Pittsburgh fans. Marino learned a valuable lesson from this disappointing season. "I think it helped me on and off the field," he told the *New York Times*. "The thing I learned ... was that you can't get down to the point where you can't perform or get so overconfident that you don't think you can do any wrong."

When he graduated from Pittsburgh with a degree in communications, Marino held school career records for passing yards (8,597), passes attempted and completed (693 of 1,204), touchdown passes (79), and total offense (8,290 yards passing and running). He finished his college career ranked fifth in passing yards, fourth in completions, and fourth in touchdown passes in National Collegiate Athletic Association (NCAA) history. Marino became only the fourth player (running back Tony Dorsett, linebacker Hugh Green, and offensive lineman Bill Fralic were the others) to have his Panthers jersey retired.

DOLPHIN DRAFTEE. Marino expected to be one of the top draft picks in the 1983 NFL draft, but because of doubts caused by his senior season, 26 players and five quarterbacks were picked ahead of him in what became known as the "Quarterback Draft." Though disappointed at being drafted lower than expected, Marino was happy to be signed with the Miami Dolphins, who had played in the Super Bowl the season before. He also looked forward to playing for Don Shula, one of the most successful coaches of all time.

In his first season, Marino started out as the backup to David Woodley, the quarterback who had led the Dolphins to the Super Bowl. When coach Shula removed Woodley because of his weak play, Marino was made the starter. He responded to the challenge, playing well enough to be named the NFL's Rookie of the Year and becoming the first rookie quarterback to be named a starter in the Pro Bowl (all-star game). He played only 10 games, but passed for 2,210 yards and 20 touchdowns and was the top-rated passer in the American Football Conference (AFC). He suffered a knee injury and missed the last two games of the regular season, but came back for the playoffs. (These would be the last games Marino would miss because of injury until the 1993 season.) Though the Dolphins lost, 27-20, Marino passed for 193 yards and two touchdowns.

SUPERSTAR

RECORD SMASHER. In his second year (1984), Marino had what was perhaps the best season a quarterback ever had. Coach Shula, realizing that Marino had a strong arm and a lightning quick release, changed the Dolphins offensive system (long based on running the football) and allowed his young quarterback to pass. Marino, who spent hours learning the Dolphins playbook and studying opposing defenses, set NFL records with 5,084 yards, 362 completions, and 48 touchdowns. "His feats this season have left NFL coaches and players gasping in amazement," reported *Newsday.* Marino was quick to credit his offensive line, which kept him from being tackled, and his speedy receivers, Mark Clayton and Mark Duper (known as the "Marks Brothers"), for his success.

SUPER BOWL. The Dolphins finished with an AFC best 14-2 record and defeated the Seattle Seahawks, 31-10, in the first round of the playoffs. In the AFC championship game, Marino set championship game records by throwing for 421 yards and four touchdowns in the Dolphins 45-28 win over the Pittsburgh Steelers. This win set up a classic Super Bowl match-up with the San Francisco 49ers and **Joe Montana** (see entry). Montana won the game, 38-16, along with the game's Most Valuable Player trophy. The 49ers stopped the Dolphins high-powered passing attack by using five defensive backs—a strategy that is common today. Marino threw for 318 yards, one touchdown, and two interceptions in his only Super Bowl appearance.

PASSING YARDAGE LEADERS

Year	Single Season	Yards
1984	Dan Marino	5,084
1981	Dan Fouts	4,802
1986	Dan Marino	4,746

Year	Career	Yards
1984	Fran Tarkenton	47,003
1981	Dan Fouts	43,040
1986	Dan Marino	40,720

In 1985 the Dolphins finished 12-4, with their biggest win coming against the Chicago Bears, 38-24—the only game the Bears would lose all year. Marino led the NFL in yards (4,137), completions (336), and touchdowns (30), but the season ended in disappointment when the Dolphins were upset in the AFC championship game, 31-14, by the New England Patriots. The following season (1986), the Dolphins fell to 8-8 and missed the playoffs even though Marino led the NFL with 4,746 yards passing (third highest total in history) and 44 touchdown passes (second highest in history). Marino threw at least one touchdown in every game during the season and had a career high of six in one game against the New York Jets.

INDIVIDUAL SUCCESS. Miami missed the playoffs for the next three seasons, hurt by a poor defense. Even though Marino continued to shine, the Dolphins had difficulty scoring enough points to keep up with the other teams. In 1988 Marino threw for an NFL leading 4,434 yards and 28 touchdowns. On October 23, he threw for 521 yards against the New York Jets—the second-highest single-game total in NFL history at that time. The Dolphins lost the game, 44-30, with Marino throwing five interceptions. He missed his fifth 4,000-yard passing season in 1989 by just 3 yards.

In 1990 Miami returned to the playoffs, finishing 12-4. Marino threw for 3,563 yards (fourth in the NFL) and 21 touchdowns, the second lowest of his career. He became only the eleventh quarterback to pass for over 30,000 yards in his career during the season, and did it in fewer games (114) than any player in NFL history. Miami won their first playoff game, 17-16, over the Kansas City Chiefs, before losing in a high-scoring shootout against the Buffalo Bills, 44-34. Marino passed for 323 yards and three touchdowns in the game.

The Dolphins were on a downslide in 1991, allowing too many points and missing the playoffs. Marino finished second in the NFL with 3,970 passing yards and fourth with 25 touchdown passes. By throwing for 3,000 yards, Marino became the first quarterback ever to pass for that many yards in eight seasons, and his touchdown total made him the first quarterback ever to throw for over 20 touchdowns in nine separate seasons.

SUPER CLOSE. Miami tied for the AFC Eastern division title in 1992 with an 11-5 record. Marino broke his own record by passing for over 4,000 yards for the fifth time (4,116) and tied the record for most times leading the NFL in passing yardage (five, tied with Washington Redskins legend Sonny Jurgenson). Miami beat the San Diego Chargers, 31-0, in the first round of the playoffs, but lost in the AFC championship, 29-10, to the Buffalo Bills. Marino completed only 22 of 45 passes for 268 yards in the game and threw two costly interceptions.

The Dolphins were off to a great start in 1993, until Marino injured his achilles tendon in a game against the Cleveland Browns on October 10. The injury broke Marino's string of 145 straight starts and surgery was needed to correct the problem. He missed the rest of the season and the Dolphins, showing the effects of losing their leader, failed to make the playoffs after seeming like a sure thing earlier in the season. The surgery on Marino's heel was successful, and he is expected to be fully recovered for the 1994 season.

OFF THE FIELD. Marino lives in Fort Lauderdale, Florida, with his wife Claire and their four children, Daniel, Michael, Joseph, and Alexandra. An outstanding golfer, Marino teamed with professional Dan Pohl to win the AT&T Pebble Beach National ProAm in February 1988. He worked as a commentator for World League of American Football games and plays himself in the movie, *Ace*

MARINO'S RECORDS

Dan Marino holds 18 NFL records and is tied for seven others. Listed below are his most impressive statistics.

Most passing attempts:
5,604 (third).

Most pass completions:
3,219 (third).

Most passing yards:
40,720 (third).

Most touchdown passes:
298 (second).

Most seasons leading NFL in pass attempts: 4 (tied for first).

Most seasons leading NFL in pass completions: 5 (tied for first).

Most seasons leading NFL in passing yards: 5 (tied for first).

Most seasons with 20 or more touchdown passes: 10 (first).

Most 4,000 yard passing seasons: 5 (first).

Most 3,000 yard passing seasons: 9 (first).

Most passing yards in a season: 5,084 (first).

Most pass completions in a season: 377 (second).

Most touchdowns in a season: 48 (first).

Ventura: Pet Detective. He established the Dan Marino Foundation, which supports many South Florida charities, and sponsors an annual golf tournament to benefit Leukemia research. Perhaps his greatest honor came in 1990 when the neighborhood field, where he'd started playing ball as a kid, was renamed Dan Marino Field.

WHERE TO WRITE

C/O MIAMI DOLPHINS, JOE ROBBIE STADIUM,

2269 N.W. 199TH ST., MIAMI, FL 33056.

MARK MESSIER

1961—

To understand how Mark Messier plays hockey, one need only hear his two nicknames: "Moose" and "The Terminator." With a rare combination of power and speed, Messier is one of the most complete players in hockey. Between 1979 and 1991, Messier did it all for the Edmonton Oilers. Skating side by side with **Wayne Gretzky** (see entry), he helped lead the club to four Stanley Cup championships in five seasons between 1984 and 1988. Then, after Gretzky was traded to the Los Angeles Kings, Messier and the Oilers captured another Stanley Cup in 1990. He was named the National Hockey League's (NHL) Most Valuable Player (MVP) that season. In the 1991-92 season Messier won a second MVP award, this time after leading the New York Rangers to the league's best record.

GROWING UP

Messier was born January 18, 1961, in Edmonton, Alberta, Canada, and grew up in Portland, Oregon. "Mark was born for hockey," his brother Paul Messier told the *Washington Post*. "He was big and strong and very, very tough. Actually, he was a little bit mean. Not toward his family. But he could get mad

"When he gets mad, it's like he's in another world. He'll look at you with those big eyes and they'll be going around in circles."—former New York Ranger Barry Beck

when he was a kid. He always played with older kids, and he'd lose his temper. When he was 17, he already was 190 pounds. He was dominating the league."

QUESTION MARK. At one time, Messier was thought to have a future in hockey only as a tough guy. Playing for his father at his first junior training camp, the 15-year-old Messier found a copy of the team's roster in the family dining room. His brother was listed as the star of the team. But next to Mark's name were three big question marks. "Back then, Mark was far from the most talented player on the team," his father, Doug, recalled in *Newsday*. "But he recognized what it takes to win—hard work, hustle, support for your teammates. Even as a teenager he had a bundle of heart [determination]. He was determined to make it in hockey and nothing was going to stop him."

TURNS PRO. When Messier was just 17, his father arranged a tryout with the Indianapolis Racers of the World Hockey Association (WHA). (The World Hockey Association was a professional league formed to compete with the more established NHL.) Mark made the team, but it soon went out of business. He then joined the Cincinnati Stingers of the WHA, scoring just one goal in 47 games.

SUPERSTAR

BECOMES AN OILER. Despite his limited record, Messier was noticed. He caught the eye of Glen Sather, general manager of the NHL's Edmonton Oilers. When the WHA went out of business in 1979, Sather used a second-round pick to draft the 18-year-old Messier, who was then a virtual unknown. The teenager was thrilled to be playing in his home town.

In his first few years in Edmonton, Messier exceeded all expectations. He could skate, he could fight, he could shoot the puck, and he quickly learned how to score. Messier's goal-scoring improved from 12 in 1979-80, to 23 in 1980-81, to 50 in 1981-82. He was named to the NHL All-Star team for the first time in 1981-82. (Through the 1992-93 season, he has played in nine All-Star games.)

By the early 1980s, the Oilers had become the best young team in hockey. In the 1982-83 season they advanced all the way to the Stanley Cup finals, but they lost to the New York Islanders, who were completing a four-year streak of Cup wins. Gretzky was the Oilers's superstar, but Messier was their hard-nosed leader. The 1983 playoffs—in which Messier scored 15 goals in 15 games—showed that he and the Oilers were on the brink of greatness.

DYNASTY. The next season, the Oilers achieved their goal. They earned the NHL's best regular-season record (winning 57 games and losing just 18, and tying five) and beat the Islanders to win the Stanley Cup. Messier's playoff scoring was down—just eight goals in 19 games—but he did an excellent job of defending Islanders's star Bryan Trottier in the final round. For his hard work, Messier was awarded the Conn Smythe Trophy as the playoff's MVP. In addition, he helped lead Canada to victory in the international Canada Cup tournament that summer.

Thus began a terrific string of success for the Oilers and for Messier. Including 1984, the club won the title four times in five years. And except for 1984-85, when he missed half the season with an injury, Messier was an All-Star each of those years. Messier averaged 35 goals and 100 points (goals, plus assists) per season during this streak. But his statistics were not the most important thing to him, as Wayne Gretzky explained to *Sports Illustrated*. "The measure of Mark's game is not in goals and assists," Gretzky said. "The statistic he cares about is number of Stanley Cups won."

GRETZKY TRADED. In 1988 Messier's character was tested. Gretzky, his fabulous teammate and best friend, was traded to

Mark Messier

the Los Angeles Kings. Messier replaced Gretzky as captain of the Oilers and faced the burden of trying to make up for the loss of his exceptional teammate. His own point totals slipped a bit, and the Oilers were knocked out in the second round of the playoffs. Coach John Muckler described the problems Messier had to *USA Today*: "When Wayne went to L.A., Mark didn't know what he should do," Muckler said. "Mark thought he had to be Wayne Gretzky. He had to learn just to be himself, to play within himself."

By the following season (1989-90), Messier had adjusted to the loss of Gretzky. He had his best season as a pro, scoring 45 goals and 129 points. Messier won the Hart Memorial Trophy as the NHL's Most Valuable Player and led the Oilers to their fifth Stanley Cup. Despite a sore hand that limited his shooting ability, Messier starred in the playoffs. His 31 points tied for the most in that season's playoffs, and made him the second-leading post-season scorer (behind Gretzky) in league history. Messier also did a superb job defensively, covering Boston Bruins's star forward Craig Janney and shutting him out in the final round.

In many ways, this was the most satisfying championship for Messier. But it was also the last. Edmonton Oilers's owner Peter Pocklington was trying to save money by selling his high-priced players—first Gretzky, then defenseman Paul Coffey, then forward Jari Kurri. Messier knew he'd have to leave the team soon. He played one more season with the Oilers, 1990-91, during which an injured left knee limited him to only 12 goals in 33 games.

BECOMES A RANGER. On October 4, 1991, the Oilers traded Messier to the New York Rangers. In return, the Oilers received $5 million and three players—center Bernie Nicholls and forwards Louie DeBrusk and Steven Rice. Almost immediately, the Rangers signed Messier to a five-year, $13 million contract. Rangers's coach Roger Neilson described his feelings about Messier at a news conference announcing the trade. "Mark has obvious skills as a player," he said. "But as a person everyone considers him a leader. The Rangers haven't had much playoff success. Mark knows how to win and we are looking for that leadership."

Messier's impact as a member of the Rangers was immediate. He killed penalties (when the Rangers had a player in the penalty box) and toiled on the power-play unit (when the other team had a player in the penalty box). When the Rangers required a big goal, he was always there. Messier was named the club's on-ice captain, and organized meetings and workshops for his teammates. "He makes you play at a higher level," teammate Tony Amonte told *Sports Illustrated*, describing Messier's effect on the Rangers. "He pushes me to give more than I ever could."

THE "BIG APPLE." Messier also became an instant celebrity in New York. Unlike most athletes, who settle in the suburbs, the hockey star lived in Manhattan. He was romantically linked to pop music star Madonna at one point and was a guest on David Letterman's television show. Messier also made many commercials and public appearances. After 12 seasons in small, faraway Edmonton, Messier found happiness in the "Big Apple." "I made the right choice to come to New York," said Messier, to the *New York Daily News*. "It's more fun than I ever thought it would be. I feel rejuvenated [refreshed] and I'm having more fun than I've had in a long time."

SUCCESS AND DISAPPOINTMENT. The New York fans loved Messier, and the Rangers sold out every home game at Madison Square Garden during the 1991-92 season. The club was reborn. Messier's talent and leadership helped the Rangers roll up a 50-25-3 record, the best in the NHL, and Messier won the Hart Memorial Trophy as the league's Most Valuable Player for a second time. "The most important thing is, the guys have responded," Messier commented in the *St. Louis Pioneer Press*. "I try to get it across what it will be like when we do win. Having been there before, I know how exciting it is. I'm always looking at the big picture."

In the end, the Rangers did not reach their goal. After a first-round playoff victory over the New Jersey Devils, the Rangers were defeated by the eventual Stanley Cup champion Pittsburgh Penguins. It was a disappointing ending to a great season for New York. The 1992-93 season brought even more disappointment to Messier and the Rangers. The team fell from an NHL-best 105 points in 1991-92 to 79 points, last in their division. Messier, bothered by nagging injuries and a running feud with coach Roger Neilson, finished with 25 goals and 91 points. Reluctant to rest, Messier played at less than full effectiveness most of the season.

At the end of the 1992-93 season Coach Neilson was fired and replaced by Mike Keenan, a proven winner who had coached successful teams with both the Philadelphia Flyers and the Chicago Black Hawks. The Rangers returned to the top of the NHL, once again earning the league's best record. Messier turned in a solid season, scoring 26 goals, adding 58 assists, and providing experience and leadership. New York entered the NHL playoffs as the team to beat for the Stanley Cup.

THE FUTURE. At the banquet announcing his second Most Valuable Player award, Messier said he planned to play for the Rangers for another ten seasons. "Winning breeds enthusiasm and positiveness and confidence," Messier told the *New York Daily News*. "Losing breeds selfishness and taking care of No. 1 and separation among the team. And when you have that, you can never win. I'm in New York to win."

WHERE TO WRITE

C/O NEW YORK RANGERS, MADISON SQUARE GARDEN, FOUR PENNSYLVANIA PLAZA, NEW YORK, NY 10001.

SHANNON MILLER

1977—

When people talk about Shannon Miller, they usually say she's cute. At four-feet-ten inches and 86 pounds, she may look fragile, but looks can be deceiving. A fierce and determined competitor, Miller made history in 1992 by winning five Olympic gymnastics medals—the most ever won by an American. In 1993 she reached the top of her sport, winning the 1993 and 1994 World Gymnastics Championships women's all-around gold medal. Tough on the inside, Miller had to overcome her shyness in order to become the best gymnast in the world.

"Shannon is the hardest worker ... and always has been."—Shannon Miller's coach, Steve Nunno

GROWING UP

Shannon Miller was born March 10, 1977, in Rolla, Missouri, but has lived her whole life in Edmond, Oklahoma. Her dad, Ron, is a college professor, and her mom, Claudia, is the vice president of a bank. Shannon began gymnastics when she was five, after receiving a special Christmas present in 1982. "My parents bought my sister and me a trampoline for Christmas," she recalled in *Sports Illustrated for Kids*. "When we started bouncing on it and trying flips, they [her parents] freaked out.

They thought we would get hurt. So they signed us up for gymnastics classes."

SHYNESS. When she began gymnastics, Miller's biggest problem was overcoming her shyness—a problem she still has today. "Shannon's always's had the talent.... She's had to overcome her shyness and learn to play to a crowd," her balance beam coach, Peggy Liddick, commented in the *Sporting News*. Her timidness hurt her in competitions, where she is judged on both her ability to complete technical maneuvers as well as entertain. Miller, a perfectionist, often became frustrated when she didn't do a routine perfectly. Many times she broke into tears at the end of an imperfect performance.

GOES FAR AWAY TO MEET COACH. When she was nine, Miller trained for two weeks at a gymnastics camp in what was then the Soviet Union. It was there that her current coach, Steve Nunno, first noticed her. "Shannon was trying so hard and getting extremely frustrated," he observed in the *Sporting News*. "I felt, There's a kid I can help if I can channel that frustration into a positive energy." Nunno, also from Oklahoma, began training Miller at his Oklahoma City gym.

It wasn't long before Miller began to attract attention. In 1988 she participated in the Junior Pan American Games in Ponce, Puerto Rico, featuring young athletes from North and South America. She finished second in the all-around and third in the balance beam. In 1989 she traveled to Yokohama, Japan, for the International Junior Gymnastics Competition, finishing sixth in the all-around competition. At the U.S. Olympic Festival in 1989, Miller won the uneven bars competition and finished third in the all-around event. She made the senior U.S. national team for the first time in 1990 at the age of 13.

WORLD CHAMPIONSHIPS. A year later Miller qualified for the U.S. team at the World Gymnastics Championships in Indianapolis, Indiana. In her first competition against the world's best gymnasts, Miller helped the United States win the silver medal in team competition and tied for a silver medal in the uneven bars. The all-around competition was won by Kim Zmeskal of the United States, who became the first American to win a world championship.

INJURED. In March 1992 Miller's Olympic dream and her career were almost ended when she fell and dislocated her elbow. She had a choice of wearing a cast for six weeks and letting the injury heal naturally (which would force her to miss the Olympics), or having surgery to fix the problem. Miller, her parents, and her coaches chose surgery. Through hard work and therapy she was ready to compete at the U.S. Gymnastics Championships just one month after the surgery. Amazingly, she won the balance beam competition and finished third in the vault.

TWISTS AND TURNS

A gymnastics competition is made up of four events, the balance beam, floor exercise, uneven bars, and vault. In the balance beam competition, a gymnast must do flips, spins, and other complicated moves on a beam only four inches wide. During the floor exercise, gymnasts combine difficult twisting jumps with beautiful dance movements. In the most dangerous event, the uneven bars, gymnasts swing quickly, moving from bar to bar in quick maneuvers. Finally, in the vault, gymnasts run and jump off a springboard, twist and turn in the air, touch what is known as the horse, and then land. Miller's two favorite events are the balance beam and the uneven bars.

FIERCE COMPETITION. Miller was expected to finish second to Zmeskal at the U.S. Olympic Gymnastics Trials held in June 1992. That prediction seemed correct when in the first event, the vault, Zmeskal won with a perfect score of 10. But then Zmeskal started to struggle. Her hand slipped on the uneven bars and she stumbled twice on the balance beam. Miller, on the other hand, performed superbly. When the final scores were added up, Miller had upset Zmeskal and taken first place at the trials. "Two months ago, she's in a hospital facing surgery, and asking me if she'll be ready," coach Nunno confided to the *Sporting News.* "It's unbelievable that she won."

SUPERSTAR

FIVE MEDALS. At the 1992 Olympics, held in Barcelona, Spain, the U.S. women's gymnastics team was, as Nunno told

Shannon Miller

the *Sporting News,* "without a doubt the strongest team ever assembled in American gymnastics." Both Miller and Zmeskal qualified for the team, and their rivalry continued throughout the Olympics. Both had fought through injuries (Miller to her elbow and Zmeskal to her wrist), to reach the top of their sport. In addition to the personal rivalry, their coaches, Nunno and Bela Karolyi, were also competing to be the U.S. Olympic women's gymnastics team coach—a competition won by Karolyi. Miller said she wasn't concerned about her rivalry with Zmeskal. "[The Olympics are] about each of us going out there and doing our best, not beating one another," she told the *Sporting News.*

Miller's main challenge in the all-around competition came not from Zmeskal, but from Tatyana Gutsu of the Unified Team (formerly the Soviet Union). Miller took the lead over Gutsu in the final event with a near-perfect vault, receiving perfect scores of ten from three judges. Gutsu needed to score 9.950 or higher to win the gold medal. She scored exactly that, barely edging out Miller to win the competition. Miller's second-place finish was the highest all-around finish by an American gymnast in an Olympics where all countries competed. (See Mary Lou Retton box.) Zmeskal finished tenth in the competition after a fall during the uneven bars competition.

HIGH EXPECTATIONS. Miller was the only American to qualify for the Olympic finals in all four individual events. She won a silver medal in the balance beam, and bronze medals in the uneven bars and the floor exercise. She added a third bronze medal when the U.S. team finished third in the team competition. Altogether Miller won five Olympic medals, the most ever earned by an American gymnast. "Other people may not have had high expectations for me," she admitted in *Sports Illustrated,* "but I had high expectations for myself."

"It was everything I dreamed of and more," Miller told *Sports Illustrated,* describing her Olympic experience. "It was fun getting there and fun being there." After her Olympic success, Miller was the crowd favorite in a tour of Olympic gymnastic stars. She tried not to let the attention go to her head. "I still go to public school," she explained in *Sports Illustrated.* "I still work out, my coach still yells at me in the gym. My brother and sister still pick on me, and I still pick on them. Many of my friends have known me since I was in fifth grade, and they still treat me the same."

WORLD CHAMP. Miller entered the 1993 world championships in a strange position—the favorite. "It was expected that we'd win," Nunno told *Sports Illustrated.* "If anybody beat Shannon, she was going to beat herself." Miller had improved since the Olympics, adding even more difficult moves to her performances. And she no longer let her shyness bother her, showing confidence during her routines and impressing both the crowd and the judges.

In 1993 Miller became the top female gymnast in the world, winning the gold medal in the all-around competition at the World Gymnastics Championships. In her final event of the competition—the vault—Miller had to make a tough choice. She could try an extremely difficult vault which could earn more points, or she could go for an easier vault worth fewer points, and try to perform it perfectly. She chose the easier vault and twice completed it beautifully. Miller took the overall lead.

Now she had to wait. Teammate Dominique Dawes might have passed Miller if she had done well on the vault, but she stumbled on both tries. The last competitor, Gina Gogean of Romania, still had a chance to win, but came up a few points short in the floor exercise. Miller had just enough overall points to win the all-around championship. "I didn't

MARY LOU RETTON

At the 1984 Summer Olympics in Los Angeles, California, Mary Lou Retton became the only American to ever win the Olympic all-around gymnastics gold medal. In a close competition, Retton edged out Ecaterina Szabo of Romania to win the gold. Unfortunately for Retton, the Soviet Union and most of its allies did not participate in the 1984 Olympics, making her accomplishment less impressive than it might have been.

Shannon Miller waves to the audience after receiving one of her 1992 Olympic silver medals in Barcelona.

worry about the score," she admitted to *Sports Illustrated* after watching Gogean compete. "I had done my job, and wherever I finished I would be happy."

Miller was again the only American to qualify for the finals in all four individual events. Despite an upset stomach, she won the gold medal in the uneven bars. The next day, still not fully recovered, she won the gold in the floor exercise. Miller became only the second American in history (the other being Zmeskal) to win the World Champion title. She now had five World Championship medals, more than any other American gymnast, male or female, in history. Later in 1993 Miller was given the Master of Sport award, one of the highest honors in gymnastics, and was a finalist for the Sullivan Award, given annually to the top amateur (unpaid) athlete in the United States. Miller repeated as the all-around champion at the 1994 World Gymnastics Championships and also won a gold medal in the balance beam. The two world championship medals increased her American record total to seven.

HARD WORK. Miller works hard in the gym and at school. During her workouts—eight hours a day, six days a week—Miller has been described as all business. "Shannon is the hardest worker in my gym," Nunno told the *Sporting News,* "and always has been." She is able to block out crowd noise and other distractions through steady concentration. "In gymnastics, I'm so focused on what I'm doing that I'm not even aware of the audience until afterward," she explained in *Sports Illustrated for Kids.*

Miller attends Edmond North High School and entered her senior year in 1993. She is a 4.0 student and a member of both the Oklahoma Honor Society and National Honor Society. Her favorite subject is math. When Miller travels she has a tutor with her. "I don't have much time for homework, with all the training," she told *Sports Illustrated,* "but somehow I make the time. I've learned through gymnastics that you can't wait until the last minute. I don't know if I'd be making straight A's if it weren't for the discipline I got from gymnastics."

OFF THE MAT. Miller still lives in Edmond with her parents. Her hobbies are swimming, shopping, playing with her dog Dusty, and watching television. Quiet and shy, Miller personally answers all of her fan mail. After her Olympic performance she did commercials for the game Trivial Pursuit. In 1992 she received the Sports Headliner of the Year award. Miller hopes to return to the Olympics in 1996 in Atlanta, Georgia, and continues to compete because she enjoys it. "It's hard to think of gymnastics as fun when you're working out eight hours a day," she explained in *Sports Illustrated for Kids.* "But when you get to a competition, you know you're having fun. I work hard here [in the gym] because that's where I want to be."

WHERE TO WRITE

C/O U.S. GYMNASTICS FEDERATION, PAN AMERICAN PLAZA, SUITE 300, 201 S. CAPITOL AVE., INDIANAPOLIS, IN 46225.

TOMMY MOE

1970—

> *"I drive fast, I bike fast, I live fast. You're a downhill racer because you like doing stuff fast."*— *Tommy Moe*

Tommy Moe was a two-time loser as a teenager. Twice he was caught smoking marijuana and kicked off ski teams. In order to help his son, his dad forced Moe to work long hours at back-breaking work. Though it was hard at the time, Moe now says it was the best thing that ever happened to him. When he stood at the top of the mountain before the Olympic men's downhill ski race, he wanted to travel as fast as he could to reach his dad at the bottom of the slope.

GROWING UP

Thomas Sven Moe was born February 14, 1970, in Missoula, Montana. His father, Tom, Sr., was a steel contractor. His ancestors were from Norway and his great-great-grandfather had come to the United States in the 1800s. Moe still has 12 relatives in Oslo, the capital of Norway. He has a brother and a sister, and when their parents divorced, his sister went to live with their mom, while Moe and his brother lived with his father's mother, Valerie Tomlinson.

LEARNS TO SKI. Moe's father was a tough, no-nonsense man who had been raised in the copper-mining town of Anaconda,

Montana. Tommy, Sr., had worked as a ski patrolman at a resort and was an excellent kayaker (a kayak is a one-person boat), so good that a part of Montana's Swan River is named Moe Hole because he was the first to navigate a kayak through it. It was his father who introduced Moe to skiing. "I first remember snowplowing with him ... when I was maybe three, but I had probably been doing it before then," Moe told *Sports Illustrated*. Moe was encouraged to try downhill skiing by his brother. "We skied to push it to the limit," Moe said in *Rolling Stone*. "I was naturally kind of wild."

FINDS TROUBLE. His father moved to Alaska, where he found steady work, and Moe continued to ski after he left. By the time he was 13, Moe was good enough to be given a contract that paid him for using Dynastar skis. With money in his pocket, Moe got into trouble. "I was not the smartest or best student," he admitted to *Time*. Moe explained to the *New York Times* that he was "experimenting, a normal kid trying to have a good time, making his father tear the hair from his head." In 1984 he was caught smoking marijuana and was kicked off his ski team. He went to Alaska, where he was able to find coaches willing to work with him. "If Tommy hadn't ended up in Alaska, he wouldn't be where he is today," his father told *Sports Illustrated*. "The coaching was a little tougher there, because everything is tougher there."

TWO STRIKES. Moe lived with his father in Alaska and began to attract attention on the slopes. When he was 15, he finished sixth at the U.S. National Alpine Championships at Copper Mountain, Colorado. He joined the U.S. Ski team, but the pressure of being a rising star was tough on him. While he was training with the national team near Anchorage, Alaska, Moe was again caught smoking marijuana.

When Moe was kicked off the national ski team, his dad decided to try something desperate to "knock his attitude out

Tommy Moe

of him." He brought his son to the Aleutian Islands of Alaska to work with his construction company. "He shoveled gravel," recalled Tom, Sr., describing Moe's 12- to 16-hour workdays. "He crawled on all fours. When he was done every day, he was one whipped pup. He was no spoiled kid and he was no rich kid. I said to him one day, 'Think about it, would you rather be here, or skiing in Argentina.'" After a few weeks of back-breaking work, Moe learned his lesson, and straightened out his life. "It was mental torture, bad news," Moe confessed to *Sporting News.* "It humbled me up pretty fast."

THE BIG TIME. In 1987 Moe won a silver medal in the downhill at the World Junior Championships. In 1988 he finished fourth at the same competition, and by the 1989 World Junior Championships, held in Alaska, Moe was an up-and-coming star. He thrilled the hometown fans, winning the Super-G and the Alpine Combined, although he finished fifth in the downhill. The next year he moved up to the international World Cup circuit, where the best skiers in the world compete.

Moe skied for six years on the international World Cup circuit, but rarely finished in the top ten. In 1992 he qualified for the U.S. Olympic ski team that would compete in Albertville, France. "I'm going to compete," Moe told *Rolling Stone* about the upcoming Olympics. "I want to make a move and be in the medals." But Moe's performance was disappointing. He finished 20th in the downhill, 28th in the Super-G, and 18th in the Alpine combined.

SHOWDOWN. His father was waiting for him at the finish line. Moe hoped for sympathy, but felt he'd let his father down. He told the *New York Times* that "Dad didn't have to say much," but Moe got the message. "I didn't yell at him," his dad recalled in the same newspaper. "I only had to look at him. He turned around and started to cry. He skied away and my wife said, 'What's wrong with you?'"

Now it was Tommy, Sr., who was learning a lesson—about being a father. Always hard on his son, he'd pushed Moe and was disappointed when his son didn't measure up to his high standards. He explained in *Sports Illustrated* that it was his wife who set him straight. "My wife told me, 'You should stop pushing him. You should be happy you have a son who is even at the Olympics. Most people never have that.' That kind of shocked me."

SUPERSTAR

COMEBACK. Moe took his Olympic disappointment very hard. "I hit rock bottom," he confessed to *Sports Illustrated*. "I was supposed to be the next superstar, but I was almost a total

---

ALPINE SKIING

Alpine skiing is made up of five events. In the downhill, skiers travel on a relatively straight course and try to go as fast as they can. In fact, the winner of the men's Olympic downhill race is usually called the world's fastest skier. The slalom is the exact opposite, because skiers have to twist and turn through gates that are placed very close together along the course. The giant slalom is a combination of the downhill and slalom, with the skiers moving faster than in the slalom but still going through gates. In the super giant slalom, or Super-G, skiers can go faster than in the giant slalom, but not as fast as in the downhill. The final event, the Alpine Combined, includes both a downhill and two slalom runs. The skier with the best total time over the three runs wins.

Tommy Moe, carried by Kjetil Andre Aamodt of Norway and Ed Podivinsky of Canada, after winning the men's downhill in Norway.

burnout." In 1992 he left the World Cup tour for a short time and returned to Alaska. He and his father spent time together and the vacation seemed to help. When Moe returned to the tour he was skiing better, finishing in second and third place. Though he'd never won a World Cup race, Moe entered the 1994 Olympics in Lillehammer, Norway, full of confidence. The course was technically difficult and Moe was an excellent technical skier. In fact, he'd won two training runs on the exact same course the year before.

Even before the Olympics started, the U.S. ski team was being written off. *Sports Illustrated* called them "Uncle Sam's lead-footed snow-plow brigade." Other publications wrote basically the same thing. Despite Moe's confidence, no one expected much success from him or the team. He felt the criticism was unfair, claiming the team had trained hard and was better than people thought. "We don't deserve to be ridiculed," Moe complained in *Time*. The entire team wanted to prove the critics wrong.

WORLD'S FASTEST SKIER. The night before the men's downhill race, Moe had a great training run. On the day of the race the temperature was cold—around one degree fahrenheit—and the crowd moved around to keep warm, clanking the cowbells that were popular in Lillehammer. The spectators were excited when Kjetil Andre Aamodt of Norway, the hometown favorite, took the lead in the downhill just before Moe was to ski. Sure that Aamodt—the World Cup leader—had won, the crowd started singing victory songs .

Moe seemed calm, yawning as he waited at the starting gate. Slow on the top of the course, and with nothing to lose, he decided to go all out. Seemingly out of control, Moe slashed down the course, rarely slowing down, making up time on the leader. "Maybe I took some unnecessary risks trying to go that much faster," he admitted to *U.S. News and World Report*. When he crossed the finish line, Moe looked at the clock. It read one minute, 45.75 seconds. Moe was in first place by .04 of a second. He danced on his skis before the silent crowd. When the last racer crossed the finish line and had not passed him, Moe knew he had won. "He was always up there," Aamodt observed to the *New York Times* after the race. "It was just a matter of time.

WHAT A DIFFERENCE. Tommy, Sr., and his third wife, Tyra, had a difficult time reaching Lillehammer, traveling through snowstorms and battling closed airports. Arriving just the night before the competition, they were at the bottom of the hill to see Moe finish the race. "This time, for the Olympics, whatever he did was fine," Tommy, Sr., not wanting to make the same mistake twice, explained to the *New York Times*. "I told him, 'No pressure, none.' But I figured he would do something here." He admitted to the same newspaper that he screamed "at the top of my lungs," until he caught his son's eye. "I owe a lot to my father," Moe confided to *U.S. News and World Report*. "I wouldn't have any of this without his guidance and support."

MEDAL NUMBER TWO. President Clinton phoned Moe after his victory in the downhill and the new champion posed for a picture with the first lady, Hillary Rodham Clinton, who was in Lillehammer attending the Olympics. "I'm having a dream Olympics," Moe told *U.S. News and World Report* after his downhill victory. But there was more to come. Moe had also qualified to ski in the super-G, which he considered his best event. Skiing on his birthday, Moe once again went all out, trying to gain as much speed as he could and still pass through the gates on the course. He made only one minor mistake on a turn near the finish line. For the second time in the Olympics, Moe looked at the clock after his race and found himself in the lead.

BILL JOHNSON

During the 1984 Winter Olympics in Sarajevo, Yugoslavia, American downhill racer Bill Johnson shocked the world when he predicted he would win the Olympic men's downhill. Most people ignored him, but Johnson backed up his prediction and won America's first downhill gold medal. It was Johnson's only moment in the sun. Satisfied with his Olympic victory, he stopped training and was soon out of shape. He never again won a major race.

This time, however, Moe could not hold on. Markus Wasmeier from Germany beat his time by .08 of a second. Moe was happy with the silver medal and explained to *Sports Illustrated* why he was doing so well at the Olympics: "I am in a zone right now where I almost can't stop myself from skiing fast." All of a sudden he was a celebrity, signing autographs for his fans. To celebrate his birthday, Moe told *Sports Illustrated* that he "went to a bar and wore Viking clothes, with horns and all, and we drank beer out of wooden cups." Even the Norwegian fans began to treat Moe like one of their own when they found out about his heritage.

RECORD BREAKER. In the final event, Moe competed in the Alpine Combined, which includes one downhill run and two slalom races. He continued his hot streak in the downhill portion, finishing third, but fell to fifth place after his two slalom runs. But Moe had already made history. His Olympic medals were the first for an American male in Alpine skiing since 1984 and he was the first American male ever to win two skiing medals at the same Olympics. He is only the second American man ever to win the Olympic downhill.

OFF THE SLOPES. Moe lives in Girdwood, Alaska. His girlfriend, downhill skier Megan Gerety, was also on the 1994 U.S. Olympic team. Moe has been the spokesperson for the Alaskan fishing industry. When asked by *Rolling Stone* to describe himself, he said: "I drive fast, I bike fast, I live fast. You're a downhill racer because you like doing stuff fast."

WHERE TO WRITE

C/O U.S. SKI ASSOCIATION,

P.O. BOX 100, PARK CITY, UT 84060.

JOE MONTANA

1956—

J oe Montana thrives on pressure. When he was young, his dad pressured him to excel in sports. At Notre Dame University, Montana was nicknamed "The Comeback Kid" for bringing the Fighting Irish back when the game seemed lost. The Montana magic continued in the National Football League (NFL) as he led his team to 29 fourth-quarter come-from-behind rallies and four Super Bowl titles. Perhaps the most accurate passer ever to play in the NFL, Montana has overcome career threatening injuries and opposing teams to become one of the best quarterbacks of all time.

GROWING UP

Joseph C. Montana, Jr., was born in New Eagle, Pennsylvania, and was an only child. The area in western Pennsylvania where he grew up is known for producing great quarterbacks including Joe's childhood idol, Hall-of-Fame quarterback Joe Namath. Montana's grandfather, "Hooks" Montana, played minor league football in the 1920s. Joseph, Sr. was his son's biggest fan. He quit a job that required out-of-town traveling, in order to coach the young Montana. A sports enthusiast, the elder Montana gave his eight-month-old son a baseball bat so

"Joe Montana is the greatest quarterback to ever play the game. Joe Montana is not human."—former Cincinnati Bengals wide receiver Chris Collinsworth

he could start practicing his swing. A few years later, Joseph, Sr. installed a basketball hoop for basketball practice and hung a tire in the yard for football practice (Montana would try to throw the football through the hole in the tire.) "Joe never really had a choice," his mom, Theresa told the *San Jose Mercury News*. "His father wanted him to play football and that was that."

Montana was a star in pee wee football (his father lied about his age to get him in the league), and threw three perfect games (no batters from the other team reaching base) in Little League baseball. At one point Montana wanted to quit playing football. "My cousins were all doing other stuff," he told *Sports Illustrated*. "I think it was Boy Scouts. And I wanted to do what they were doing." But his dad wouldn't let him quit, and Montana went on to star in several sports at Ringgold High School. North Carolina State University offered him a basketball scholarship, but he chose to play football for the legendary University of Notre Dame.

"THE COMEBACK KID." Montana did not find instant success at Notre Dame. Extremely shy, he ranked last among three quarterbacks when he was a freshman. He did not practice as hard as he should have and admitted to being homesick. Remembering his dad's advice, though, Montana refused to quit. In his second season he earned the nickname "The Comeback Kid" by entering as a late-game substitute and passing the Fighting Irish to come-from-behind victories over North Carolina and the Air Force Academy. Montana sat out the entire 1976 season with a separated shoulder, but in the fourth game of the 1977 season he got his chance to win the starting job after leading Notre Dame to another late rally by beating Purdue University. Montana led the Irish to the national championship that season after routing previously number-one ranked Texas 38-10 in the Cotton Bowl.

It was not until his senior season that NFL scouts began to consider Montana a professional prospect. Again Montana performed miracles, rallying his team from a 17-7 deficit with eight minutes remaining to beat the University of Pittsburgh 26-17. Then, trailing 24-6 against Southern California, Montana brought the Irish back to lead 25-24 before a last-second field goal defeated Notre Dame 27-24.

The Irish finished the season 8-3 and were invited to play for the second straight year in the Cotton Bowl, where Montana had his greatest college game. Suffering from the flu and lowered body temperatures caused by the cold weather at the game, Montana's team trailed the University of Houston 34-12 in the fourth quarter. With 7:37 remaining in the game, the comeback began. By the time it was over the Irish had won, 35-34, with Montana throwing the winning touchdown pass with two seconds remaining on the clock. In 1994 Montana's performance was voted the best ever in a college bowl game by the *Sporting News*.

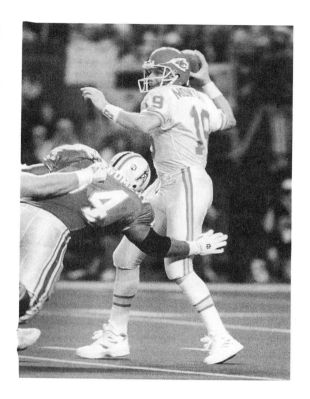

Joe Montana

JOINS 49ERS. During his college career Montana threw for 4,121 yards and twenty-five touchdowns. Despite his heroic comeback victories, most NFL teams were not sure Montana's arm was strong enough or accurate enough for him to be a professional quarterback, and at six-feet-two inches and 192 pounds, Montana was small for an NFL passer. The San Francisco 49ers drafted Montana in the third round of the 1979 NFL draft. "I knew about his inconsistency [up and down play]," 49ers coach Bill Walsh told *Sports Illustrated*. "I also knew about his competitiveness. If he could be great for one game, why not two.... He was willing to learn. That was easy to tell. I knew he would improve."

The 49ers were terrible in 1979, Montana's rookie season, finishing 2-14. Montana sat on the bench and learned from veteran quarterback Steve DeBerg. In his second season Montana split time with DeBerg, throwing for 1,795 yards, 15 touchdowns, and completing 65 percent of his passes—the best in the NFL. He worked his come-from-behind magic again, bringing the 49ers back from being behind—winning 38-35 over the New Orleans Saints in overtime. San Francisco finished the season 6-10, but Montana won the starting quarterback job.

SUPERSTAR

SUPER SEASON. In 1981 the 49ers had the best season in their history to that point, and Montana was a big reason. He threw for 3,565 yards and 19 touchdowns and provided the leadership needed to keep a young team together. San Francisco finished the season 13-3 and won the National Football Conference (NFC) West division championship. The inexperienced 49ers entered the playoffs as underdogs, but defeated the New York Giants 38-24 in the first round, with Montana throwing for 304 yards and two touchdowns. The victory put the 49ers in the NFC Championship game against the Dallas Cowboys.

Entering the fourth quarter with a 21-17 lead, the 49ers lost the lead and trailed 27-21. They had the ball with just under five minutes left in the game, but were on their own 10-yard line. Mixing short passes with running plays, Montana moved San Francisco to the Dallas six-yard line. On third down Montana, moving to his right to avoid being tackled, leaped and threw a bullet to wide receiver Dwight Clark, who jumped and pulled down the pass in the back of the end zone. Montana had done it again and San Francisco was going to the Super Bowl, where they would meet the Cincinnati Bengals. San Francisco led 20-0 at halftime, but had to hold on for a 26-21 victory. Montana, who completed 14 of 22 passes for 157 yards was named the game's Most Valuable Player.

The 1982 season was cut short by a players' strike and the 49ers missed the playoffs. They finished 10-6 in 1983 and Montana had a great season, throwing for 3,910 yards and 26 touchdowns. The 49ers lost, however, in the NFC Championship game to the Washington Redskins, 24-21. Another Montana-led rally came up just short when Mark Mosley kicked a 25-yard field goal to win the game after three fourth-quarter Montana touchdown passes.

ALMOST PERFECT. The next season San Francisco was nearly perfect. Their 15-1 record was one of the best of all time, with the only loss coming against the Pittsburgh Steelers, 20-17. Montana was nearly as perfect, throwing for 3,630 yards, 28 touchdowns, and completing 65 percent of his passes. San Francisco defeated the Chicago Bears 23-0 in the NFC Championship game and faced the Miami Dolphins in the Super Bowl. This time no comebacks were necessary, as the 49ers rolled to a 38-16 victory. Montana threw for a then Super Bowl record 331 yards, passed for two touchdowns, ran for another, and won his second Super Bowl MVP award.

The 49ers were kept out of the Super Bowl the next three seasons, but Montana continued to shine. He threw for 3,653 yards and 27 touchdowns in 1985, but San Francisco lost in the first round of the playoffs to the New York Giants. In the first game of 1986 Montana suffered a back injury and underwent career-threatening surgery. Doctors said he would miss the entire season, but Montana was back in two months, throwing for 270 yards and three touchdowns in a 49ers win. His remarkable comeback sparked the team, and the 49ers went 5-2 at the end of the season to win the NFC West division title. But they ran into a red-hot New York Giants team and lost in the first round of the playoffs, 49-3.

The 1987 season was again interrupted by a player's strike, and Montana played only 13 games. He still threw for a career-high 31 touchdowns and set an NFL record by completing 22 consecutive passes. The 49ers went 13-2 and won the NFC Western division title, but were upset in the first round of the playoffs, 36-24, by the Minnesota Vikings. Montana was replaced in the game by backup quarterback, **Steve Young** (see entry) after the Vikings had taken a 27-10 lead. Montana completed only 12 of 26 passes for 46 yards, probably the worst playoff performance of his career.

COMPETITION. During the 1988 season Coach Walsh decided to give more playing time to Young at quarterback, and Montana worried about being replaced. "I've never doubted myself, but sometimes you wonder a little," he told the *Boston Globe*. Amid rumors that he was going to be traded, Montana became more determined to prove that he should be the starting quarterback. In the end Montana was the 49ers's main man, again coming back from injuries and leading the team to another Western division title. He threw six touchdown passes in blowout playoff wins over the Minnesota Vikings and the Chicago Bears to put the 49ers in the Super Bowl against the Cincinnati Bengals.

THIRD RING. "This trip to the Super Bowl is more gratifying [better] than the others because the road has been harder," Montana told the *Mercury News*. The game was one of the best ever, and once again Montana was the late-game star. The Bengals led 16-13 with only 3:20 remaining on the clock. San Francisco had the ball, but they were on their own eight-yard line. Montana, showing great poise under pressure, moved the 49ers downfield, the big plays being three passes to game MVP **Jerry Rice** (see entry). Finally, with 34 seconds left in the game, Montana threaded the needle with a pass to wide receiver John Taylor in the back of the end zone. San Francisco won 20-16, and Montana added to his legend, passing for 357 yards and two touchdowns.

MAKES HISTORY. After the 1988 season, Coach Walsh decided to retire, saying he was worn out from the pressure of coaching. Defensive coach George Siefert took over and the 49ers hardly slowed down. It helped Siefert to have Montana, who had a record breaking year, completing an amazing 70.2 percent of his passes (third highest in NFL history) for 3,521 yards and 28 touchdowns. When the NFL put all of these statistics into their complicated rating system, they discovered that this was the best season a quarterback had *ever* had. (His rating was 112.4.) Montana was named Player of the Year by the *Sporting News*.

The 49ers were unstoppable in the playoffs, winning their three games by a combined score of 126-26. In the NFC Championship game Montana completed 26 of 30 passes (86.7 percent) for 262 yards and two touchdowns as the 49ers routed the Los Angeles Rams 30-3. The Super Bowl was a super-blow-out with the 49ers winning 55-10 over the Denver Broncos. Montana won his third Super Bowl MVP award after completing 22 of 29 passes for 297 yards and a Super Bowl record five touchdowns. Only two other teams have ever won four Super Bowls (Dallas Cowboys and Pittsburgh Steelers) and only one quarterback other than Montana has ever won four Super Bowl games (Terry Bradshaw of the Steelers). The 49ers had made history.

The 49ers were going for a Super Bowl "three-peat" in 1990, and they again dominated the NFL, going 14-2 during regular season. Montana passed for a career best 3,944 yards and also threw for 26 touchdowns. Leading 13-9 with nine minutes remaining in the NFC Championship game against the New York Giants, Montana broke his finger. Young came in and performed well, but a fumble by running back Roger Craig gave the Giants a break. Matt Bahr hit a 42-yard field goal, his fifth of the game, to give New York a 15-13 win. Though he didn't know it at the time, this would be the last game Montana would start for the 49ers.

BIG TRADE. At the 49ers's 1991 training camp, Montana injured his elbow and had to have surgery. Despite hard work he would miss the next two seasons and Young would become an NFL superstar quarterback. Near the end of the 1992 season Montana said he was ready, and played the second half of the 49ers's last regular season game against the Detroit Lions. He played well, throwing for 126 yards and two touchdowns, but when the playoffs started, Young remained the 49ers quarterback. When the season ended Montana told San Francisco that he would only stay with them if he was given an opportunity to be the starting quarterback.

SUPER BOWL QUARTERBACKS

In the history of the Super Bowl, only four quarterbacks have played in the game four times. The following chart shows the Super Bowl career statistics for each of these quarterbacks. (P=Passes, C=Completions, Y=Yards, T=Touchdowns; numbers in bold indicate a Super Bowl record.)

Player	P	C	Y	T
Joe Montana	122	**83**	**1142**	**11**
Terry Bradshaw	84	49	932	9
Roger Staubach	98	61	734	8
Jim Kelly	**145**	81	829	2

JOE, MONTANA

Fans in Kansas City were so happy to have Montana join the Chiefs that radio station KYYS thought of a unique way to honor their new quarterback: have a city named after him. In return for a five day vacation in Kansas City, including tickets to a Chiefs game, the town of Ismay, Montana—population 26—changed its name to "Joe" for one year.

The 49ers, forced to choose between Young and the legendary Montana, chose Young—mainly because Montana was five years older. Montana, who didn't want to cause problems, asked to be traded to the Kansas City Chiefs in April 1993. Many fans in San Francisco, who remembered all the great games Montana had played for the 49ers, felt the team had made a mistake and mourned the loss of their favorite player. Montana was sad about leaving, but realized it was best for him and the 49ers.

BIG CHIEF. The Chiefs who had won only one playoff game since 1970, were glad to have Montana. (Because his number 16 had been worn by Hall-of-Fame quarterback Len Dawson and retired by the Chiefs, Montana now wears number 19, a number he last wore in pee wee football.) Even though he missed all or parts of six games during the regular season due to assorted injuries, Montana threw for 2,144 yards and 13 touchdowns. The Chiefs finished 11-5 and Montana was completely healthy for the playoffs. In the Chiefs's first game, against the Pittsburgh Steelers, Kansas City trailed 17-10 entering the fourth quarter. This was no problem for Montana, who threw a touchdown pass with under two minutes left in regulation time to tie the score 24-24. The Chiefs won in overtime, 27-24.

The Chiefs's second playoff game was against the Houston Oilers, a team that had won 11 straight games. Kansas City fell behind again, losing 13-7 with less than ten minutes left in the game. Montana took over, throwing two touchdown passes in the fourth quarter while leading the Chiefs to a 28-20 victory. His luck ran out, however, in the American Football Conference (AFC) Championship game against the Buffalo Bills when he suffered a concussion and was knocked out of the game. The Bills won, 30-13.

OFF THE FIELD. Montana lives with his wife, Jennifer, and their three children. A shy person, Montana says it's hard sometimes to be famous, but he always tries to be polite to fans and reporters. He is a spokesperson for Sega video games and LA Gear athletic equipment. Through the 1993 season, Montana was the NFL's all-time highest ranked and most accurate passer, completing 63.4 percent of his passes. He is fifth all-time in passing yardage (37,268) and fourth in touchdown passes (257). But for Montana, helping his team win is still the most important thing. Even though the Chiefs did not reach the Super Bowl, Montana was satisfied with his season. "It feels as good as ever," he told the *Sporting News*. "Especially when a lot of people were counting you out, that you could never make it this far [again]. It feels good to be playing, to be staying in one piece and still playing and still winning. It's as good as I've ever felt."

WHERE TO WRITE

C/O KANSAS CITY CHIEFS, ONE ARROWHEAD DR.,
KANSAS CITY, MO 64129.

WARREN MOON

1956—

"I just want to be looked at as a guy who is trying to help as many people as he can. I definitely want to excel in my sport, and I think I do."—Warren Moon

Warren Moon has always been a fighter. Passed over by major colleges after high school and the National Football League (NFL) after a successful career at the University of Washington, Moon went to Canada to prove that he could be a professional quarterback. Now one of the best quarterbacks in the NFL, Moon also had to fight the racist feelings of others who thought that African Americans could not play quarterback. Instead of quitting, Moon has always fought hard. "I've been told all my life that I didn't have what it took," he told the *Rocky Mountain News.* "It was the people who told me I couldn't do things that kept me going."

GROWING UP

Harold Warren Moon was born November 18, 1956, in Los Angeles, California. He was the middle child and only boy in a family of seven children. He was seven when his father died of liver disease. His mother, Pat, a nurse, raised the family by herself. Like his sisters, Moon had to help cook and clean and also worked after school in restaurants and as a paperboy to help support the family. His neighborhood was rough, but his mother always told him to stay away from drugs and crime, and he obeyed. Growing up in a house full of women, Moon learned to cook, sew, and bake cookies.

STRONG ARM. As a kid, Moon played hide-and-seek, built soapbox race cars out of shopping carts, and played electric football—a machine with a vibrating field that moves the players. He played every sport possible when he was young, but in high school had to chose just one sport, because the rest of his time would be spent studying and working. He decided on football, mainly because he had a strong arm and could throw a ball farther than anyone he knew.

Trying to stay out of trouble, Moon left his neighborhood to attend Hamilton High School, which had a better academic and athletic program. In his first game for the freshman football team, Moon threw the ball 80 yards, too far for the intended receiver, but far enough to impress the varsity football coach, Jack Epstein. "I'll remember that pass until the day I die," Epstein told the *Houston Post*. "He was just a little skinny kid and he threw the ball so hard there was smoke coming off the back of the ball. The ball went about a mile over the receiver's head. I knew then he would be a great one."

FIGHTING TO SUCCEED. Taking over as varsity quarterback, Moon led Hamilton to the 1973 city playoffs as a senior and was named to the all-city team. But colleges showed little interest in him as a quarterback because of his size—five-feet-eleven inches and 165 pounds. When coach Epstein became offensive coordinator at West Los Angeles Junior College, Moon followed him there, and a freshman, Moon was named the Western State Conference Player of the Year. He sent tapes of his performances to major colleges, and caught the attention of University of Washington coach Don James, who offered Moon a chance to transfer to a school that played big-time college football in the Pacific 8 (now Pacific 10) Conference. Moon went to Washington, despite his worries about

SCOREBOARD

LED THE EDMONTON ESKIMOS TO FIVE STRAIGHT GREY CUP CHAMPIONSHIPS IN THE CANADIAN FOOTBALL LEAGUE (1978-82).

TWICE LED NFL IN PASSING YARDAGE (1990 AND 1991).

SET NFL RECORDS IN 1991 WITH 655 PASSING ATTEMPTS AND 404 COMPLETIONS.

HAS OVERCOME MANY OBSTACLES TO BECOME ONE OF THE BEST QUARTERBACKS IN THE NFL.

SUDDEN DEATH

Before a game between Hamilton High and Crenshaw High, an opposing player said that Moon would be killed if Hamilton beat Crenshaw. Moon took the threat seriously, since gangs were strong in his neighborhood, and told his mom, his coach, and the police. He then went out and led Hamilton to a stunning victory over Crenshaw. Nothing happened to Moon, but at the celebration party, a fight broke out between Hamilton and Crenshaw students.

attending a school with a history of racial tension and where less than 4 percent of the students were African American.

REAL GENTLEMAN. As a sophomore, Moon was a bench warmer. As a junior he was the starting quarterback, and the Huskies stumbled to a 5-6 record. The fans took the losing record out on Moon. "There's always a big question whether they were booing the guy because he was the quarterback and we weren't winning, or whether they were booing him because he was black," coach James told the *Seattle Times*. "I'm sure they were tough times for Warren to go through. I'm sure it did bother him.... But Warren was a real gentleman. He didn't lash out at any of the fans publicly. He took everything he got and he turned around and got more determined to prove that he was a good quarterback." Moon was helped by Thelma and Willie Payne, a Seattle couple who took him in and treated him like their son. Willie became the first father-figure Moon had ever had.

ROSE BOWL HERO. Moon proved he was a good quarterback in 1977. After a slow 2-2 start and more calls for the coach to change quarterbacks, he led the Huskies to the conference championship and a 27-20 upset over the University of Michigan in the 1978 Rose Bowl game. He was named the Rose Bowl's Most Valuable Player and the Pacific 8 Conference Player of the Year after passing for 1,584 yards and 11 touchdowns. Overall, Moon passed for 3,277 yards and 19 touchdowns in his college football career.

HEADS TO CANADA. Even after his Rose Bowl success, NFL scouts still did not believe Moon would make a good professional quarterback. So, once again, Moon decided to prove himself elsewhere, signing with the Edmonton Eskimos of the Canadian Football League (CFL). During his six seasons in Canada, Moon became a star, throwing for 21,228 yards and running for 1,700 more. His 5,648 passing yards in 1983 remains an all-time record for professional football. With Moon at quarterback, the Eskimos won five straight Grey Cup trophies as champions of the CFL (1978-82). Moon liked playing in Canada, especially since he never felt that anyone judged him by his race.

BECOMES AN OILER. By 1984 Moon had nothing left to prove to NFL scouts. When his contract with Edmonton expired, seven NFL teams wanted to sign him. Moon at first wanted to play with the Seattle Seahawks, where he could play in his college town. Eventually, he chose the Houston Oilers for two reasons. First, Houston offered him the chance to rejoin his Edmonton coach, Hugh Campbell, whom Houston had hired a month earlier. Second, the Oilers offered Moon a contract that made him the highest paid player in the NFL.

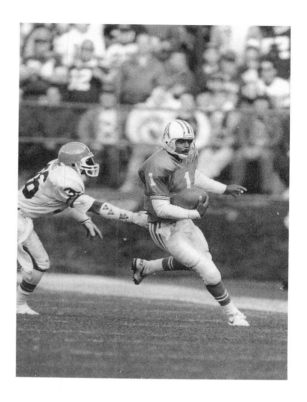

Warren Moon

When Moon joined Houston, it was one of the worst teams in the history of the NFL, having won just three games in two seasons. In 1984 Moon was a rookie sensation. His six years in the CFL gave him a head start on other rookies just out of college, and he threw for a then-club record of 3,338 yards. Still, the Oilers went 3-13, finishing last in the American Football Conference (AFC) Central division. The next season (1985), after the club won just five of its first 14 games, Campbell was fired and Jerry Glanville, a more defensive-minded coach, was hired.

"BLACK" QUARTERBACK. Moon faced pressure as the only African American starting quarterback in the NFL. Before Moon, many people in the NFL felt that African Americans could not play quarterback in professional football because their arms were not strong enough and they ran too much. "The opportunities haven't been given [to African American quarterbacks]," Moon told the *Los Angeles Times.* "But I think

I've been accepted pretty well throughout the league. As I improved, you started not to hear the word 'black' put in front of quarterback all the time. And now I'm pretty much recognized as just another quarterback in the league."

In 1986 Glanville's first year as coach, the Oilers focused on their running game rather than passing. After eight consecutive losses, Moon complained, saying the team needed to throw the ball more. Glanville agreed, and Moon went on to break his one-season Oilers's passing record with 3,489 yards. In 1987 using an offense that stressed passing, the Oilers won nine games and made the playoffs for the first time since 1980. Houston defeated the Seattle Seahawks, 23-20, in overtime in the first round of the playoffs before losing to the Denver Broncos, 34-10. Moon averaged 250 yards passing in the two playoff games.

"RUN-AND-SHOOT." The Oilers made the playoffs in both the 1988 and 1989 seasons with records of 10-6 and 9-7, but in both years they failed to advance beyond the second playoff round. Moon was named to his first All-Pro (all-star) team in 1988 (despite missing five games with a broken shoulder), after passing for 2,327 yards and 17 touchdowns. In 1989 he passed for 3,631 yards and 23 touchdowns, but with the Oilers's repeated playoff failures, it was clear that the team needed a change. Glanville was fired following the 1989 season, and Houston hired Jack Pardee, coach of the University of Houston, who had developed the "run-and-shoot" offense, a system based on speedy receivers and a strong-armed quarterback. Moon was thrilled, knowing he would finally have a chance to show his passing talents.

SUPERSTAR

LEAGUE LEADER. Moon became an NFL superstar in 1990, having his best season ever. In 15 games he led the league with 362 completions in 584 attempts for 4,689 yards and 33 touchdowns. At the end of the season, he was voted NFL Offensive Player of the Year by the Associated Press. In the season's 14th game, against the Kansas City Chiefs, Moon threw for 527 yards—just 27 yards short of the all-time single game record. The Oilers finished 9-7, making the playoffs, but Moon was injured in the next-to-last game of the season and sat on the sidelines during the Oilers 41-14 loss to the Cincinnati Bengals in the first round of the playoffs.

In 1991 Moon set league records in passing attempts (655) and completions (404), and led the NFL with 4,690 passing yards. The Oilers finished 11-5, winning their first AFC Central division title. Moon threw for 271 yards in the Oilers 17-10 first round playoff victory over the New York Jets. In the next game against the Denver Broncos, he threw for 325 yards and three touchdowns, only to see his team lose once again, 26-24.

HISTORIC DEFEAT. Moon's frustration continued in 1992, as he missed five games with a separated shoulder. The Oilers finished 10-6, and faced the Buffalo Bills in the first round of the playoffs. Everything went Houston's way in the first half of the game. The Oilers led 28-3 at halftime and Moon had completed 19 of 22 passes for 218 yards and four touchdowns. The Oilers increased their lead to 35-3 in the third quarter, but Moon was nervous. "I went around, telling guys, 'It's not over,'" he told *Sports Illustrated.* "Thirty-five to three, you could feel it on the sidelines, everyone just letting down. Then it all fell apart." In one of the greatest comebacks in NFL history, Buffalo tied the game 38-38, and won in overtime, 41-38.

In 1993 for the first time in his career, Moon was benched after throwing four interceptions in a 18-17 loss to the San Diego Chargers. The Oilers began the season 1-4 and appeared headed for their first losing season since 1987. With Moon back at quarterback, however, the Oilers started to roll, winning 11 straight games to run away with the AFC Central division title. Moon threw for 3,485 yards and 21 touchdowns, and the Oilers

ROLE MODEL

When 12-year-old Keythan Daniels was having problems in school, getting into fights, staying out late, and trying to start his own gang, his mother called Warren Moon's Crescent Moon Foundation, asking for help. Moon talked to Keythan one-to-one. "It made me feel special," Keythan told *Sports Illustrated for Kids.* "Warren told me he didn't get to the NFL by being stupid or making trouble. My momma told me to work hard and be good too, but hearing it from Warren was different because he's an NFL quarterback. Now I want to be a doctor and an NFL quarterback. And when I make it, I want to help another kid follow his dreams, too."

were a favorite to go to the Super Bowl. But once again, Houston was disappointed, losing 28-20 to **Joe Montana** (see entry) and the Kansas City Chiefs, despite 306 yards passing by Moon. This would be Moon's last game with the Oilers. He was traded to the Minnesota Vikings in the off-season.

OFF THE FIELD. Moon lives in Missouri City, Texas, outside of Houston, with his wife, Felicia, whom he met in high school, and their four children. When he retires from football, Moon would like to enter politics or own a professional sports team. One of the most active NFL players in charitable organizations, in 1989 he established the Crescent Moon Foundation which raises money for college funds, as well as field and camping trips. Moon travels the country, crusading against poverty and disease, and promoting quality education for young people. In 1989 he was named the NFL's Man of the Year for his charitable work, and in 1993 *Sports Illustrated for Kids* gave him their Good Sport award. "I hope people see more into me than just football," Moon told the *St. Louis Post Dispatch*. "I just want to be looked at as a guy who is trying to help as many people as I can. I definitely want to excel in my sport, and I think I do."

WHERE TO WRITE

C/O MINNESOTA VIKINGS,

9529 VIKING DRIVE, EDEN PRARIE, MN 55344

MARTINA NAVRATILOVA

1956—

M artina Navratilova ran away from home in 1975. She wasn't mad at her parents, she was mad at the Communist government of Czechoslovakia that told her where and when she could play tennis. She became one of the greatest women's tennis players in history and won more tournaments than any player, male or female. In 1986 Navratilova returned to Czechoslovakia and was given a hero's welcome by the country she was forced to leave behind.

Navratilova is "arguably the greatest player of all time"—tennis commentator Bud Collins

GROWING UP

Martina Navratilova was born October 10, 1956, in Prague, Czechoslovakia. Her stepfather, Miroslav, was an economic advisor in a factory, and her mother, Jana, was an office worker. Navratilova was part of a tennis-playing family. Her grandmother, Agnes Semanska, was the number-two ranked women's tennis player in Czechoslovakia before World War II and her parents were tennis administrators for the Czechoslovakian government. Her younger sister, Jana, was also a tennis player.

Navratilova grew up in the Krkonose Mountains and learned to snow ski at an early age. When she was five years old her family moved to Revnice, a suburb of Prague. Her parents were active tennis players. "They were at the courts every day and they took me with them," Navratilova told *Sports Illustrated*. "I had an old racquet that my father cut down and I hit the ball against a wall. I could do it for hours. They would make me stop and sit me on a chair, but whenever they didn't watch me I would go to the wall again." Navratilova's stepfather saw his daughter's talent and began to coach her.

TENNIS NUMBER ONE. Navratilova played her first tournament at age eight, where she advanced to the semifinals. She won her first national tournament when she was 14 years old. Over the next two years she won three national women's championships and the national junior title and was the number-one ranked female tennis player in Czechoslovakia. Navratilova also swam, skied, and played soccer and ice hockey. School did not interest her. "I was the third-best student in my class but I never studied," she told *Sports Illustrated*. "By the time I was fifteen and sixteen I didn't have time to study anyway. But I loved geography, and I imagined myself in places like New York and Chicago."

JUNK FOOD JUNKIE. In 1973 Navratilova traveled to the United States for the first time. She loved American junk food, especially pancakes, pizzas, and hamburgers. She gained 20 pounds. "I was really fat and really slow, but I didn't know I was fat," Navratilova told an interviewer. She also began her 16-year rivalry with Chris Evert, losing to the then number-one player in the world in a close match in Akron, Ohio. "She was overweight, but eager and gifted," Evert said after the match. Navratilova earned her first victories over the best players in the world in 1974. She defeated the legendary Margaret Court, 6-4, 6-3, in the quarterfinals of the 1974 Australian Open and defeated Evert for the first time at the Virginia Slims Championship.

FREEDOM. The Communist government in Czechoslovakia told Navratilova where and when she could play tennis. She resented their control and wanted the freedom to play wherever she chose. "They [the government] told me they didn't want me to play in the United States as much," Navratilova explained to *Sport.* "I was under tension all the time ... I realized I would never have the ... freedom to play the best tennis as long as I was under their control."

On September 6, 1975, Navratilova asked the American government for permission to stay in the United States. "Politics had nothing to do with my decision," she said in an Associated Press story. "It was strictly a tennis matter." Navratilova felt she had to defect in order to develop as a tennis player and as a person, but the decision was a painful one. She knew it would be years before she would be able to see her parents and younger sister again. Navratilova was not allowed to return to Czechoslovakia and her family could not leave the country. "I miss my family badly," she told the *New York Times Magazine.*

Martina Navratilova

Navratilova had a hard time adjusting to her new freedom. "Just a year ago, she was in prison," her manager, Fred Barman, explained to *Newsday.* "She wants to do this, she wants to do that." Navratilova consistently won singles tournaments over the next few years and by 1977 was the number-three player in the world. But she had not been able to win one of the Grand Slam tournaments—the Australian Open, French Open, Wimbledon, or U.S. Open. Navratilova lost in the finals of both the French Open and Australian Open in 1975. In 1976 she lost in the semifinals at Wimbledon to Evert, but won the doubles title with the woman who had defeated her in the singles tournament. Navratilova won four singles tournaments in

1977 and took the U.S. Open doubles title with her partner, Betty Stove, of the Netherlands.

WIN AT WIMBLEDON. In 1978 Navratilova began to challenge Evert for the number-one ranking. She won the first seven tournaments and 37 matches throughout the year. In July Navratilova finally broke through and won a Grand Slam title—Wimbledon, the most important tournament in the world. She defeated Evert in the final in a tough, three-set match, 2-6, 6-4, 7-5. Navratilova won 12 of the last 13 points.

"I don't know if I should cry or scream or laugh. I feel very happy that I won, but at the same time I'm very sad that I can't share this with my family," said Navratilova, who had not seen her parents or her 15-year-old sister since coming to live in the United States. Her victory was ignored by the government-controlled media of Czechoslovakia, but her parents watched the match on German television by driving to a town near the German border. Navratilova became the number-one player in the world for the first time in 1978, a position she would hold off-and-on for the next nine years.

SEES MOM. Navratilova returned to Wimbledon in 1979 to defend her title. Her mother, whom she had not seen since 1975, was at the tournament. "Winning here last year was the greatest moment of my career," Navratilova said, "but yesterday [her airport reunion with her mother] was one of the greatest moments in my life." She won both the singles and doubles titles at Wimbledon.

In 1980 Navratilova led the tour in money-winnings but could not win a Grand Slam singles title. She lost in the Wimbledon semifinals to her old nemesis, Evert, 4-6, 6-4, 6-2. Navratilova had a great year in 1981, both on and off the court. She won 10 singles tournaments, including her first Australian Open title and teamed up with Pam Shriver to win 11 doubles championships, including the Wimbledon title.

BECOMES CITIZEN. The most important event in Navratilova's year occurred on July 21, 1981, when she became a U.S. citizen. She broke down in tears when her new countrymen in the crowd at the U.S. Open gave her a standing ovation after losing in the singles finals. "I want to thank each and every one of you who was pulling for me today," Navratilova told the crowd.

Navratilova split the Grand Slam singles tournaments with Evert in 1982. She won the French Open for the first time and won again at Wimbledon. She lost to Evert in the finals of the Australian Open and lost to her doubles partner, Pam Shriver, in the quarterfinals of the U.S. Open—the only time all year she did not reach the finals of a tournament. Navratilova won 15 singles titles and 14 double crowns. She became the number-one ranked women's singles player in the world and stayed there until 1987, a record 150 straight weeks. (This record was later broken by **Steffi Graf** [see entry].)

SUPERSTAR

BEST EVER. In 1983 Navratilova had the greatest year ever by a tennis player. She won 16 of her 17 singles tournaments and lost only one *match* all year (she won 86). Her only loss was at the French Open, where she fell to Kathy Horvath, the 33rd-ranked player in the world. "I knew I had to lose sooner or later," Navratilova admitted after the upset.

Navratilova won Wimbledon, the Australian Open, and her first-ever U.S. Open title, where she defeated Evert, 6-1, 6-3, in the final. She became only the eleventh player, male or female, to win all of the Grand Slam titles in a career. "If I don't win another tournament in my life," a happy Navratilova said after her victory at the U.S. Open. "I can still say I've done it all." She also won 13 doubles titles, including Wimbledon and the U.S. Open. When asked if she was the best player in the world, Navratilova asked, "Is there any doubt in anybody's mind?" She also won the doubles titles at Wimbledon and the Australian and U.S. Opens.

ALMOST AS GOOD. In 1984 Navratilova was almost as good as the year before. She extended her match winning streak to 74, breaking the record Evert had set in 1974. She won the French Open, Wimbledon, and the U.S. Open, but was denied a Grand Slam (winning all the Grand Slam tournaments in one calendar

Another championship trophy for Martina Navratilova—this one came from the 1988 Bausch and Lomb Tournament.

year) when she lost in the semifinals of the Australian Open in December. Her streak of six straight Grand Slam singles victories tied a record set by Margaret Court from 1969 through 1971. Navratilova won 13 singles titles and her match record was an amazing 78-2. She and her partner Shriver did achieve a Grand Slam in doubles, winning all four of the major titles.

Over the next three years, Navratilova went unchallenged as the best women's player in the world. She added three Wimbledon, two U.S. Open, and the Australian Open titles to her list of singles victories. She and Shriver also dominated in doubles, continuing a winning streak that reached a record 109 consecutive matches. In 1987 she won her sixth straight Wimbledon title, breaking the record for most consecutive wins. Navratilova accomplished a rare feat at the 1987 U.S. Open when she won the singles, doubles, and mixed doubles titles.

HARD WORK. Rather than taking it easy after her success, Navratilova worked even harder to be the best tennis player she could be. She ate a special diet and trained hard—lifting weights, running sprints, and studying every aspect of the game. She asked for and accepted advice from coaches and other players. Her training allowed her to dominate both women's singles and doubles when most of the top competitors played only singles. She began to wear glasses in 1985 to correct her vision. Her most famous coach was Billie Jean King (see box), who helped Navratilova develop the attacking serve-and-volley game that was so successful in the early 1980s.

GOES HOME. In 1986 Navratilova came back to her home country for the first time since her 1975 defection, returning as a member of the U.S. Federation Cup team that eventually defeated Czechoslovakia. (The Federation Cup is an international tournament in which teams representing many countries compete against one another.) "They [Czechoslo-vakians] may know about me," she said, "but they haven't actually seen me—not for a very long time, anyway. I want to show them what I can do." Navratilova was greeted as a hero by the Czechoslovak people. "The whole experience was beyond my wildest dreams," she said after receiving a heartwarming reception.

SLIPS FROM TOP. Navratilova's time at the top of women's tennis came to an end in 1988. Steffi Graf took over the top ranking in 1987 and won the Grand Slam in 1988, defeating Navratilova in the finals of Wimbledon. "Steffi's number one, no doubt about that," Navratilova confessed. In 1991 **Monica Seles** (see entry) took over from Graf as the most dominant player on the tour. Navratilova still won her share of tournaments, but could not regain the top spot.

BILLIE JEAN KING

Billie Jean King was one of the greatest women's tennis players of all time. She holds the record for most Wimbledon titles—singles, doubles, and mixed doubles—with 20. Only Margaret Court and Navratilova have won more Grand Slam titles than King's 39. More importantly King was a trailblazer for women's sports. She was the first woman to win over $100,000 in a season and was an outspoken fighter for equal recognition of women athletes. In 1973 King struck a blow for women's rights when she defeated 55-year-old ex-Wimbledon men's champion Bobby Riggs in a nationally televised exhibition match.

RECORD WINS. The last great Grand Slam singles win of Navratilova's career came in 1990 at Wimbledon. She won her record ninth Wimbledon singles title, defeating American Zina Garrison, 6-4, 6-1, in the final. "It was my match to win," Navratilova said after her victory, "and I wasn't afraid of it [the record]." She also set a Wimbledon record with her ninth consecutive appearance in the single's finals. In 1991 she once again made history by breaking Evert's record for match wins with her 1,309th victory. She followed that up in 1992 by breaking Evert's record for most singles titles in a career (157).

OFF THE COURT. Navratilova lives in Aspen, Colorado. She supports many non-profit groups and charitable causes and works to benefit underprivileged and abused children in cities throughout the world. She contributes to scholarship funds for needy children and the Women's Sports Foundation, set up to support the development of women's athletics. She is a member of the Sierra Club, a wildlife and nature organization.

MARTINA AND CHRIS

The rivalry between Navratilova and Chris Evert was one of the best in sports history. Evert was a great player who won 18 Grand Slam singles titles in her career and set a record by winning at least one Grand Slam singles title in 13 consecutive years. For 10 years, she and Navratilova battled each other for the number-one world ranking. "Martina and I have pushed each other to get better and better," Evert said. The two met 14 times in the finals of Grand Slam tournaments, with Navratilova winning 10 of the matches. Navratilova and Evert played for the last time in 1988, with Navratilova winning. Their career record against each other was 43-37, in favor of Navratilova. The two players are friends off the court and often play exhibition matches to raise money for charity.

Navratilova enjoys snow skiing, golf, basketball, and horseback riding. She has five dogs and her favorite music is by k.d. lang, Elton John, Hothouse Flowers, Neneh Cherry, Arrested Development, Melissa Ethridge, Indigo Girls, and Annie Lennox. She also likes to read literary classics and watch Katherine Hepburn movies.

At the end of 1993 Navratilova announced that she would retire after the 1994 season. She holds the record for most singles titles, male or female, with 166. She has also won a record 163 doubles titles. Navratilova's 18 Grand Slam singles titles are third on the all-time list (tied with Evert) behind Margaret Court (24) and Helen Wills Moody (19). She has won 54 total Grand Slam titles (including singles, doubles, and mixed doubles), trailing only Court, who won 62. Navratilova was named the Female Athlete of the Decade for the 1980s by *National Sports Review,* United Press International, and the Associated Press. As tennis commentator Bud Collins said, she is "arguably the greatest player of all time."

WHERE TO WRITE

C/O WOMEN'S TENNIS ASSOCIATION, STOUFFER VINOY RESORT, ONE FOURTH ST., N., ST. PETERSBURG, FL 33701.

HAKEEM OLAJUWON

1963-

Hakeem "The Dream" Olajuwon is considered one of the best centers playing in the National Basketball Association (NBA). While most of his teammates and rivals got involved with the sport in grade school, Olajuwan didn't play the game until his senior year in high school. Basketball was almost unknown in Olajuwon's homeland of Nigeria, Africa, and he did not come to the United States until he entered college at the University of Houston. He learned quickly, however, and has been named five times to the All-NBA first team in ten seasons. Olajuwon took his place among the game's great players when he was named the NBA's Most Valuable Player following the 1993-94 season.

GROWING UP

Olajuwon was born January 21, 1963, in Lagos, Nigeria. His parents, Salaam and Abike Olajuwon, owned a concrete business in Lagos. Olajuwon was their third child and he has four brothers and one sister. The name Hakeem means "doctor" or "wise one," and Olajuwon means "being on top." Olajuwon's parents taught him to be respectful of adults. "In Nigeria," Hakeem told *Sports Illustrated for Kids,* "if you are impolite to adults, they can punish you, even if they aren't your parents."

> *"It's the movement, there's a feel to it. When you shoot it and make the basket, it's just a good feeling.... Basketball is a cool game."— Hakeem Olajuwon*

AKEEM AND HAKEEM

*The "H" in Hakeem is
silent in Olajuwon's
native language.
Because of this, his
name was listed as
"Akeem" until 1991
when he corrected
the mistake.*

It makes Olajuwon angry when people make fun of Nigeria, saying that all of Africa is made up of jungle. Olajuwon remembers his hometown, Lagos, the capital of Nigeria, as a thriving city. "I do not like it when TV only shows the bad things and then says, 'This is Lagos,'" Olajuwon told *Ebony* magazine. "There are bad things, sure, but in Lagos we have designer clothes, big buildings, videos, and many other things that people enjoy in America."

TOO TALL? Olajuwon has made a lot of money because he is tall, but when he was six-feet-nine-inches at age 15 it was not that easy. Not knowing as much about basketball as teenagers in the United States, his friends teased him. "They would tease me all the time in Nigeria, and I would get into fights every day," he told the *Chicago Tribune*. "Sometimes I would be ashamed of being so tall. I would wish I was normal height so I can be friendly just like everyone else. Everywhere I went, people were looking. My parents knew why I was always fighting, and they tried to encourage me about my height."

DISCOVERS BASKETBALL. Olajuwon didn't play basketball until his senior year in high school, at the Moslem Teacher College. Before then he had been a goalie on the soccer team, and he also played team handball. Recognizing Olajuwon's athletic skill, coach Oscar Johnson of the Nigerian national basketball team talked Olajuwon into trying the American game. "Once I start playing basketball I don't play those other sports again," he told *Sport*. The adjustment to basketball was hard for Olajuwon. "They don't show you basketball on TV [in Nigeria]," Hakeem told *Sport*. "If you turn it on to watch sport they will show you soccer game, that's what you will see. So I had just to learn the rules of basketball and the form, how to shoot."

Although he had to teach Olajuwon the simplest moves, like how to dunk, Richard Mills, the coach of the Nigerian national basketball team, made Olajuwon the team's center. It wasn't long before the six-feet-eleven-inches, 17-year-old Olajuwon was leading the Nigerian basketball team in the All-African games. In 1979 the Nigerian team won third place in the All-African tournament. During this time, Olajuwon was discovered by a U.S. State Department employee, Chris Pond, who arranged for him to visit colleges in the United States.

COMING TO AMERICA. Olajuwon arrived in New York City on a chilly October day in 1980. "I thought it was too cold for me to live in this country," he told *People* magazine. He liked the warm weather in Houston, Texas, much better. At the University of Houston he met coach Guy Lewis, who Pond had said was a good man. Lewis wasn't sure about how good Olajuwon was before he met him. "I've had hundreds of foreign kids referred to us over the years," Lewis told *People*. "Frankly, they just don't play basketball in most countries the way they play it in the U.S."

Hakeem Olajuwon

At nearly seven feet tall, Olajuwon possessed more speed and moved around better than most players his size. He was also undisciplined, underweight, and out of shape. Lewis offered Olajuwon a full athletic scholarship to Houston, but did not put him on the team his first year in order to teach him the game and help him gain some weight. He ate plenty of steak and ice cream and tried to learn the American style of basketball play. Professional basketball star Moses Malone, then with the Houston Rockets, played one-on-one with him to improve his defensive ability.

COLLEGE. His first year on the Cougar basketball team was difficult for Olajuwon, who was in constant foul trouble and only averaged eighteen minutes of the forty-minute college game. Houston reached the semifinal game of the National Collegiate Athletic Association (NCAA) tournament, where Houston lost to eventual national champion, the University of

North Carolina, 68-63. The next season Houston was nearly unstoppable. Led by a front court of **Clyde Drexler** (see entry), Larry Micheaux, and Olajuwan, a trio also known as the "Phi Slamma Jamma" (a take off on college fraternity names), the Cougars won twenty-five straight games and spent much of the season ranked number one. Olajuwon lead the country in blocked shots and averaged more than 13 points and 11 rebounds per game.

Olajuwon scored 21 points, grabbed 22 rebounds, and blocked eight shots as Houston defeated the Louisville Cardinals, 94-81, in the semifinals of the NCAA tournament. Heavily favored to defeat North Carolina State University in the final game, Houston was upset, 54-52, on a buzzer-beating tip-in by Lorenzo Charles of a desperation shot. Olajuwan scored 20 points and had 18 rebounds in the losing cause. Olajuwan was named Most Valuable Player (MVP) of the Final Four, a rare feat for a player from the losing team.

Drexler and Micheaux were gone for the 1983-84 season, but Olajuwon was prepared to carry the Houston team. And carry them he did, averaging 16 points and a nation-leading 13.5 rebounds per game. Houston advanced to the Final Four of the NCAA tournament for the third straight season. In the semifinals, Houston defeated the Virginia Cavaliers, 49-47 in overtime, setting up a national championship matchup between Houston and the Georgetown Hoyas, with their fine center **Patrick Ewing** (see entry). In the first of many meetings between Olajuwon and Ewing, Ewing and the Hoyas won, 84-75. Ewing was named the tournament's MVP, but Olajuwon also made the all-tournament team.

SUPERSTAR

FIRST PICK. Having proved he could play with the best in the world, Olajuwon gave up his last year at Houston. The Houston Rockets held the first pick in the draft, and used it to pick Olajuwon. (Picked third in the same draft was **Michael Jordan** [see entry]). In his first years with the Rockets, Olajuwon was paired with seven-feet-four-inches tall Ralph Sampson, a frontcourt known as the "Twin Towers." Olajuwon averaged

20.6 points and 11.9 rebounds a game, finished second to Jordan in Rookie of the Year voting, and lead the Rockets to a second-place finish in the NBA Midwest division. Houston lost in the first round of the playoffs to the Utah Jazz, three games to two.

Olajuwon became a true star in his second season (1985-86), averaging 23.5 points and 11.4 rebounds and being named to the All-NBA second team. Houston won their division and then defeated the Los Angeles Lakers, led by **Magic Johnson** (see entry), in the Western Conference finals. In the NBA finals, against the Boston Celtics, Olajuwon faced two All-Star centers, Robert Parish and Bill Walton. Led by **Larry Bird** (see entry), the Celtics used a well-balanced attack to defeat the Rockets four games to two.

Considered a contender for the NBA crown in 1986-87, the Rockets instead did poorly, finishing third in their division and losing in the second round of the playoffs to the Seattle Supersonics. After a slow start in 1987-88, the Rockets gave up on the "twin tower" idea, trading Ralph Sampson. Olajuwon finished the season in the top ten in scoring (22.8 per game), rebounding (11.4 per game), and blocked shots (3.39 per game), but the Rockets lost in the first round of the playoffs to the Dallas Mavericks. Frustrated, Olajuwon became angry at his teammates and blamed the team's management for not finding quality players.

INJURED. Houston's problems continued the next two seasons, losing in the first round of the playoffs both years. Olajuwon still dominated, winning back-to-back rebounding titles (13.5 per game in 1988-89 and 14 per game in 1989-90), scoring over 24 point per game, and leading the league in blocked shots in 1989-90 (4.59 per game), but his supporting cast was weak. Olajuwon's career almost came to an end on January 3, 1991, when Chicago Bulls' center Bill Cartwright elbowed him in the face, breaking the bone around his right eye. Olajuwon missed 25 games, but, surprisingly, the Rockets won 15 of them. When Olajuwon returned the Rockets won 13 straight games. Their success was short-lived, however, as they once again lost in the first round of the playoffs to the Los Angeles Lakers.

HAKEEM "THE DREAM"

How does Hakeem Olajuwon stack up with the other NBA great centers? The following chart shows how they compare in scoring and rebounding averages.

Player	Average Scoring	Rebounds
H. Olajuwon	23.7	12.5
K. Abdul-Jabbar	24.6	11.2
W. Chamberlain	30.1	22.9
B. Russell	15.1	22.5

The 1991-92 season was difficult for Olajuwon, who feuded with Houston management, trying to renegotiate his contract. When Olajuwon said he had a pulled hamstring muscle and refused to play a game in March 1992, he was suspended for five games, all of which the Rockets lost. (Doctors later said that Olajuwon actually was injured.) Houston failed to make the playoffs for the first time in Olajuwon's career, so he asked to be traded.

BEST SEASON. New coach Rudy Tomjanovich urged the Houston owners not to trade Olajuwon, and during the 1992-93 season Olajuwon played the best basketball of his career. He scored a career-best 26.1 points per game, pulled down 13 rebounds, and led the league in blocked shots with 4.17 a game. Most importantly, Olajuwon showed a new willingness to not do everything himself and to trust his teammates. Named the NBA's Defensive Player of the Year, Olajuwon finished second to **Charles Barkley** (see entry) of the Phoenix Suns in MVP voting. The Rockets won a team record 55 games and won the Midwest division, but lost in the second round of the playoffs to the Seattle Supersonics in a tough seven-game series.

The Rockets opened the 1993-94 season by tying an NBA record by winning their first 15 games, and Olajuwon was the early favorite to win MVP honors. During his career Olajuwon has been named to the All-NBA first team five times and has been an All-Star player nine out of ten seasons.

OFF THE COURT. Over the years Olajuwon has become a devout Muslim. He prays every day and carries a compass to find the direction of Mecca, the Muslim holy land. Olajuwon speaks English, French, and four African languages. He lives in a suburb of Houston and has a daughter, Abisola. In summing up Olajuwon's ability, Seattle Supersonics coach George Karl said simply, "[He] is the second best basketball player in the world, and I never thought anyone would even get close to Michael [Jordan]."

WHERE TO WRITE

C/O HOUSTON ROCKETS, THE SUMMIT,

10 GREENWAY PLAZA EAST, HOUSTON, TX 77046.

SHAQUILLE O'NEAL

1972—

"Believe me, I'm going to be the man in this league someday. Five years from now, I don't know what they'll be saying about me."—Shaquille O'Neal

Basketball player Shaquille O'Neal has the potential for superstardom on the same level as all-time great centers Wilt Chamberlain, Kareem Abdul-Jabbar, and Bill Russell, all players who dominated the National Basketball Association (NBA). O'Neal signed a multimillion dollar contract with the Orlando Magic when he was only twenty years old. He won the National Basketball Association's Rookie of the Year award and is currently the most popular player in the league.

O'Neal's college statistics were impressive: "The Shack," or just Shaq, as he is known, led the National Collegiate Athletic Association (NCAA) in rebounding and finished near the top in scoring, blocked shots, and shooting percentage. University of Texas Coach Tom Penders told the *Atlanta Constitution*, "He's as big as Jabbar, if not bigger, stronger than Chamberlain and runs like **Magic Johnson** (see entry)." If all the experts' predictions of greatness come true, O'Neal will dominate the NBA for years to come.

GROWING UP

Shaquille Rashaun O'Neal was born on March 6, 1972, in Newark, New Jersey. His first name means "little one" in Arabic, and his middle name means "warrior." Since his parents, Philip Harrison and Lucille O'Neal, didn't marry until he was three, O'Neal took his mother's maiden name as his last name. The son of an army sergeant, O'Neal's early years were spent in the rough areas of Newark and nearby Jersey City. "It's kind of rough in Newark," he told the *New York Daily News*. "I'm glad my father took me out of there. If I'd have stayed, I think I would have been a troublesome kid, hanging around, doing the wrong thing."

MEETS COACH BROWN. When O'Neal was 12, his father transferred to an army base in Wildflecken, West Germany. When he was 13, he met Dale Brown, head coach of the Louisiana State University (LSU) basketball team. Brown was in Germany conducting coaching clinics, and O'Neal went to one. "I asked him if he had any information on how to improve my vertical jump," O'Neal told the *Rocky Mountain News*. "As he reached in his briefcase, he asked me, 'How long have you been in the Army, soldier?' I told him I was 13. He said, 'Where's your father?' My dad was in the sauna. Coach Brown had a nice suit on, but he went right in the sauna, found my dad, shook his hand and said, 'It's nice to meet you, Mr. Harrison.'"

Brown made a sales pitch for O'Neal to attend LSU, but his father stopped him . "He said to me, 'Well, basketball, that's fine. But I'm concerned with this young man's education,'" Brown recalled in the *Philadelphia Daily News*. "Then, he went on to tell me he thought it was about time for blacks to become managers, not laborers; to become generals, not sergeants; head coaches, not assistants. I told him, 'Sergeant, we're going to get along just fine.'"

SERGEANT DAD. Throughout his young life, O'Neal has been strongly influenced by his father, a career soldier and strict disciplinarian. O'Neal also has two younger sisters and a younger brother. "In junior high in Germany I fought kids all the time," O'Neal remembered in *Sports Illustrated*. "I had such a bad temper, I almost got thrown out of school. A few lickings from my dad got me out of that scene. He wore me out with a paddle." One time his father grabbed O'Neal during half-time at a high school basketball game and ordered him to tuck in his shirt. "I always told Shaquille the world has too many followers," Harrison said in *Sports Illustrated*. "What he needed to be was a leader. He'd see guys hanging out on the corner, and he'd know they were followers. I told him I'd whup him rather than have the guys on the corner whup him. I told him there's no half-stepping in this life."

HIGH SCHOOL. In 1987, the O'Neal family moved to San Antonio, Texas, where Harrison was stationed at Fort Sam Houston. O'Neal attended Cole High School, was a B student, and continued to grow, reaching six-feet-ten-inches tall and 250 pounds. He led Cole High's basketball team to a 32-1 win/loss record, but he was still not considered an outstanding college prospect. During O'Neal's senior year, his father told him if he was not going to play his hardest, then he may as well not play at all. That same night O'Neal scored 52 points in a tournament game in Lubbock, Texas. The next week, he received letters from Georgetown and North Carolina, two college basketball powerhouses, asking him to play for them.

Cole High went 36-0 in O'Neal's senior season and won the Texas state title. Several colleges offered O'Neal scholarships, and he chose LSU, where Brown was still coach. "I chose LSU, first, because Coach Brown was honest. Second, the players were like family. They were close. Other places, one goes this way, one goes that way. Here, they're together," O'Neal said in the *Houston Post*.

JOINS LSU. LSU was expected to contend for a national title when O'Neal joined them in 1989. The Tigers featured Stanley Roberts, a seven-feet tall freshman power forward, and Chris Jackson, a high-scoring All-American. O'Neal found himself the third wheel on the team, and it was a difficult transition for him. Jackson did most of the shooting on the team, and O'Neal was forced to concentrate on rebounding. He still averaged 13.9 points and 12 rebounds per game, and he established a Southeastern Conference record of 115 blocked shots. He also fouled out of nine games. The year ended when LSU lost in the first round of the NCAA tournament.

A year later O'Neal played in the National Sports Festival, an event featuring the country's top amateur (unpaid) athletes. During the tournament he dominated players that were three and four years older. He finished by averaging 24.5 points and 13.8 rebounds per game and was named the tournament's Most Valuable Player.

When O'Neal returned to LSU that year, he found himself in a better position. Jackson had left college to join the Denver Nuggets of the NBA and Roberts went to play in Spain. Coach Brown made O'Neal co-captain. During the summer O'Neal had increased his vertical jump from 16 inches in his senior year in high school to 42 inches. With his arms outstretched, he could touch a spot two-and-a-half feet above the rim.

Shaquille O'Neal

BECOMES A STAR. His new jumping ability helped make O'Neal the dominant player in college basketball. During the 1990-91 season, he led the NCAA in rebounding with 15.2 a game. He was also sixth among all college players in scoring (28.5 points per game), fourth in blocked shots (4.8 per game), and fourteenth in shooting percentage (63.9 percent). After a January game, in which O'Neal scored 34 points and snared 16 rebounds, discouraged Georgia coach Hugh Durham admitted in *Sports Illustrated*: "Shack may be unguardable."

The key to O'Neal's success has been using his size to overpower opponents. Tim Povtak, an *Orlando Sentinel* writer, called O'Neal "a powerful giant with a feathery [soft] touch who can control a basketball game in so many ways. He blocks shots like [New York Knicks] center **Patrick Ewing** [see entry], but runs the floor like [Utah Jazz forward] **Karl Malone** [see entry]. He is strong enough to knock down anyone, but is graceful enough to dribble the length of the court and athletic enough to take an errant [off-target] alley-oop pass, change his course in midflight and still slam it."

HALL-OF-FAME HELP. In 1991, Coach Brown asked two teachers to help O'Neal with his game—Hall-of-Fame centers Kareem Abdul-Jabbar and Bill Walton. Abdul-Jabbar showed him his sky hook, while Walton taught him offensive moves and shot-blocking. The training improved O'Neal's already great game. Brown told the *Rocky Mountain News*: "Bill and Kareem did many things we'd been trying to teach Shaquille. But it's like raising a child. You can keep telling him something. But when somebody he respects tells him the same thing, it makes an indelible impression."

TURNS PRO. Professional scouts and coaches tried to convince O'Neal to leave college and join the NBA. There was no doubt that he could challenge the Houston Rockets' **Hakeem Olajuwon** (see entry), the San Antonio Spurs' **David Robinson** (see entry), and the New York Knicks's **Patrick Ewing** (see entry) as the top center in professional basketball. O'Neal resisted, announcing plans to stay at LSU for another season before considering turning pro. His goal, he said, was to improve his game and try to win an NCAA championship. "I'm just a big kid right now, and I'm in no hurry to grow up," O'Neal told the *Philadelphia Daily News*. "Like my dad always said, 'College can be the best four years of your life,' and so far it is."

O'Neal changed his mind, however—against the wishes of his parents, who longed to see him finish college—and in April 1992 decided to give up his senior year at LSU to be available for the upcoming NBA draft. In June, to no one's surprise, he was the first overall draft pick, chosen by the Orlando Magic. O'Neal signed with the Magic for a reported $40 million over seven years.

SUPERSTAR

ROOKIE OF THE YEAR. Becoming professional basketball's highest-paid rookie, O'Neal had to live up to great expectations in his first year. He didn't disappoint anyone. O'Neal was the first rookie to start in the NBA All-Star game since **Michael Jordan** (see entry) in 1985. He was also the only player in the league to finish in the top ten in scoring (23.4 points per game; eighth), rebounding (13.9 per game, second), field-goal percentage (.562; fourth), and blocked shots (3.53 per game, second). O'Neal pulled down backboards in two cities with the monster dunks that became his trademark and was a near-unanimous choice as the NBA's Rookie of the Year.

PLAYOFF BOUND. The Magic qualified for the NBA playoffs for the first time in their history during the 1993-94 season. The addition of point guard Anfernee Hardaway helped O'Neal have a fantastic season. O'Neal finished second in the NBA in both scoring (29.3 points per game) and rebounding (13.2 per game). Orlando won 50 games, good for second place in the NBA Eastern Division. The season ended in disappointment for O'Neal, however, when the Indiana Pacers upset Orlando in the first round of the NBA playoffs. Despite the loss the Magic established themselves as one of the elite teams in the NBA.

OFF THE COURT. O'Neal's success led to numerous opportunities off the court. His $4 million annual basketball salary is less than half of what he will make from other activities. During the summer between the 1992-93 and 1993-94 NBA seasons, O'Neal released an autobiography, *Shaq Attack*, and a rap album, *Shaq Diesel*. He also made a movie, *Blue Chips*, with Nick Nolte. One of the most popular product endorsers in sports, O'Neal stars in television commercials for Pepsi and Reebok athletic equipment, featuring the "Shaq Attack" line of shoes (O'Neal wears size 21). In addition, Shaq basketballs,

SHAQ vs. MOURNING

O'Neal's rookie season was marked by the beginning of a rivalry between him and fellow rookie center Alonzo Mourning of the Charlotte Hornets. While O'Neal won the Rookie of the Year award and got most of the attention, Mourning has stayed out of the spotlight. "I could care less about all these commercials," Mourning told the *Sporting News*. "I'll leave all that stuff and the big money to Shaq."

action figures, trading cards, video games, t-shirts, and pre-shattered backboards are also being sold.

Shaq lives with his Rottweiler dog, Shazaam, in Orlando, Florida, and bought his family a house there. His hobbies include rapping and going to water parks and amusement parks, where he likes to ride go-carts and roller coasters. (O'Neal says he wants to build the world's largest roller coaster and call it "Shaq Mountain.")

THE FUTURE. While the opportunities for making money are great, some people worry that O'Neal may be doing too much. "This is the sort of thing that probably has people around the league worried," Charlotte Hornets President Spencer Stolpen told the *Sporting News*. "Is he [O'Neal] more concerned with being the best player he can be, or the best rapper he can be?" O'Neal answered his critics by telling the *Sporting News*: "I'm too young to get out of bed in the morning with nothing to do. I can relax when I get older. Guys like me set their goals real, real high. And I expect to reach them."

WHERE TO WRITE
C/O ORLANDO MAGIC, ORLANDO ARENA,
ONE MAGIC PLACE, ORLANDO, FL 328001.

SCOTTIE PIPPEN

1965—

S cottie Pippen is a rare superstar, an outstanding basketball player who arrived from Arkansas as an almost complete unknown. Pippen—a versatile player who averaged 18.6 points, 7.7 rebounds, 6.3 assists, and 2.13 steals per game in the 1992-93 basketball season for the three-time National Basketball Association (NBA) champion Chicago Bulls—was not even asked to play basketball on the major college level. Instead he began his college days as a team manager, not knowing that some day he would be a part of the 1992 U.S. Olympic "Dream Team," considered the greatest basketball team ever assembled.

"Pippen is one of the rare athletes in professional basketball, which features the most athletic players in sport," wrote Sam Smith in the *Chicago Tribune*. "He's tall yet both strong and quick. He can jump with big men and outrun smaller ones.... He fills numerous roles for the Bulls. He's a playmaker and a rebounder, a scorer and defender. He is one of the few players in the game who can take the ball off the backboard on one end, travel the length of the court and finish with a score on the other end." Teamed with **Michael Jordan** (see entry), Pippen has helped make the Chicago Bulls one of the best teams in NBA history.

"He's tall yet both strong and quick. He can jump with big men and outrun smaller ones."—Chicago Tribune *writer Sam Amith*

GROWING UP

Pippen was born September 25, 1965, in Hamburg, Arkansas, the youngest of 12 children born to Preston and Ethel Pippen. Hamburg, with its population of little more than 3,000, is located in the southeastern corner of Arkansas. Pippen's father worked at the major company in town, a paper mill plant.

With six boys in the family, the Pippens had their own basketball team at the local playground. When Pippen was a freshman in high school, his father suffered a severe stroke, forcing him to stay in a wheelchair and making him unable to talk. As his family tried to deal with this illness, Pippen joined the high school basketball team. At 15 he was still not as tall as his mother, and, as he told *Sports Illustrated*, "I didn't have any big plans for basketball."

HIGH SCHOOL. Pippen played so little as a sophomore at Hamburg High that he skipped the basketball team's off-season training program and served as manager of the football team. "I was responsible for taking care of the equipment, jerseys, stuff like that," he told *Sports Illustrated*. "I always enjoyed doing that, just being a regular manager."

Pippen enjoyed being the manager so much, in fact, that he was almost cut from the basketball team during his junior season. It took a vote from the other players to convince the coach to put him back on the team. Pippen rarely played that season, but he grew during the summer, and was the starting point guard in his senior season. Despite his growth, he was still small for a basketball player at five-feet-11-inches tall and 145 pounds. Following his senior season, Pippen did not receive a single college scholarship offer.

HELPING HAND. Luckily for Pippen, his high school coach, Donald Wayne, had played basketball for Donald Dyer, the basketball coach at Central Arkansas University. Wayne was able to talk Coach Dyer into giving Pippen at least some financial assistance to attend college— as manager of the basketball team. "Skin and bones," Dyer remembers. "You never would have thought he would make any kind of a player. I mean, he had some talent, but he was so small and skinny."

To Pippen's surprise, he continued to grow taller throughout college. Soon he was playing for, not managing, the basketball team. By the middle of his freshman year he was six-feet-three-inches tall, and by the beginning of his sophomore year he had grown an additional two inches, to become one of the tallest players on the team. Pippen played point guard, forward, and center, moving around to confuse the opposition and take advantage of his many skills.

Scottie Pippen

SMALL COLLEGE STAR. In his senior season at Central Arkansas, Pippen averaged 23.6 points, 10 rebounds, and 4.3 assists a game, while shooting almost 60 percent from both the field and three-point range. Professional scouts began to hear about Pippen's ability, but it was difficult finding out much information about him. Central Arkansas was a small school that played weak competition and few scouts were willing to go to Arkansas to see Pippen play. One person who was convinced about Pippen's talent was Marty Blake, the NBA's head of scouting. "I advised as many teams as I could to go see him play," Blake told *Sports Illustrated*, "but when you're dealing with a player they've never heard of from a small college, the trick is to make people believe he is bona fide [the real thing]. Some believe, some don't."

Pippen graduated with a degree in industrial education. Even though professional teams were not showing much interest, Pippen was sure he could play in the NBA. Scouts began to believe in him, too, when he starred at several tournaments against quality opponents. Suddenly he was no longer an unknown player, but rather a promising athlete who was going to be a high first-round draft choice. Jerry Krause, an official of the Chicago Bulls, was very impressed with Pippen, especially since the young player held his own with talented players from bigger schools.

BECOMES A BULL. In order to make sure he could draft Pippen, Krause made a deal with the Seattle Supersonics, who had the fifth pick in the NBA draft. Seattle drafted Pippen, and then traded him to the Bulls for center Olden Polynice and other considerations. Pippen was proud to be drafted fifth overall, and when he called home, as he told the *New York Times*, his mother said: "Your daddy watched you on TV. He's got tears running down his face."

Pippen's first professional season got off to a slow start when he had surgery to repair a spinal disc in his back. He played 79 games his rookie year, but averaged only 7.9 points per game. In his second season (1988-89) Pippen established himself as a starter, averaging 14.4 points per game, second only to Michael Jordan on the Bulls. He helped the Bulls advance to the Eastern Conference finals against the Detroit Pistons, but suffered a concussion when he collided with Piston center Bill Laimbeer. The Bulls lost in six games to the Pistons.

WHAT A HEADACHE. In the 1989-90 season, Pippen showed the wide range of talents he possessed. He raised his scoring average to 16.5 points per game—second on the team to Jordan—and averaged 6.7 rebounds and 5.4 assists per game. He was named to the All-Star team for the first time. (He would also make the team in 1992 and 1993.) Once again the Bulls earned the right to play the Pistons for the Eastern Conference title. Pippen's performance was hurt by a mysterious migraine headache (a very painful headache), which he suffered before the seventh and deciding game of the series with the Pistons. His vision became blurred and he suffered throbbing pain. "I thought maybe I'd eaten something and gotten poisoned," he told the *Chicago Tribune*. Pippen played in the game, but he wasn't very effective, and the Pistons won the conference championship.

Critics of Pippen questioned his toughness after the Pistons series. They said that he played well when everything was going well for him, but had problems when he faced difficulties. Pippen felt that he was not voted onto the 1991 All-Star team because of those opinions. He was afraid the headache might come back. "It [his fear] stayed with me a long while, long into the season," he told the *Chicago Tribune*. "I'd come to games and sit there and wait sometimes, almost like I expected it to happen. And then it wouldn't. But I always had that fear. Nothing like that had ever happened to me before."

SUPERSTAR

COMEBACK. After a slow start, Pippen had his best season to date in 1990-91. Shooting better than 50 percent from the floor, Pippen averaged 17.8 points, 7.3 rebounds, and 6.2 assists per game. Refusing to be denied, the Bulls rolled through the playoffs, winning 15 out of 17 games on their way to the NBA championship. In an Eastern Conference finals rematch against the Pistons, Pippen averaged 22 points, 7.8 assists, and 5.3 rebounds per game. In the finals against the Los Angeles Lakers, Pippen guarded **Earvin "Magic" Johnson** (see entry) and disrupted the Lakers offense, then scored 32 points in the game that clinched the championship. The Bulls beat the Lakers four games to one.

Pippen told the *Chicago Tribune* that the Bulls's great season helped him overcome his disappointment over his past playoff performances. "It does make it better," he said. "That gave us an opportunity to redeem ourselves, and I, and my teammates, all got back into a position where we thought we should be last year. We've had a lot of guys step up their efforts to get us here [to the championship]. It's just been a great season."

REPEAT. The 1990-91 season was great for Pippen and the Bulls, but the 1991-92 season was even better. Pippen's individual statistics were career bests (21 points, 7.7 rebounds, and 7 assists per game) and the Bulls came within two victories of tying the NBA record for most wins in a season, finishing with 67. (The 1971-72 Los Angeles Lakers won 69 games.) The Bulls repeated as NBA champions, defeating the Portland Trail Blazers, four games to two, in the finals.

DREAM TEAMER. Now recognized as one of the best players in the NBA, Pippen was named to the 1992 U.S. Olympic "Dream Team." The strain of the extra games during the summer showed on Pippen, whose statistics slipped slightly (18.6 points, 7.7 rebounds, and 6.3 assists per game) during the 1992-93 NBA regular season. "I would say the season was O.K. under the circumstances," he said. "But I have too much pride to be satisfied. I always want to be looked at as being one of the elite players in the game."

THREEPEAT. Entering the playoffs, the Bulls were not favored to win. The Phoenix Suns, led by NBA Most Valuable Player **Charles Barkley** (see entry), had earned the league's best regular season record. More importantly, only two teams in NBA history—the Minneapolis Lakers (1951-54) and the Boston Celtics (1958-66)—had ever won three or more consecutive NBA championships. The Bulls were trying to make history, and they did. When Jordan had an off series against the New York Knicks in the Eastern Conference semifinals, Pippen raised the level of his play. In the NBA finals against the Suns, Pippen averaged 21.2 points per game and the Bulls defeated Phoenix, four games to two.

MAIN MAN. When Jordan retired prior to the 1993-94 season, Pippen became the Bulls's main man. He won the Most Valuable Player Award at the NBA All-Star Game and led the Bulls to 57 wins, good for second place in the NBA Central Division. Pippen averaged a career-best 22 points per game and also grabbed 8.7 rebounds a contest. The Bulls fell short of winning their fourth straight NBA title, however, losing in the Eastern Conference semifinals to the Knicks. The season was a success for Pippen, despite the playoff loss, because he proved he could be a team leader and be a great player without Jordan at his side.

OFF THE COURT. Success has brought financial security to Pippen. He signed a five-year, $18 million contract with the Bulls in 1991 and was hired by Nike to star in advertisements for their shoes. Pippen is ready to meet any challenges. "I like the idea of expectations being so high," he told Paul Ladewski, a writer for the *Southtown Economist*. "It keeps me wanting to continue to improve and wanting to be one of the top players."

WHERE TO WRITE

C/O CHICAGO BULLS, ONE MAGNIFICENT MILE,

980 N. MICHIGAN AVE., SUITE 1600, CHICAGO, IL 60611.

KIRBY PUCKETT

1961—

Kirby Puckett is living proof that one doesn't have to be tall and thin to be a baseball superstar. For over a decade the five-feet-eight-inch tall Puckett has been both a star hitter and fielder for the Minnesota Twins and has helped his team win two World Series titles (1987 and 1991). A .318 lifetime hitter (and 1989 American League batting champion with a .339 average) and six-time Gold Glove winner for fielding excellence, Puckett is one of the best all-around players in major league baseball.

"Little guys can be giants in the big leagues," wrote Roy Blount in *Sports Illustrated*. From the time he was a teenager, Puckett knew that he would never hit six-feet in height. "So I figured if I can't be tall, I'll be strong," Puckett told *Sports Illustrated*. "A bodybuilder, like Arnold Schwarzenegger." Although Puckett is shorter than many major leaguers, he weighs over 200 pounds—and it's mostly muscle. "You don't get to pick your body," he told *Esquire*. "God just hands 'em out as he sees fit. Would I like to be six-four or six-five, be tall and thin, look like [Los Angeles Dodger outfielder] Darryl Strawberry? Sure, that would be cool. Didn't work out that way, though. I got what I got."

GROWING UP

Kirby Puckett was born March 14, 1961, in Chicago, Illinois. The youngest of nine children of William and Catherine Puckett, he spent the first twelve years of his life in the Robert Taylor Homes, a rough housing project in Chicago's inner city. Puckett ignored the gangs and the drugs that surrounded him, because his life was baseball. He spent most of his childhood on baseball diamonds that he and his friends made with stones and chalk. After dark he would spend hours in his room with rolled-up socks and aluminum foil bats, playing out imaginary games. "I was a kid enjoying myself," he told *Sports Illustrated*. "I'd come home from school, do my homework, then look for kids to play ball with.... I loved baseball so much I was always thinking of ways I could keep playing."

Puckett calls his mom and dad his "heroes in life." They encouraged him to play baseball and helped him survive the tough conditions in which he grew up. "I can see some of these guys in the big leagues who came from those nice grassy fields in the suburbs and I just want to say, 'You have no idea.' But I wouldn't have wanted to grow up any other way." When he was eight, Puckett was already a star who played with older children.

UNNOTICED. Puckett did not play on an organized team until he went to high school. He played third base at Calumet High School in Chicago and for a semipro team called the Chicago Pirates. Puckett began his weight training in high school when it seemed certain that he wasn't going to be tall. The training helped increase his speed on the base paths and his endurance. Still, major league scouts were not impressed with his ability, and he did not receive any contract offers from professional teams. After high school graduation, Puckett went to work at a local Ford automobile manufacturing plant.

Kirby Puckett

Not giving up, Puckett participated in a tryout for the Kansas City Royals. Even though he didn't get any professional offers, he did receive a scholarship to play baseball for Bradley University in Peoria, Illinois. The Bradley coach, Dewey Kalmer, moved Puckett from third base to center field and worked with him on his offense. By the end of his first year, Puckett had earned the first of a string of awards—he was named to the all-Missouri Valley Conference team.

SIGNS WITH TWINS. After his father's death, Puckett left Bradley University to be nearer his mother. He enrolled at Triton Community College. Puckett hit .472 with 42 stolen bases in his one season at Triton, led his team to the national junior college finals, and finally attracted professional scouts. The Minnesota Twins drafted Puckett in the first round of the January 1982 draft. Puckett was sent to the minor leagues, first to Elizabethton in the Appalachian League. There he hit .382 and led the league in seven categories, including batting average, at-bats, hits, runs, total bases, and stolen bases. *Baseball America* named him that league's Player of the Year. In 1983 he was promoted to Visalia, California, where he batted .314 and was selected the California League's Best Major League Prospect. He was called up to the major leagues by the Twins in the spring of 1984.

MAJOR LEAGUER. In his first game, on May 8, 1984, Puckett had four hits in five at bats. By the end of the year, he was a starter and the Twins's Rookie of the Year. He batted .296 his first season and .288 his second season (1985), with 74 runs batted in. Puckett proved he could hit for a high average, but he had little or no power, hitting a total of only four home runs in his first two seasons. Hall-of-Famer Reggie Jackson, making fun of Puckett, called him a "Punch and Judy" hitter, someone who is too weak to hit home runs. Realizing he had to improve his power, Puckett worked during the off-season and spring training to make better use of his strength.

ALL-STAR. In 1986 Puckett hit 31 home runs and had 96 runs batted in, statistics matching those of the best power hitters. He also batted .328 (third in the league), stroked 223 hits (second in the league), scored 119 runs (second in the league) and won his first Gold Glove award for fielding excellence in center field, the most difficult outfield position. (The centerfielder is usually one of the fastest players on the team and is responsible for covering the largest area of the field. Puckett, even though he is not thin, is one of the Twins's fastest runners.) Puckett was named to his first All-Star team (he would be on the team every year through 1992) and finished sixth in the voting for Most Valuable Player, won that year by **Roger Clemens** (see entry) of the Boston Red Sox.

SUPERSTAR

WORLD CHAMPS. Puckett's individual improvement, however, did not help make the Twins a better team. In his first three seasons, Minnesota's win total dropped from 81 in 1984, to 77 in 1985, to 71 in 1986. But everything came together in 1987, as Puckett had another outstanding season (.332 average, 28 home runs, 99 runs batted in, and a league leading 207 hits), leading the Twins to their first American League Western division title since 1970. Facing the powerful Detroit Tigers, winners of 98 games in the regular season, in the American League Championship series, the Twins pulled off an upset, winning their first American League pennant since 1965, four games to one. In the World Series against the St. Louis Cardinals, Puckett was a star, batting .357. The Twins, winning all four games in the noisy Metrodome, defeated the Cardinals to win their first ever World Series championship.

> ### KIRBY BEAR
>
> Kirby Puckett became so popular in Minnesota in 1987 that the Twins sold a Kirby Bear, a stuffed doll wearing Puckett's number 34 jersey. The bears sold so fast that the Twins had a hard time making enough of them. Matt Hoy of the Twins told the *Minneapolis Star*: "Nobody had even seen the bears, but it's the kind of thing that everybody wants, because Kirby is so popular. He's just a huggable looking guy. That's where the teddy bear [idea] came from."

THE 1980S

Kirby Puckett had the third-highest batting average of any major league player during the decade of the eighties. The top five are as follows:

Player	Hits	Average
Wade Boggs	1597	.352
Tony Gwynn	1354	.332
Kirby Puckett	1243	.3234
Don Mattingly	1300	.3232
Rod Carew	838	.314

BEST HITTER. For the next three seasons, the American League Western division was dominated by the Oakland Athletics. By 1990, Minnesota had fallen all the way to last place. The Twins's fall was not Puckett's fault, however, as he continued to perform at a superstar level. In 1988, he acheived career-best records in batting average (.356, second in the league), hits (234, first in the league), and runs batted in (121, second in the league). The next season Puckett won the American League batting championship, hitting .339 and again leading the league in hits with 215. In 1989 Puckett briefly became the highest-paid player in baseball.

BACK ON TOP. 1990 was an off year for both Puckett and the Twins. Minnesota finished last in their division, and Puckett's average dropped below .300 (.298) for the first time in five seasons. No one expected much from the Twins in 1991, but, helped by the addition of pitcher Jack Morris, Minnesota was the surprise team in the American League, going from worst (last place) in 1990 to first in 1991. The Twins won 95 games and the Western division crown, and Puckett, with his .319 batting average, was a big reason for their success. In the American League Championship Series, Minnesota defeated the Toronto Blue Jays four games to one, with Puckett batting .429.

The World Series was a classic battle between the Twins and the Atlanta Braves. Three games were decided in extra innings and four games were won in a team's last at bat. Puckett batted only .250 in the Series, but one of his hits was one of the biggest of all time. In Game Six, with the Twins facing elimination, Puckett hit a home run deep into the left-center-field seats of the Metrodome to give Minnesota a 4-3 win in 11 innings. The next night, Minnesota won its second world championship, as Morris pitched a 1-0 shutout, with Dan Gladden scoring the winning run in the bottom of the tenth inning.

STAYS AT HOME. Minnesota won 90 games in 1992 but finished second in their division to the Oakland A's. Puckett finished second in the league in batting average (.329), first in hits (210), and fourth in runs scored (104). He also drove in 110 runs. Puckett became a free-agent (able to sign with any team) following the 1992 season, and many thought he would leave Minnesota. In a major surprise, Puckett accepted less money from the Twins than he could have gotten from other teams and re-signed with Minnesota. Explaining his decision, Puckett said "I thought about my family. I didn't only think about baseball. Who's to say that you will be much happier elsewhere? The grass isn't always greener on the other side. I'm happy to be a Minnesota Twin for the rest of my career." Describing the Minneapolis-St. Paul area to *Sports Illustrated*, Puckett said: "There is no prejudice in Minneapolis at all. It's one of the best places for interracial things, the kind of place that you want your kids to grow up in. Even if I get traded I'll keep a house in Minneapolis."

Trying to save money, Minnesota began trading away many of its higher-priced players. The Twins won only 71 games in 1993 and Puckett batted .296. Puckett's five-year, $30 million contract will keep him in Minnesota for several more seasons. His teammates call him "Puck," because he is shorter than other players, and Puckett shaves his head before every season. Puckett lives near Minneapolis with his wife Tonya and their daughter, Catherine. Success has not changed Puckett, who is considered one of the nicest and most easygoing players in the major leagues. "I'm living out my dream every day," Puckett told *Esquire* magazine. "I think of myself as an average person. I've never thought I was God's greatest gift to the game of baseball. But I came in smiling and I'm gonna leave smiling."

WHERE TO WRITE

C/O MINNESOTA TWINS,

HUBERT H. HUMPHREY METRODOME,

501 CHICAGO AVE., S., MINNEAPOLIS, MN 55415.

JERRY RICE

1962—

When Jerry Rice was in college, the experts said he wasn't fast enough to be a star receiver in the NFL. Nine seasons and 124 touchdowns later, not many players who have tried to cover Rice will question his speed. As a vital part of the San Francisco 49ers high-powered offense, Rice has caught 708 passes in the regular season for 11,776 yards and an NFL record 118 touchdowns. Many other receiving records are within his grasp and his position as one of the greatest receivers in NFL history is unquestioned. As New York Jets General Manager Dick Steinberg told the *Sporting News:* "From the standpoint of what he has accomplished, he is the best. There might have been players who were faster or maybe some who have had better hands [for catching the ball] but for the games he has won, the big plays he has made, I don't think you will get an argument if you call him the best.... It puts him in a class by himself."

GROWING UP

Jerry Rice was born October 13, 1962, in the African American community of Crawford, Mississippi. His father, Joe Nathan, was a bricklayer who built a home for his large family on the edge of a pasture. When his dad had a lot of work, Rice helped by carrying bricks and mortar. "I always did have good work habits," Rice told *Newsday*. "I guess it's from my parents. I take a lot of pride in everything and try to be the best in what I'm doing. Every time I step on the football field, it's not like a job to me; I really enjoy it. Working with my father taught me the necessity of hard work. On my mother's side, I'm a caring person. I guess that's why I've been successful."

LEARNS LESSON. Rice and his five brothers played sports, made up games of their own, and chased horses in the pasture until one could be caught and ridden. Rice was also known to play pranks, and his football career began when he tried to skip school. As he tells the story, he was sneaking out of the school building when the vice principal saw him and told him to stop. Rice didn't stop—he ran, with the vice principal right behind him. He was caught, whipped, and sent to the gym for football practice. Rice told the *Los Angeles Times* that the principal "made me go out for the [football] team, and that's how I started playing the game. Until the day I played hooky [skipped school], I had no intention of playing football."

TOO SLOW? In high school Rice played just about every position, from quarterback to lineman, and though he was a good athlete, few colleges showed interest in him. But one college coach *was* interested—Archie Cooley, then with tiny Mississippi Valley State in Itta Bena. Cooley saw in Rice a graceful, speedy, and nearly unstoppable wide receiver. He had caught over 100 passes in each of his last two seasons at Mississippi Valley, and had 28 touchdown catches as a senior. Professional scouts, however, were not convinced. "The only question you had about him was that he didn't have the blazing speed," scout Dick Steinberg told the *Sporting News*. "You knew he

Jerry Rice

would be a productive receiver in the league [NFL]. But you couldn't see the greatness."

His college feats drew the attention of San Francisco 49ers coach Bill Walsh who wanted Rice so badly that he traded in order to be able to select him in the sixteenth pick of the first round of the NFL draft. Even though Rice had played at a small school, Walsh saw that he had the ability to be a great receiver. "Jerry's movements were spectacular for a pass receiver, no matter the levels," Walsh told the *Los Angeles Times.* "He'd been catching 100 passes year after year. We felt that if they'd throw to him that much, and if he'd catch that many, he must have the basic instincts for the job." Walsh also realized that even though Rice wasn't as fast as some receivers in sprints, he had good "football" speed, the ability to run pass patterns and know when to run his fastest.

JOINS 49ERS. At first drafting Rice seemed a mistake. As a rookie in 1985, he dropped 15 passes—a problem which came from trying to learn the complicated 49ers offense. He simply had to learn the moves he said, so that he could run a play without thinking about it. Once he felt comfortable, he began to catch passes, 49 by the end of the season for 927 yards (an average of 18.9 yards per catch) and three touchdowns. He broke the 49ers's single game receiving record with 241 yards. He was a unanimous choice for the 1985-86 NFL All-Rookie team.

In 1986 Rice caught 86 passes and led the NFL with 1,570 yards and 15 touchdowns. Following the season he was named to play in his first Pro Bowl (all-star game), a game he would play in every season but one (1988). Rice had an even better season in 1987 when he set NFL records for receiving touchdowns in a single season (22) and touchdown catches in consecutive games (13). His regular season scoring total of 138 points led the league and set a team record. At season's end Rice won Most Valuable Player honors from the Pro Football Writers of America, the *Sporting News,* and *Pro Football Weekly.* Rice's season ended in disappointment, however, when the 49ers lost their first playoff game to the Minnesota Vikings, 36-24. "I don't think about how many touchdowns I scored," he told the *San Jose Mercury News.* "I don't think about the yardage. I guess a lot of people sit down and look at stats. But not me. I just want to go to the Super Bowl."

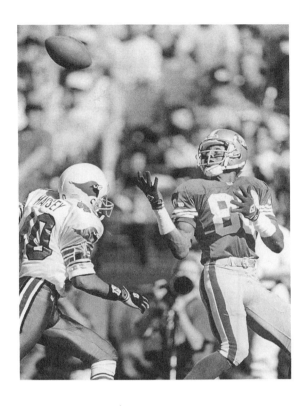

Jerry Rice waits for a pass.

SUPERSTAR

SUPER BOWL STAR. Rice got his wish following the 1988 season, when the 49ers met the Cincinnati Bengals in the Super Bowl and won a dramatic 20-16 victory. **Joe Montana** (see entry) threw ten yards to John Taylor for the last-minute winning touchdown—a play set-up by a 27 yard catch by Rice. That was just one of 12 catches Rice made that day (for 215 yards), despite injuring his ankle before the game and being double-covered on almost every play. When the votes were counted for the Most Valuable Player in the game, Rice came out the winner.

REPEAT. Claiming that he was tired of coaching, Bill Walsh retired following the 49ers Super Bowl victory. He was replaced by defensive coach George Siefert and San Francisco kept on winning, earning a NFL leading record of 14-2. His ankle bothered him throughout the 1989 season, but Rice led the league in receiving yards (1,483) and receiving touchdowns (17). The 49ers defeated their first two playoff opponents, the Minnesota Vikings and the Los Angeles Rams, by a combined score of 71-16. Returning to the Super Bowl to play the Denver Broncos, the 49ers and Rice were unstoppable. Rice caught seven passes against the frustrated Denver

TOUCHDOWN CATCHES

Jerry Rice is the all-time NFL leader in touchdown catches and adds to his record every season. Here is a list of the top five touchdown catchers in NFL history.

Player	Years Played	TD Catches
Jerry Rice	1985-	118
Don Hutson	1935-45	100
Steve Largent	1976-89	100
Don Maynard	1958, 1960-73	88
Lance Alworth	1962-72	85
Paul Warfield	1964-74, 1976-77	85

defense for 148 yards and the 49ers won, 55-10. The final score set records for most points scored by a team in the Super Bowl and the biggest margin of victory. With four Super Bowl championships in the decade, the 49ers were the "Team of the 80s."

The 49ers repeated their 14-2 record in 1990, but were denied a third straight trip to the Super Bowl by the New York Giants, who defeated them, 15-13, in the National Football Conference (NFC) championship game. Rice reached the century mark in catches (100) in 1990, leading the NFL, and also led the league in receiving yards (1,502) and receiving touchdowns (13). San Francisco lost more than their chance to play in the Super Bowl in the game against the Giants—Joe Montana injured his back and missed the entire 1991 season, replaced by **Steve Young** (see entry) at quarterback. After a slow start the 49ers missed the playoffs, but Rice once again led the NFL in touchdown catches (14).

RECORD BREAKER. During the 1992 regular season the 49ers earned the best record (14-2) in the NFL and Rice earned a place in history. Although he caught only ten touchdown passes in 1992, he passed legendary Green Bay Packer great Don Hutson and former Seattle Seahawks's star Steve Largent to become the NFL's all-time leader in touchdown catches with 103. "I love to score touchdowns," Rice told the *Los Angeles Times*. "There's nothing like the feeling you get in the end zone. When you score a touchdown, it feels like winning $6 million in the lottery." Because he is such a scoring threat, Rice is able to scare opposing teams. "With all the great receivers, you know they would catch the ball," San Diego Chargers General Manager Bobby Beathard told the *Sporting News*. "But with him, every time he catches it, there is a good chance he could end up scoring." Rice's ability to gain yards *after* he catches the ball sets him apart from other receivers. He has often turned five-yard passes into 70-yard touchdowns.

The 1992 season ended in frustration for the 49ers, with a 30-20 loss to the eventual champion Dallas Cowboys in the NFC Championship game. After the season San Francisco had to make a decision—whether to keep Steve Young at quarterback or give the job back to Joe Montana, whose injuries had healed. They chose to keep Young, trading Montana to the Kansas City Chiefs. No matter who the quarterback is, Rice catches passes and scores touchdowns. In 1993 he caught 98 passes (second in the NFL), for 1,503 yards (first in the NFL), and 16 touchdowns (first in the NFL). The 49ers won the NFC West division with a 10-6 record, then blew out the New York Giants, 44-3, in the first round of the playoffs. For the third straight season, the 49ers were stopped one game short of the Super Bowl, losing once again in the NFC Championship game to the Dallas Cowboys, 38-21.

OFF THE FIELD. In the off-season Rice, his wife Jackie, and their daughter Jacqui, spend time in Crawford, where Rice has built a new home for his parents. To stay in shape, he exercises when not playing football. "I don't sit on my butt, I really work," he told the *Sporting News*. "What you have is 50 percent natural and the other 50 percent you have to work at developing. People think you are born to be a receiver, but that is not true. You have to be willing to put the extra work in." Even though most football experts rate Rice as one of the best receivers in NFL history, he will not stop working hard. "I'm convinced that I still haven't reached my potential," Rice told the *Sporting News*. "I

RICE'S RECORDS

During the 1994 season, Rice will likely break the all-time record for total (both rushing and passing) touchdowns of 126 held by Hall-of-Fame running back Jim Brown. (At the end of the 1993 season Rice had a total of 124, 118 receiving and six rushing.) Rice already holds the record for most receiving touchdowns (118), most receiving touchdowns in one season (22), most consecutive games catching a touchdown pass (13), most consecutive seasons with at least 1,000 yards receiving (eight), is tied for first for most 1,000-yard receiving seasons (eight), and is fifth on the all-time NFL list of total catches with 708 and sixth in total receiving yards with 11,776. In the regular season Rice has gained 100 yards receiving in 44 games and caught passes in 127 consecutive games. In two Super Bowls Rice has caught 18 passes for 363 yards and four touchdowns. He has gained over 100 yards receiving in five playoff games and has scored 12 touchdowns in the playoffs. Rice has never missed a game in the regular season or in the playoffs.

can still learn, I still can get better … I'm just not ready for anyone to take over my territory. Their time will come. But it won't be for a while."

WHERE TO WRITE

C/O SAN FRANCISCO 49ERS, 4949 CENTENNIAL BLVD., SANTA CLARA, CA 95054.

CAL RIPKEN, JR.

1960—

In July 1995 Cal Ripken, Jr., may break one of baseball's most important records: Lou "The Iron Horse" Gehrig's 2,130 consecutive game playing streak. Even without breaking the record, Ripken will join Gehrig in the Hall of Fame as winner of two American League Most Valuable Player (MVP) awards and establishing himself as one of the hardest hitting and smoothest fielding shortstops of all time. Baseball has always been a way of life for the Ripken family, and Cal has given a lot to the game he loves, often playing when other players would have asked for a day off, and working to be a good role model off the field for his fans. Just like Lou Gehrig.

GROWING UP

Calvin Edwin Ripken, Jr., was born August 24, 1960, in Harve de Grace, Maryland. Baseball was in his blood—his dad Cal, Sr., was a minor league player in the Baltimore Oriole farm system. During Ripken's childhood his father spent 20 years as a minor league coach and manager before finally making the big leagues as a coach for the Orioles. His dad's job helped Cal, Jr. choose a career. "From the time Cal Jr. was a little tyke," his mom, Vi, told *Sports Illustrated*, "all he ever wanted

"I'd like it if there were some eight-year-old kid out there now imitating my batting stance. That's what I always did."—Cal Ripken, Jr.

SCOREBOARD

AMERICAN LEAGUE MOST
VALUABLE PLAYER
(1983 AND 1992).

AMERICAN LEAGUE ALL-STAR
(1983-93).

HOLDS MANY ALL-TIME
SHORTSTOP FIELDING AND
HITTING RECORDS.

HOLDS RECORD FOR PLAYING
EVERY INNING IN THE MOST
CONSECUTIVE GAMES (904).

AT THE END OF THE 1993 SEASON,
HAD PLAYED IN 1,897
CONSECUTIVE GAMES, SECOND ON
THE ALL-TIME LIST.

ONE OF THE BEST, AND MOST
DURABLE, SHORTSTOPS IN MAJOR
LEAGUE HISTORY.

to be was a ballplayer." Ripken says his mom was even more important than his dad in encouraging him to play sports. "Everybody talks about how much of an influence my dad must have been on me, but the truth is I really didn't see that much of him at all," Ripken told *Sports Illustrated*. "When I look back on [my childhood], I really have to tip my hat to my mom. She took me to all of my games, congratulated me if I did well, consoled me [made me feel better] if I didn't." Since his dad didn't get to see many of Ripken's Little League games, it was his mother who taught her son how to hit.

BASEBALL SCHOOL. Even though his dad traveled a lot, Ripken says his family was close and he had a good relationship with his two brothers and sister. "Three of us kids were only about a year apart," Ripken told *Sports Illustrated*. "We played together all the time.... We were always in strange places and always together. As soon as school was out, we'd be off to where dad was." Going to his dad's games was like going to school for Ripken. "I'd watch those games intently [seriously]," Ripken told *Sports Illustrated*. "Other kids would be wandering through the stands, but I'd be sitting behind the screen finding out what the pitchers were throwing. After the game ... I'd start asking my dad questions. I always wanted to know why he did something. By the time I was ready to play, I knew the proper way to do things."

In high school Ripken won a letter in soccer and was a pitcher and shortstop on the Aberdeen High School baseball team. He batted .492 his senior season, had a 7-2 record as a pitcher, allowing only two hits in winning the state championship game. After graduation his dream came true when he signed with the Orioles, the team his dad worked for. "The Orioles were my only team—for obvious reasons," Ripken told *Sports Illustrated*. "I grew up around them. But there was a side of me that hoped when I was ready for the draft, that somebody else would take me. I didn't want to think that I was only being drafted because of my dad. But what it finally boiled down to was that I wanted to be an Oriole.... [But] I had to prove to everyone that I wasn't there just because of my father."

ROOKIE OF THE YEAR. Ripken worked his way through the minor leagues and kept in touch with his father for advice. During his first professional season he did not hit a single home run. But three years later he hit 23 and in 1981 received a late-season call to the majors. In 1982 the Orioles traded starting third baseman Doug DeCinces to make room for Ripken. On opening day, Ripken went two for three with a home run, but by May 1 his average had dropped to .117. At this point that Ripken got a good piece of advice from Hall-of-Famer Reggie Jackson. "The Orioles traded away a fine player in Doug DeCinces so they could bring you up," Jackson recalled telling Ripken in *Baseball Digest*. "They [the Orioles] know you're going to be great. So just do what you know you can do, not what everybody else tells you to do."

By the end of his first full year in the majors Ripken had raised his average to .264 and led American League rookies in home runs (28), runs batted in (93), doubles (32), runs (90), games (160), and at-bats (598). In addition to these offensive feats, Ripken changed positions, moving from third base to the much more difficult shortstop position. Ripken's accomplishments earned him the American League Rookie of the Year award by a 24 to 4 vote. Baltimore was also in the pennant race, finishing one game behind the Milwaukee Brewers, and Ripken played well under pressure.

SUPERSTAR

MVP. The next season (1983) the Orioles were favored to win the World Series. Ripken became a superstar and was the Orioles's team leader. He led the major leagues with 211 hits and 47 doubles, he led the American League with 121 runs, and

Cal Ripken, Jr.

finished among American League leaders in batting average (.318), home runs (27), and RBIs (102). Ripken did all this while playing every inning of every Orioles game at the physically demanding shortstop position. When the Orioles won 98 games and ran away with the American League East division title, it was obvious that Ripken was the American League's Most Valuable Player, an award he was given at the end of the season.

The Orioles faced the Chicago White Sox in the American League Championship Series. Ripken continued his great play, batting .400 in the series, which the Orioles won three games to one. Their victory set up a World Series showdown with the Philadelphia Phillies. Philadelphia won the first game of the series, but the Orioles swept the last four games to win the championship. Ripken, appearing in his first, and so far only, World Series, batted only .167 with one RBI.

In 1984 the Orioles failed to repeat, quickly falling behind the Detroit Tigers, who set a major league record by starting the season with a 35-5 record. Though his statistics were not as good as the year before, Ripken still had a great season. He batted .304, hit 27 home runs, and had 86 RBIs. He also set an American League record for shortstops with 583 assists (an assist is a play that leads directly to an out being recorded), and played every inning of every game the Orioles played.

THE BALTIMORE RIPKENS. The Orioles continued to struggle during the next two seasons, finishing fourth in 1985 and last, for the first time in team history, in 1986. Ripken batted .282 in each season, had 110 RBIs in 1985, hit 26 home runs in 1985 and 25 in 1986. When the 1987 season started, there were three Ripkens in Orioles uniforms. His dad was made team manager and his brother, Billy, was trying out for second base—a job he didn't win until mid-way through the season.

When Billy joined the Orioles, Cal Sr. became the first major-league manager to have two of his sons on his team.

The Ripkens's time together wasn't successful. The team finished in sixth place in 1987 and when they lost their first six games; in 1988, Cal Sr. was fired as manager. (He stayed on the team as third base coach.) The team's new manager was former Orioles star and Hall-of-Famer Frank Robinson. The Orioles lost another 15 straight for Robinson, setting a record with 21 straight losses at the beginning of the season. Ripken batted only .252 in 1987, but had 27 home runs and 98 RBIs. Even as the rest of the team collapsed in 1988, Ripken held steady, batting .264, with 23 homers and 81 RBIs. He continued to play every day, but in 1987 his dad insisted he sit out part of a meaningless game on September 14, breaking his consecutive inning streak after 904 games (believed to be the longest such streak in history).

The Orioles made a remarkable comeback in 1989, leading the American League East division by seven-and-a-half games at the All-Star break. But poor pitching caught up with the young team in the second half of the season, and they lost the pennant to the Toronto Blue Jays on the next-to-last day of the season. Ripken led the way, hitting 21 home runs—making him the first shortstop in history to have eight straight twenty-homer seasons. He also drove in 93 runs and led American League shortstops in several defensive categories.

BREAKS RECORD. Ripken reached a major milestone on June 10, 1990, when he played in his 1,308th consecutive game, passing Everett Scott and moving into second place on the all-time list behind the legendary Lou Gehrig. He also broke Scott's record for most consecutive games played at one position. "What some people don't understand is that I never set out to play all these games in a row," Ripken told the *Sporting News*. "It's just something that happened.... I've just never believed in

TALL-STOP?

Ripken has always been such a good hitter that his defensive play has been overlooked. At six-feet-four inches tall and 220 pounds, he is one of the largest shortstops ever to play in the major leagues. Not as quick as smaller shortstops, Ripken uses his head to outguess hitters, usually knowing where they will hit the ball before they do. "The fact is most of my plays look routine [easy] ... because I'm already standing in the general area where the ball's hit," Cal told *Baseball Digest*.

THE STREAK

Ripken is the only player to seriously challenge legendary Yankee great Lou Gehrig's record of playing in 2,130 games. What makes Ripken's streak even more amazing is that he has played almost every inning of the 1,897 straight games he has played (Gehrig played every inning of every game in only one season—1931) and has played all but a handful of those games at shortstop—next to catcher the hardest position physically to play. (Gehrig played first base, maybe the easiest to play.) Both Ripken and Gehrig have forced themselves to play with injuries that surely would have kept other players out of the lineup. It will take until July of 1995 for Ripken to break Gehrig's record, if he can play every game until then. The streak is important to him, but not if it hurts the team. "I approach the game day to day from a standpoint that I'm going to play from the start of the game and contribute," Ripken told *Sport.* "If I was tired or hurt or whatever ... hurting the team ... I'd have to say that that's it, I can't do it."

taking a day off for the sake of taking a day off." When he broke Scott's record, Ripken was in one of the worst slumps of his career, and many people said he was too tired because he insisted on playing every game. Even though he was having trouble at the plate, Ripken continued to improve in the field, setting major league records for shortstops by making only three errors in 1990 and going 95 games without an error. And even though a .250 average, 21 homers, and 84 RBIs were an off-season for Ripken, they are great statistics for most shortstops, a position usually played by weaker hitters.

MVP II. In 1991 Ripken took his play to new heights, silencing all his critics with an outstanding season. First he won the MVP award at the All-Star game when he hit a 3-run homer that won the game for the American League, 4-2. At season's end, his statistics added up to one of the greatest seasons a shortstop ever had. He batted .323, hit 34 home runs, had 114 RBIs, and struck out only 46 times. Ripken continued to be an outstanding shortstop and won his first Gold Glove award for fielding excellence. Though the Orioles finished with a losing record, Ripken won the American League MVP award for the second time.

Ripken was unable to repeat his MVP performance in either 1992 or 1993. He struggled in 1992, failing to hit over 20 homers for the first time in his career (14) and batting only .251. He was back over the 20 home run mark in 1993 (24) and drove in 90 runs, but critics insisted that he needed rest, though he continued to be a standout defensively. Ripken, a free agent who could sign with any team after the 1992 season, decided to take less money and stay in Baltimore. "If the good Lord wants him to have an off day, He'll let it rain," Orioles's manager Johnny Oates told *Sports Illustrated*. "If Cal stays healthy, he'll break the record. The decision's out of my hands now."

OFF THE FIELD. Ripken lives in Reisterstown, Maryland, with his wife, Kelly, and their daughter, Rachel. When not playing baseball, he likes to play basketball and racquetball. Remembering how he felt about baseball players when he was a kid, Ripken never turns down an autograph request and tries to be a good role model for his fans. "I recognize that as a baseball player you are instantly a role model," he told *Sport*. "Some people don't accept that. I choose to accept it because I remember vividly [clearly] what baseball players meant to me and how they influenced my life. It's a responsibility, but I'm happy they [kids] perceive [see] me as a good role model." Ripken is also involved in charitable work, donating $250,000 to build a literacy center and participating in programs promoting education. His "Because We Care" program has supplied thousands of tickets to underprivileged children and adults. In the end, though, baseball is still most important to him. "I want to be known as a good ballplayer.... I'd like it if there were some eight-year-old kid out there imitating my batting stance. That's what I always did."

WHERE TO WRITE

C/O BALTIMORE ORIOLES,

ORIOLE PARK AT CAMDEN YARDS,

333 WEST CAMDEN ST., BALTIMORE, MD 21201.

DAVID ROBINSON

1965—

> *"I'm a good player right now, but if I approach the game as if there is always something to learn, I can always keep climbing."—David Robinson*

When David Robinson was young, he had one goal—he wanted to be a student at the United States Naval Academy. He reached that goal, and along the way earned his nickname, "The Admiral." After growing to seven-feet-one-inch tall, he set another goal—to be the best player in the National Basketball Association (NBA). Voted the College Basketball Player of the Year in 1987, NBA Rookie of the Year in 1990, and NBA Defensive Player of the Year in 1992, Robinson has come a long way toward reaching his new goal. An example of how to play basketball on the court, and a role model in his personal life, Robinson may soon be the NBA's "commander in chief."

GROWING UP

David Maurice Robinson was born August 6, 1965, in Key West, Florida, and grew up in Virginia Beach, Virginia. His father, Ambrose, was a naval officer, and his mother, Freda, was a nurse. Robinson and his brother and sister were responsible for many of the household chores at an early age, since their dad was away from home—on duty in the navy—much of the time and their mom worked all day. From the age of six,

Robinson was placed in programs for gifted children at school. His idea of fun was to take televisions apart, repair them, and put them back together. As a high school senior, Robinson scored among the top five percent nationally on the Scholastic Aptitude Test (SAT). His favorite subjects in high school were mathematics and science.

TO THE NAVY. Robinson played many sports when he was young, including tennis, golf, pool, and baseball. Only five-feet-nine-inches tall as a freshman in high school, Robinson quit the basketball team because he rarely got a chance to play. Robinson did not really become involved in competitive basketball until he had grown to be a six-feet-seven-inches tall high-school senior at Osbourn Park High School in Manassas, Virginia. He became the starting center on Osbourn Park's team, but did not have the skills to attract the attention of many colleges. This didn't bother Robinson, though, because he had already been accepted to the Naval Academy in Annapolis, Maryland.

Basketball was not a top priority for Robinson when he started at the Naval Academy. "I didn't care if I played basketball at the academy," he told *Gentleman's Quarterly*. "I just wanted to get good grades and fit in." Robinson played on the academy's basketball team his freshman year, but saw only limited action. During the summer between his freshman and sophomore seasons, Robinson grew five inches and now stood seven-feet tall.

Robinson had a solid, but unspectacular season his sophomore year. After that second season, Robinson had to make a decision. If he stayed at the Naval Academy, he would be forced to serve a two-year military assignment after he graduated, delaying his playing in the NBA. Many colleges tried to talk him into transferring to their schools, but Robinson decided to stay at the academy. "Something could happen,

SCOREBOARD

COLLEGE PLAYER OF THE YEAR (1986-87).

NBA ROOKIE OF THE YEAR (1990-91) AND NBA DEFENSIVE PLAYER OF THE YEAR (1991-92).

LED NBA IN SCORING (1993-94) REBOUNDING (1990-91) AND BLOCKED SHOTS (1991-92).

MEMBER OF 1988 U.S. OLYMPIC BASKETBALL TEAM AND 1992 U.S. OLYMPIC "DREAM TEAM."

CONSIDERED ONE OF THE BEST OFFENSIVE AND DEFENSIVE PLAYERS IN THE NBA.

David Robinson

and you'd stop being a basketball player," Robinson told the *Charlotte Observer*, explaining his decision. "You'll always benefit from being an officer."

NAVY SAILS. In his junior season (1985-86), Robinson and the Navy Midshipmen went 30-5. Robinson averaged 22.7 points per game and led the nation in rebounding (13 per game) and blocked shots (207). Navy reached the East Regional final of the National Collegiate Athletic Association (NCAA) tournament, but lost to Duke University, 71-50. Robinson averaged 27.5 points and 12.3 rebounds per game in the tournament, scoring 30 points in a first-round victory over Tulsa University and 35 in a second-round victory over Syracuse University.

PLAYER OF THE YEAR. As a senior, Robinson continued to get better. He set 33 Naval Academy records, and broke NCAA records for blocked shots in a game (14), season (207), and career (516). When he graduated, Robinson was the tenth-leading scorer in NCAA history. He was the first player in major college history to score more than 2,500 points (2,669), grab 1,300 rebounds, and shoot better than 60 percent from the field (not including free throws) for his career. Robinson won every major award as the best player in college basketball, including the Wooden Award and the Rupp Award. Navy lost in the first round of the NCAA tournament to the University of Michigan, 97-82, but Robinson scored 50 points and had 13 rebounds.

ROLE MODEL. A fine basketball player on the court, Robinson was also a role model off the court. "He has become a folk hero," said John Feinstein in the *Washington Post*. "He is on magazine covers, his handsome features lighting up the page with a big smile that reveals a set of braces he will have to endure [put up with] until April. Braces at 22. How All-American can you get? He gets letters from kids who say they want to grow up to be David Robinson, and he writes them back." Robinson graduated in four years from the Naval Academy with a degree in mathematics.

TOP PICK. The San Antonio Spurs had the first pick in the 1987 NBA draft. They used it to pick Robinson, knowing that he would not be able to play for two full years. (Most graduates of the Naval Academy must serve for five years, but since Robinson was too tall to work on naval ships his service was reduced to two years.) Many experts thought that San Antonio made a mistake, feeling that Robinson might lose his basketball skills in two years. In addition to this fear, Robinson had the option of waiting to be drafted again in the 1988 draft. At first, Robinson did not want to play in San Antonio, as he told *Sports Illustrated*: "There are obvious disadvantages [to playing in San Antonio] if you have a lot of other interests you want to get into. If you're going to work in a small pond [city] there are sacrifices you make."

DOES HIS DUTY. To make sure they signed Robinson, the Spurs made him an offer he couldn't refuse—$26 million for eight years, a record contract at the time. Robinson signed, then prepared for his navy service. He was stationed at the Trident submarine base in King's Bay, Georgia, an area where he experienced the effects of racism for the first time. "I was scared to death," he told *Gentleman's Quarterly*. "It was real life. I had always been judged on my abilities, never on whether I was black or white." Eventually he earned the rank of lieutenant, junior grade, and worked as a civil engineer. With his free time during his military service, Robinson studied religion and Spanish. He also bought a keyboard synthesizer, which he still takes with him on road trips.

OLYMPIC DISAPPOINTMENT. During his time in the navy, Robinson was able to play competitive basketball. He was a

ROGER STAUBACH

Before Robinson, the best athlete to come from the Naval Academy was football great Roger Staubach. In 1963 Staubach won the Heisman Trophy as the best college football player in the country. Staubach served five years in the navy before joining the Dallas Cowboys in 1969. In his 11-year career, Staubach quarterbacked the Cowboys to four Super Bowls (1971, 1975, 1977, and 1978), winning two (1971 and 1977). Staubach was elected to the Professional Football Hall of Fame in 1985.

member of the 1987 U.S. team in the Pan-American Games, a team that finished a disappointing second to Brazil. Robinson also played on the 1988 U.S. Olympic team. During the tournament in Seoul, South Korea, the U.S. team lost to the Soviet Union and finished third, winning a bronze medal, the lowest finish ever by an American basketball team in the Olympics. Robinson did not play well during the Olympics, averaging only 12.8 points and 6.8 rebounds per game. Many experts, including Olympic coach John Thompson of Georgetown University, wondered if his time off had hurt Robinson.

SUPERSTAR

ROOKIE OF THE YEAR. Robinson decided to prove the doubters wrong. "One of the best lessons I learned over the last two years is how to motivate myself," he told the *Los Angeles Times*. "I couldn't train by myself before." When his service in the military was over, Robinson was ready to enter the NBA. The San Antonio Spurs hired a new coach, Larry Brown, who had just led the Kansas Jayhawks to an NCAA championship, and drafted the College Player of the Year, Sean Elliot of the University of Arizona.

San Antonio, a team that had won only 21 games the year before, won 56 games in Robinson's first season (1989-90) and capped the biggest turnaround in NBA history by winning the NBA Midwest division title. Robinson averaged 24.3 points (tenth in the league), 12 rebounds (second in the league), and 3.89 blocked shots (third in the league) per game. The Spurs lost in the second round of the playoffs to the Portland Trail Blazers, four games to three, with Portland winning one game in overtime and another in double-overtime. Robinson was fifth in the voting for league Most Valuable Player and was the unanimous choice for NBA Rookie of the Year. "Some rookies are never really rookies, and he's one of them," **Earvin "Magic" Johnson** (see entry) told the *Chicago Tribune*. "He's a man."

BEST SEASON. 1990-91 was Robinson's best season to date. He scored a career best 25.6 points per game (ninth in the league), led the league with 13 rebounds per game, and blocked 3.9 shots per game (second in the league). He was the leading All-Star vote-getter for the Western Conference and was named to the All-NBA and All-NBA Defensive first teams. The Spurs repeated as Midwest division champion, but were upset in the first round of the playoffs by the Golden State Warriors, three games to one. Robinson averaged 25 points per game in the series, but it wasn't enough.

The Spurs, considered a NBA title contender, started to stumble during the 1991-92 season. Robinson continued to star, leading the league in blocked shots (4.49 per game), grabbing 12.2 rebounds per game (fourth in the league), and averaging 23.2 points per game. (He also finished in the league's top ten in steals and field goal percentage, becoming only the third player in NBA history to place in the top ten in five statistical categories during one season.) He was honored as NBA Defensive Player of the Year and was once again named to the All-NBA first team. The Spurs finished second in their division, but then disaster struck, as Robinson had surgery on his left hand. Without their star, the Spurs lost in three straight games to the Phoenix Suns in the first round of the NBA playoffs. Robinson was given a chance to make up for his 1988 Olympic disappointment when he was named to the 1992 U.S. Olympic "Dream Team," which dominated the competition from the rest of the world.

After starting the 1992-93 season with a 9-11 record, the Spurs hired John Lucas to coach. Lucas was a former NBA star who had once had drug problems and who had previously been working with drug-addicted basketball players to coach. The Spurs finished the season second in the Midwest division, and Robinson had another standout year (23.4 points, 11.7 rebounds, and 3.22 blocked shots per game). San Antonio won its first playoff series, four games to one over the defending Western Conference champion Portland Trail Blazers, before losing to **Charles Barkley** (see entry) and the Phoenix Suns, four games to two. Robinson averaged 23.1 points and 12.6 rebounds per game in the playoffs. He won the 1993-94 NBA scoring title (29.8 points per game) over **Shaquille O'Neal** (see entry) by scoring 71 points in the Spurs final game. The Spurs lost in the first round of the playoffs.

WHO'S BEST

David Robinson, **Patrick Ewing** (see entry) of the New York Knicks, and **Hakeem Olajuwon** (see entry) of the Houston Rockets are considered the top three centers in the NBA. The following chart will help you decide which one is best.

Player/ Seasons	Scoring	Rebounding
Ewing 9	23.8	10.3
Olajuwon 10	23.7	12.5
Robinson 5	25.3	11.9

OFF THE COURT. Robinson lives with his wife, Valerie, and his son, David Maurice, Jr. His Nike shoe commercials, featuring "Mr. Robinson's Neighborhood," are very successful, and Robinson also is a spokesperson for Coca-Cola and the Casio watch company. Robinson supports many community organizations, including the I Have a Dream Foundation, through which he has donated $100,000 for the college education of an entire class of inner-city school children.

When he is finished with basketball, Robinson would like to be a scientist or musician. In his spare time Robinson plays the piano and saxophone, reads science fiction, and studies the Bible. A "born again" Christian, Robinson says his faith helps him get through the tough NBA season. Robinson is a founding member of Athletes for Abstinence, along with basketball player A.C. Green of the Phoenix Suns and football players **Barry Sanders** (see entry) of the Detroit Lions and Darrell Green of the Washington Redskins. The group has made a video called "It Ain't Worth It," and works to convince teenagers not to have sex before they are married. A quiet person, Robinson tries to be a role model by leading a good life. "Some people think my life is boring," he told *Gentleman's Quarterly*, "but I wouldn't trade places with anyone. I think I'm having the best time in the world."

WHERE TO WRITE

C/O SAN ANTONIO SPURS,

600 E. MARKET ST., SUITE 102, SAN ANTONIO, TX 78205.

NOLAN RYAN

1947—

A hard-throwing pitcher is the closest thing sports has to the gunslinger made famous in tales of the Old West. Alone on the mound, the pitcher winds up and tries to throw the ball past the batter. It only makes sense that Nolan Ryan, the pitcher who was the best at doing this, was born and raised in Texas. After dueling with Ryan, major league batters went back to the dugout as strikeout victims 5,714 times, unable to make contact with the "Ryan Express," the nickname given to his fastball. Blessed with a strong right arm that can throw a baseball 100 miles-per-hour, Ryan shattered the all-time major league strikeout record and won 324 games. Seven times he threw no-hitters—three times more than anyone else. When the sun finally set on Ryan's career, he rode off into the sunset, on his way to the Hall of Fame.

"Others will throw harder, but no one will throw harder for longer."—former Texas Rangers pitching coach Tom House

GROWING UP

Nolan Ryan was born January 31, 1947, in Refugio, Texas. The youngest of the six children of Lynn Nolan Ryan, an oil company executive, and his wife, Martha, Ryan grew up in a small town where it was hard to find things to do. He told *Sports Illustrated* that he and his buddies passed the time by throwing rocks at snakes on long summer afternoons when school was out. Young Ryan had a paper route and played baseball, although he didn't consider himself a very good player. He attended Alvin High School, where he played both basketball and baseball. Basketball was his favorite sport, but as a pitcher for the baseball team he developed a fastball that could go "through a wall," according to his high school coach, Jim Watson.

NO CONTROL. Even though he could throw the ball hard, he had trouble getting it over the plate, but struck out a lot of batters who were afraid of getting hit. "He didn't have any idea where the ball was going," coach Watson told *Sports Illustrated,* "but he didn't have to exactly thread the needle back then. Those kids were so scared, they'd swing at anything just to get out of there."

BECOMES A MET. Seeing great potential in Ryan, New York Mets scout Red Murff told the major league team about the youngster with the rocket arm. When Ryan graduated from high school, the Mets drafted him in the 14th round. He was disappointed to be drafted so low, but his dad talked him into accepting the Mets's offer. Ryan was called up to the Mets's big-league team in 1966, but still had problems with his control. In four seasons with the Mets Ryan went 29-28 and struck out almost a batter per inning. The problem was that he walked a lot of batters, too.

In 1969 the "Miracle Mets," who finished second to last in the National League with 45 wins in 1968, won 100 games and the National League's East division title. Ryan contributed only six wins during the regular season, but pitched seven strong innings in the final game of the National League Championship series against the Atlanta Braves to earn the victory. He pitched only once in the World Series against the highly favored Baltimore Orioles, earning a save in Game Three of a five-game Mets Series victory—one of the biggest upsets of all time. This would be the only World Series in which Ryan would pitch during his career.

JOINS ANGELS. Over the next two seasons it became obvious to Ryan that he did not fit into the Mets future plans. He also found it difficult, having been raised in a small town, to adjust to living in New York. After the 1971 season he asked to be traded and the Mets sent him to the California Angels, a move they would come to regret. For the next eight seasons Ryan ranked as one of the best pitchers in the American League, twice winning twenty games (21 in 1973 and 22 in 1974) and 19 twice (1972 and 1977). Four times he finished with earned run averages (ERAs) under 3.00 and led the major leagues in strikeouts six times in eight seasons. (The two years he did not lead the major leagues, he finished second.) In 1973 he set a major league record with 383 strikeouts, struck out over 300 batters four times, set a record by striking out more than 300 batters in three straight seasons (1972-74), and on August 12, 1974, he struck out 19 Boston Red Sox, tying the major league record at the time for strikeouts in one game.

Nolan Ryan

SUPERSTAR

NO NO'S. Ryan credited his new-found success to Angels pitching coach Tom Morgan. His fastball still hummed at close to 100 miles per hour, and Ryan had learned better control. He also learned how to throw a slow breaking pitch—a throw that is almost impossible for a batter to hit if he's expecting the "Ryan Express" fastball. His improved control was most obvious in the four no-hitters he threw while with the Angels. On May 15, 1973, he beat the Kansas City Royals, 3-0, and two months later, on July 15, he beat the Detroit Tigers, 6-0, striking out 17 batters. In his third no-hitter he walked eight batters, but beat the Minnesota Twins, 4-0, and in his fourth, a 1-

0 win over the Baltimore Orioles on June 5, 1975, Ryan's catcher, Ellie Rodriguez, told *Sports Illustrated* that Ryan didn't have "his good stuff." His fourth no-hitter tied the major-league record set by Hall-of-Famer Sandy Koufax.

But even with Ryan the Angels were not a very good team, finishing last twice and next-to-last three times. Finally, in 1979, the Angels won the weak American League West division. For only the second time in his career Ryan pitched in the playoffs, this time against the East division champion Baltimore Orioles. Ryan started Game One, pitching seven innings and leaving with the game tied 3-3. The Angels lost the game in the 10th inning and lost the series, three games to one. This would be the last time Ryan would pitch for the Angels.

GOES HOME. After the 1979 season Ryan became a free-agent and could go with the team of his choice. Not surprisingly, Ryan signed with the Houston Astros and was able to move his family back to his home town of Alvin, less than fifty miles from Houston. Ryan pitched nine seasons for Houston, but never won more than 16 games in a season. He did lead the major leagues in strikeouts (270) and ERA (2.79) in 1987, even though he finished with an 8-16 record. On September 6, 1981, Ryan again made history when he pitched his fifth no-hitter, beating the Los Angeles Dodgers, 5-0.

ALL-TIME LEADER. On August 27, 1983, Ryan broke his most important record of all. When he struck out Brad Mills of the Montreal Expos, Ryan moved ahead of the legendary Walter "Big Train" Johnson and into first place on the all-time strike-out list. Then, on July 11, 1985, he struck out Danny Heep of the Mets to become the first major-league pitcher with more than 4,000 career strikeouts. Well past the age of 30, when most hard-throwing pitchers begin to lose their speed, Ryan was still overpowering, his fastball clocked regularly at 95 miles per hour. "I don't know why I've been able to maintain my velocity [speed] this long," Ryan admitted to the *Philadelphia Daily News*. "I think people think I do something different than anybody else has done. But it's not true.... Believe me, I'm as surprised as everybody else."

In his first year with Houston (1980), Ryan finished 11-

Nolan Ryan adds another victim to his strike-out total.

10 and the Astros won the National League West division title. He started Game Two and Game Five of the National League Championship Series against the Philadelphia Phillies. He didn't get a decision (win or loss) in either game, but lost a 7-2 lead in the eighth inning of the fifth and deciding game—a game the Astros lost, 8-7, in ten innings. The 1981 season was interrupted by a player's strike, and each division had a champion for the first and second half of the season. The Astros won the National League West second half title, and played the Los Angeles Dodgers in a first-ever divisional playoff series. Ryan won Game One of the series, going the whole nine innings in a 3-1 win. He started, and lost, Game Five, 4-0, as the Astros once again fell just short.

Nolan Ryan's final playoff appearance came in 1986. He went 12-8 and the Astros won the National League West division by 10 games. The Astros faced the New York Mets in the National League Championship Series, and the two teams played an incredible series. Four games were decided by one run and two were decided in extra innings. Ryan started and lost Game Two, giving up five runs in five innings. In Game Five, with the teams tied at two games apiece, Ryan pitched the best game of his playoff career, going nine innings, giving up only one run and two hits, while striking out 12. But the Astros could score only one run for him, and Houston lost the game, 2-1, in 12 innings. Game Six was one of the most exciting of all time, with the teams tied through 15 innings. Then, in the top of the 16th, the Mets scored three runs. But the Astros wouldn't quit, and scored two in their half of the 16th, with the tying and winning run on base and two outs. Mets reliever Jesse Orosco, exhausted after the long night, struck out Kevin Bass to give the Mets the pennant and deny Ryan a return trip to the World Series.

TEXAS RANGER. After the 1988 season Ryan was a free-agent again. Wanting to stay in Texas, but disappointed in the salary offered by Houston, Ryan went to the Texas Rangers. Now 42 years of age, most experts believed Ryan was washed up. Once again he proved the experts wrong, going 16-10 and again exceeding the 300 strikeout mark (301). On June 11, 1990, Ryan pitched his sixth no-hitter, a 5-0 win over the Oakland A's. He became the oldest player (43) to pitch a no-hitter and the first to pitch no-hitters in three different decades. In August of that year he won his 300th game (one of only 20 pitchers to accomplish this feat), and struck out his 5,000th batter—the only pitcher to ever reach this milestone. Finally on May 1, 1991, Ryan pitched his seventh and last no-hitter, striking out Toronto Blue Jay's second baseman Roberto Alomar to win the game, 3-0. Making Ryan's seven no-hitters even more remarkable is the fact that he also has 12 career one-hitters—another major league record.

RETIRES. Ryan announced that the 1993 season would be his last. Although he was planned to retire, the end came sooner than expected, when he tore a ligament in his right elbow on September 22. When he left the game after 27 seasons, he held or shared 53 major-league records. He had won 324 games, lost 292, pitched 5,319 innings, and recorded 5,714 strike outs (by 1,175 different batters), a record average of 9.7 every nine innings. (He also holds the major league record with 2,795 walks.) Ryan's hard work, great physical shape, and near-perfect pitching motion no doubt helped him to pitch as long as he did. Although he lost almost as many games as he won in his career, Ryan is a guaranteed Hall of Famer when he is eligible to be inducted.

OFF THE FIELD. Ryan lives in his hometown of Alvin with his wife Ruth, his high school sweetheart. They have three children: Reese, Wendy, and Reid. Because he is such a hometown hero, the Nolan Ryan Expressway was named in his honor, as was his old baseball field in Alvin. A quiet man, Ryan has always tried to set a good example off the field. He is a spokesperson for several products, including Nike and Advil pain reliever, and continues to work for the Rangers organization. He is also the sponsor of the Nolan Ryan Baseball Scholarship program at Alvin Community College. Ryan plans to spend more time working on his ranch, where he raises cattle, and though he has become a national hero, his heart has always remained in Alvin. "I grew up in this town [Alvin]," Ryan told *Sports Illustrated*. "I was blessed with a good childhood. When I left home, I never really found a place I wanted to live in except Alvin." His heart may be in Alvin, but his accomplishments belong to baseball fans everywhere.

STRIKEOUT KING

Nolan Ryan tops both of the following lists for strikeouts in a season and in a career.

Single Season

Player	Strikeouts
Nolan Ryan	383
Sandy Koufax	382
Nolan Ryan	367

Career

Player	Strikeouts
Nolan Ryan	5,714
Steve Carlton	4,136
Bert Blyleven	3,701

WHERE TO WRITE

C/O TEXAS RANGERS,

1000 BULL PARK WAY, ARLINGTON, TX, 76011.

PETE SAMPRAS

1971—

In 1990 Pete Sampras surprised the world of tennis by becoming the youngest man ever to win the U.S. Open men's singles title with a serve that often travelled over 120 miles per hour. When he couldn't repeat his success during the next two years, some said he'd been lucky at the U.S. Open, that he really didn't deserve to be considered a great player. Instead of letting what people said get him down, Sampras just worked harder. In 1993 he became a superstar, first earning the world's number-one ranking and then winning the famous Wimbledon tournament and the U.S. Open once again. A very quiet and shy person, Sampras is a fierce opponent on the court.

GROWING UP

Pete Sampras was born August 12, 1971, in Washington, D.C. His dad, Soterios, is of Greek descent and was a civilian aerospace engineer with the U.S. Air Force when Pete was a boy. His mom, Georgia, is a housewife and he has a brother, Gus, and two sisters, Stella and Marion. At the age of three, Sampras could "both throw and kick a ball in a straight line," his dad told *World Tennis*. "I didn't know that Pete would play tennis, but I knew he was an above average athlete." When

Sampras was seven, his family moved to Rancho Palos Verdes, California, when his dad accepted a new job. Because the weather was nice so much of the year, Sampras and his sister Stella began to play tennis, a game they'd hardly ever played in Washington. "[In Washington] the only tennis Pete and I had played was against the basement wall and at the local high school tennis courts," Stella once told *World Tennis*.

FIRST COACH. As a child, Sampras's hero was legendary Australian tennis star, Rod Laver (see box). When Sampras was nine he met Peter Fischer, his first coach. Fischer was a pediatrician—a doctor who specializes in caring for children—who also taught tennis. He encouraged Sampras to learn all aspects of the game, changed his backhand from a two-handed to one-handed stroke, and taught him how to compete on the tennis court. "He didn't teach me strokes," Sampras once said. "I already had those—but he taught me strategy." Fischer encouraged Sampras set his goals as high as possible. "The goal has always been [the famous English championship] Wimbledon, the competition has always been Laver," Fischer told *Tennis*. "I always told him he was going to be the greatest tennis player ever."

Sampras describes himself in the *USTA Yearbook* as "A good but not outstanding junior player." In 1987 he advanced to the finals of the U.S. Tennis Association (USTA) National Boys' 18 Hardcourt Championships, for players under 18 years of age. He lost in the finals to **Michael Chang** (see entry), but won the 1987 USTA National 18 Grasscourt doubles championship with his partner, Matt Lucena. Sampras was 16 years old at the time.

TURNS PRO. Later in 1987 Sampras won $7000 at the *Newsweek* Champions Cup. When he accepted the prize money, he became a professional player. He decided to leave high school in order to train full-time. The 16-year-old Sampras was ranked only 311th in the world. But he showed steady improvement and moved up to number 12, though he did not win a tournament in 1987, 1988, or 1989. In 1990 Ivan Lendl, one of the top-ranked players in the world, invited Sampras to his Connecticut home to practice. "The guy practically killed me," Sampras told *World Tennis*. "[He] had me biking 20 miles a day, talking to me about discipline and working hard and practicing until I couldn't walk home. I'll never forget that."

SUPERSTAR

YOUNGEST CHAMP. The extra work started to pay off. Sampras won three tournaments and reached the semifinals in another. His biggest win came in the 1990 U.S. Open, one of tennis's "Grand Slam" tournaments. (The others are the Australian and French Opens, and Wimbledon.) Displaying an overpowering serve, clocked at 120 miles per hour, Sampras defeated Lendl in the quarterfinals and American superstar John McEnroe in the semifinals to earn the right to play **Andre Agassi** (see entry) in the finals.

The finals match-up with Agassi provided a contrast in styles, both on and off the court. Agassi wore flashy clothes, had long hair, and was very outgoing and controversial. Sampras wore the traditional white tennis clothes, had very short hair, and was very shy and quiet. On the court, Agassi was patient, standing at the back of the court and waiting for the other player to make a mistake. Sampras, with his powerful serve, liked to move up toward the net and end points more quickly. In the finals, Sampras was the better player, winning 6-4, 6-3, 6-2, in what Agassi called "a good old-fashioned street mugging." With the win, Sampras became the youngest-ever U.S. Open champion (19 years and 28 days old). "I'm just a normal 19-year-old with an unusual job, doing unusual things," Sampras said.

The win in the U.S. Open earned Sampras $350,000 and the world's number-five ranking. He followed this success with a win in the Grand Slam Cup, a tournament with the highest prize money ever given— $2 million to the winner. Now a celebrity, Sampras found out that not everything about being a star was fun. Naturally shy, he now had to talk to reporters, which made him uncomfortable. He was paid $2 million by Sergio Tacchini, an Italian sportswear company, to wear their shoes and clothes. But the shoes gave him shinsplints (a leg injury) and they had to be redesigned. He also had a contract with Wilson to use their racquets, and was a spokesperson for a watch company and a sunglasses manufacturer. The *New York Times* reported that Sampras made $6.5 million in 1990.

Pete Sampras

WORKS ON GAME. Much was expected of Sampras in 1991 but, because of a series of injuries, he failed to repeat his U.S. Open success. He won four tournaments in 1991, but came up short in the Grand Slam tournaments. "The Grand Slams have always been my top priority," Sampras told the *New York Times*. "Wimbledon is very important to me.... It's nice to make money, but that's not what my tennis is all about."

Sampras left coach Fischer and began training with Tim Gullikson, a former professional player. To improve Sampras's game, Gullikson convinced him to play more clay court tournaments. On clay, where the ball bounces more slowly, Sampras was forced to hit more shots and not rely as much on his powerful serve. "If it takes five hours to win, it takes five hours to win," Sampras told *Sports Illustrated,* expressing his new, more patient, attitude.

The strategy worked, as Sampras began moving up the world rankings in 1992. He lost in the semifinals at Wimbledon to another hard-serving player, Goran Ivanesevic of Croatia. He defeated **Jim Courier** (see entry) in the semifinals of the U.S. Open despite a serious stomach problem. A win in the finals would have made Sampras the number-one ranked player in the world, but he lost to Stephan Edberg of Sweden, 3-6, 6-4, 7-6, 6-2. Sampras called the match "the most devastating loss in my career."

NUMBER ONE. Sampras got his revenge on Edberg in the Davis Cup semifinals, as the United States defeated Sweden, 4-1. (The Davis Cup is an international tennis tournament in which national teams compete.) The U.S. team was outstanding, made up of Agassi, Courier, McEnroe, and Sampras. They went on to defeat Switzerland to win the Davis Cup title. After the U.S. Open Sampras won 19 straight matches and, on April 23, 1993, became the number-one ranked player in the world, passing good friend and one-time doubles partner Jim Courier. "I just hope I can maintain it," Sampras told *USA Today.*

WINS WIMBLEDON. He not only stayed number one in the world in 1993, he blew away the competition. In July Sampras reached another of his goals by winning the legendary Wimbledon title, considered the most important tournament in tennis. Despite a sore shoulder, Sampras defeated Agassi, the defending champion, in the quarterfinals, and Boris Becker, a three-time Wimbledon champion, in the semifinals. In the finals he defeated Courier, a player with whom Sampras has a good-natured rivalry, 7-6, 7-6, 4-6, 6-3. The victory was the biggest of his career and proof that Sampras was the best player in the world.

WHO'S BORING? Sampras was so good at Wimbledon that the big story of the tournament was that newspapers in London said that Sampras was dull, especially compared to Agassi. "Pete's a Bore" read one headline. "I'm not very controversial, and controversy definitely sells tickets and causes [TV] ratings to go up," Sampras told *Sports Illustrated.* "But I'm not going to change my style." Players and tennis experts came to Sampras's defense. "I look to a guy like Pete Sampras," American MaliVai Washington, a top tour player, told *Tennis* magazine. "A few years ago, it was said that he was too laid-back or too flaky or whatever. But he's become one of the most consistent guys on the tour."

U.S. OPEN. At the 1993 U.S. Open, Sampras was unstoppable. While many of the top players—including Agassi, Courier, Edberg, and Boris Becker—lost in the early rounds, Sampras fought his way to the finals. There he faced French player Cedric Pioline, a surprise finalist who had never won a tournament but who had earlier defeated Courier. Sampras easily defeated Pioline in the finals, 6-4, 6-4, 6-3, winning his second U.S. Open title. "It has been a great year," Sampras told the *Sporting News*. "The Wimbledon victory was really big for me, and now I have won the two biggest tournaments in the world."

Sampras continued his great play in the first part of 1994. In January he won his first Australian Open title, defeating Courier in the semifinals and American Todd Martin in the finals. With that win Sampras had won three of the Grand Slam tournaments—the only one he hasn't won is the French Open. He's earned over $8 million in his career, and his hold on the number-one ranking is secure. Sampras seems ready to take his place with the best players in the history of the game.

OFF THE COURT. When he's not travelling around the world, Sampras lives in Tampa, Florida. And when he's not playing tennis, he enjoys playing basketball and other sports. His favorite football team is the Dallas Cowboys. When people accuse Sampras of being boring, he tries not to care. He told *Sports Illustrated:* "I let my racquet do the talking.... I just go out and win tennis matches."

SLAM SHORTAGE

Since Sampras's hero Rod Laver won the Grand Slam—winning the Australian Open, French Open, Wimbledon, and the U.S. Open in the same year—in 1969 (he had also won the Grand Slam in 1962), no other male player has been able to win all four tournaments in his *career!* Here's a list of the men who have won three of the Grand Slam tournaments since 1969 and the name of the one tournament they haven't been able to capture.

Player	Hasn't Won
Arthur Ashe	French Open
Boris Becker	French Open
Bjorn Borg	U.S. Open
Jimmy Connors	French Open
Stephan Edberg	French Open
Ivan Lendl	Wimbledon
John McEnroe	French Open
Pete Sampras	French Open
Guillermo Vilas	Wimbledon
Matts Wilander	Wimbledon

WHERE TO WRITE

C/O PROSERVE, 1101 WILSON BLVD., ARLINGTON, VA 22209.

ARANTXA SANCHEZ VICARIO

1971—

Arantxa Sanchez Vicario is a complete tennis player. She plays both singles and doubles—unlike most stars, who only play singles—and she stars in every tennis match she plays. Sanchez Vicario is the second-ranked women's singles player in the world and the winner of the 1989 and 1994 French Open women's singles championships. She is a fierce competitor on the court and a bubbly and energetic person in her everyday life. Sanchez Vicario is one of the best and most popular women's tennis player in the world.

GROWING UP

Arantxa (pronounced ah-RAHN-cha) Sanchez was born December 18, 1971, in Barcelona, Spain. She was named after Saint Aranzazu, the patron saint of the Basque region of Spain. Her father, Emilio, is an engineer, and her mother, Marisa, is a teacher. Her mother wanted the family to take up skiing, but her father preferred tennis. Her father won and tennis became the family sport.

BEST FRIEND. Arantxa began playing tennis when she was two years old. "She was always crawling on the court," her mother remembered in *Sports Illustrated,* "always getting in the way." Her mother gave her daughter a tennis racquet to keep her occupied. The racquet, not her dolls, became her favorite toy. Sanchez Vicario took it with her wherever she went. "That racquet was my first partner," she admitted to the same magazine. She spent many hours hitting tennis balls against a wall. At the age of eight Sanchez Vicario began wearing the ball holder she has made famous. The holder clips on the back of her skirt and holds the extra ball when she serves.

Sanchez Vicario began practicing at the Club Real de Tenis, which was close to her home. The club has clay courts, which are still Sanchez Vicario's favorite surface on which to play. (On clay the ball bounces higher and more slowly than on hardcourts or grass.) She was the number-one ranked female player in Spain by the age of 13, and turned professional at the age of 14 in 1986.

EARLY SUCCESS. Sanchez Vicario beat three established players in her first professional tournament. She won her first doubles tournament in Athens, Greece, and reached the singles final of the Argentinean Open. At the end of her first year as a professional, she ranked 124th in the world. She was a quarter-finalist in the singles tournament at the 1987 French Open and had climbed to 47th in the world by the end of that year. Sanchez Vicario was given the Women's Tennis Association (WTA) Most Impressive Newcomer award.

In 1988 Sanchez Vicario earned her most impressive victory so far when she defeated the American legend Chris Evert, 6-1, 7-6, in the third round of the French Open. She won her first singles tournament, the Belgium Open, by defeating Raffaella Reggi, 6-0, 7-5, in the final. By the end of the year Sanchez Vicario was number 18 in the world and won the WTA Most Improved Player award.

SCOREBOARD

1989 AND 1994 FRENCH OPEN WOMEN'S SINGLES CHAMPION.

NUMBER-TWO RANKED WOMEN'S SINGLES PLAYER IN WORLD DURING 1993 AND 1994.

STARS IN BOTH SINGLES AND DOUBLES TOURNAMENTS, MAKING HER ONE OF THE WORLD'S BEST ALL-AROUND WOMEN'S TENNIS PLAYERS.

Arantxa Sanchez Vicario

THE SWINGING SANCHEZES

All four Sanchez children became tennis players. Marisa, the oldest daughter, attended Pepperdine College in California and played competitive tennis. She now works as a television sports reporter. Brothers Emilio and Javier both play on the men's tour. (Emilio was named as one of *People* magazine's 50 Most Beautiful People in the World in 1992.) The family is very close and spends a great deal of time together. They practice together, eat meals together, and watch each other's matches. Sanchez Vicario's mother travels with her on the tour, washing her clothes and attending all of her matches. Sanchez Vicario added her mother's maiden name, Vicario, to the end of her own in 1989. "I wanted both sides of my family to see their names in the paper," she explained in *Sports Illustrated*. Sanchez Vicario has had many tennis coaches but always looks to her brother Emilio for guidance. "He knows my game best," she told *Sport Illustrated*.

SUPERSTAR

UNBEATABLE? Sanchez Vicario was the seventh-seeded woman at the 1989 French Open. (The French Open is one of tennis's Grand Slam tournaments. The other Grand Slam tournaments are the Australian and U.S. Opens and the Wimbledon tournament in England.) She was then the 10th-ranked player in the world, but ranked more highly on clay surfaces like those at the French Open. Sanchez Vicario played well and surprised the experts by working her way into the final of the women's singles tournament against the number-one player in the world, **Steffi Graf** (see entry). Graf had won five straight Grand Slam singles titles, a gold medal at the 1988 Summer Olympics, and 117 of her previous 121 matches. She was the overwhelming favorite to defeat Sanchez Vicario in the final.

Teenager **Michael Chang** (see entry) was also a surprise in the men's tournament. He upset Ivan Lendl, the number-one ranked men's player, in the fourth round. Sanchez Vicario was inspired by Chang's victory. "I see Michael beat Lendl and ask, 'Why not I am beating Number One?'" she asked *Sports Illustrated* in her fractured English. She added in *Time:* "Plus, look what Monica did." **Monica Seles** (see entry) had won a set against Graf before losing 6-3, 3-6, 6-3, in the semifinals. "That gave me hope," She explained. Sanchez Vicario also had a secret weapon—a lucky wristband given to her by her brother Emilio.

BIG MATCH. The first set of the final match was very close. Sanchez Vicario frustrated Graf by running fast enough to chase down her powerful shots. Trailing 5-6, Sanchez Vicario fought off two set points to tie the first set, 6-6. She was then able to win the tiebreaker that decided the first set. Graf took the second set, 6-3, and led 5-3 in the third set. Her superior power seemed to be too much for Sanchez Vicario. But Sanchez Vicario wouldn't quit. "I knew I don't lose even before then," she told *Sports Illustrated*. "I was gonna run down everything."

"WINS STEFFI." In an amazing turnaround, Sanchez Vicario won 16 of the last 19 points. She won the last four games of the third set and won the championship, 7-6, 3-6, 7-5. She threw her racquet in the air, did a somersault, and hugged Graf after the final point. "I am very joyed," Sanchez Vicario said after the match. "I am so excited to win Steffi."

Arantxa Sanchez Vicario

"Arantxa is a wonderful girl and she played unbelievable to win," Graf said after her loss. "She was making some unbelievable shots, so close to the lines." Graf seemed ill during the match and complained of stomach cramps caused by eating "bad pizza." Sanchez Vicario explained to *Sports Illustrated* that the secret to her win was playing "Steffi very sneaky-smart." She hit a variety of different shots to confuse Graf and used her speed and stamina to wear out her opponent. "Everybody else lose to Steffi in their head before they step on court," Sanchez Vicario added. "I say, 'I beat her. It is possible, no?' They say, 'Arantxa, you crazy.' I say, 'No, it is all in the mentality. I come to play her, not pray to her.'"

MAKES HISTORY. With her victory, Sanchez Vicario became the first Spanish woman to win a Grand Slam singles tournament. She was also the youngest player at the time to win the French Open. (Seles was younger when she won in 1990.) Sanchez Vicario was the lowest-ranked woman player to win a Grand Slam since 1962. "This is a great day for me," she said after the match. "This is the tournament I wanted to win all my life. This is the one I've been dreaming about." (Sanchez

WHAT'S HER SECRET?

At five-feet-six inches tall and 124 pounds, Sanchez Vicario is small for a tennis player, but makes up for her lack of size with determination. "Inch for inch, I think she gets more out of her game than any competitor," former player Pam Shriver explained in *Sports Illustrated*. Sanchez Vicario trains hard and is a fierce competitor. "If you don't practice and you don't want to play, you go down," she commented in the same magazine. "But me, I run [for] all the balls and really enjoy playing." Tennis commentator Ted Tinling described Sanchez Vicario: "She's feisty and fiery and laughs back at the public [crowd] when she misses an easy shot. But beneath all the fun and the giggles, she's a lion."

Vicario was also a finalist in the French Open mixed doubles, but lost.) To celebrate her French Open victory, Sanchez Vicario went to a disco for the first time. "You can go," her dad told her, according to *Sports Illustrated,* "but you have to be back by three in the morning."

Sanchez Vicario became a hero in Spain where she and her family met privately with King Juan Carlos and Queen Sofia. "It was neat, kinda," She told *Sports Illustrated,* "but I feel uncomfortable a little bit." Later in 1989 Sanchez Vicario reached the singles quarterfinals at both the famous Wimbledon tournament and the U.S. Open. She won the tournament held in her home town of Barcelona and was given the WTA Most Improved Player award for the second consecutive year. She entered the world's top-ten rankings and finished the year as the number-six ranked player in the world.

CHANGES NAME. After her French Open victory, Sanchez announced she was adding her mother's maiden name to her own, becoming Arantxa Sanchez Vicario. She won two singles tournaments in 1990, but failed in her attempt to defend her French Open singles title. Sanchez Vicario also won four women's doubles tournaments and the mixed doubles title at the French Open. Her biggest victory of the year came at the Hamburg Open, where she defeated **Martina Navratilova** (see entry) in the semifinals of the tournament, 6-1, 6-7, 6-2. It was the first time in seven meetings that she had beaten Navratilova.

In 1991 Sanchez Vicario returned to the singles finals of the French Open. She defeated Graf in the semifinals, 6-0, 6-2. The two games that Graf won were the lowest totals in her professional career. "That [losing so badly] hasn't happened in a long, long time," Graf admitted after the match. Sanchez Vicario lost 6-3, 6-4, in the finals to Seles, who was then the number-one ranked player in the world. Sanchez Vicario won only one singles titles in 1991, but won three women's doubles tournaments.

WIN FOR SPAIN. Sanchez Vicario helped lead Spain to its first Federation Cup championship in 1991. (The Federation Cup is an international tournament made up of national teams.) Spain defeated the U.S. team in the finals. Sanchez Vicario defeated Mary Joe Fernandez in singles and she and her partner, Conchita Martinez, defeated Zina Garrison and Gigi Fernandez in doubles, 3-6, 6-1, 6-1.

HOME TEAM. The 1992 Summer Olympics were held in Sanchez Vicario's home town of Barcelona, Spain. The Olympics were very important to the Sanchez family. "Ah, the Olympics ... in our city.... You cannot imagine what a feeling," her father told *Sports Illustrated*. Sanchez Vicario and her brother Emilio made the Spanish Olympic team, but Javier did not. Sanchez Vicario was second-seeded in the singles tournament and played doubles with countrywoman Conchita Martinez. She won the silver medal in doubles and the bronze medal in singles.

Sanchez Vicario had a year of near-misses in singles in 1992. She defeated Graf, 6-0, in the first set of their semifinal match at the French Open. But unlike the year before, Graf came back to win the next two sets, 6-2, 6-2. Sanchez Vicario was frustrated after the match because she had played so poorly in the last two sets. She beat Graf in straight sets in the semifinals of the U.S. Open, but lost to Seles in the final, 6-3, 6-3. She did win two singles tournaments and was the number-four ranked woman in the world by the end of the year.

Sanchez Vicario had a better 1992 season in doubles. She and her partner, Helen Sukova, won ten women's doubles tournaments. Together they won the Australian Open doubles title and were named the WTA Doubles Team of the Year. Sanchez Vicario also won the French Open mixed doubles tournament with her partner, Todd Woodbridge of Australia.

BEST SEASON. Nineteen ninety-three was a great year for Sanchez Vicario. She won four singles tournaments and made the quarterfinals in 17 of the 18 singles tournaments in which she played. She reached the singles semifinals in three of the

Arantxa Sanchez Vicario

four Grand Slam tournaments—the Australian Open, French Open, and U.S. Open. She had a 77-14 singles match record and also won four doubles tournaments. She won the Australian Open mixed doubles championship with Woodbridge and the U.S. Open women's doubles with Sukova. Sanchez Vicario ended the year ranked second in the world in singles and fifth in doubles. Sanchez Vicario topped off 1993 by helping Spain win its second Federation Cup title.

SECOND FRENCH TITLE. Sanchez Vicario battled her way to the finals of the 1994 French Open women's singles tournament, where she expected to face her old foe Steffi Graf. Graff was upset, however, by American Mary Pierce in the semifinals. Pierce had played outstanding throughout and hit the ball as hard as any woman tennis player in the world. Sanchez Vicario would have to play her best to win.

Pierce opened the match by earning a 3-1 lead in the first set. A rain storm forced the match to be delayed until the next day; the rest seemed to help Sanchez Vicario. She returned to the court and frustrated Pierce with her ability to return the hardest hit shots. Sanchez Vicario won in straight sets, 6-4, 6-4, earning her second French Open women's title.

OFF THE COURT. Sanchez Vicario lives in the country of Andorra. She has two dogs—Roland, named after Roland Garros Stadium in Paris, France, and Crac. "In Spanish, *crac* is like a boom! It means big champion," she told *Sports Illustrated*. "My brother Emilio tell the newspapers, 'Arantxa is Crac!'" Sanchez Vicario enjoys cycling, playing cards, reading, soccer, and basketball. Her favorite music group is the Beatles and she also likes Phil Collins and Bruce Springsteen. She enjoys eating chicken, pasta, and vegetables, and her favorite flower is the rose. Sanchez Vicario does not let anything get her down, as she said in *Sports Illustrated:* "No matter what, I always smiley."

WHERE TO WRITE

C/O WOMEN'S TENNIS ASSOCIATION, STOUFFER VINOY RESORT, ONE FOURTH ST., N., ST. PETERSBURG, FL 33701.

RYNE SANDBERG

1959—

Ryne Sandberg is a quiet man who lets his bat and glove do the talking. He won the National League Most Valuable Player award in 1984 and has set numerous major league offensive and defensive records for second basemen. He has won ten Gold Glove awards for fielding excellence and once hit 40 home runs in one season. Many experts consider Sandberg to be the best second baseman to ever play the game. But you'll never hear that from him.

"I never dreamed of this. Never. Not at all. I'm a lucky guy."—Ryne Sandberg

GROWING UP

Ryne Dee Sandberg was born September 18, 1959, in Spokane, Washington. His father, Derwent, was a mortician, and his mother, Elizabeth, a nurse. The youngest of four children, Sandberg and his family lived on West Augusta Street in Spokane. His parents couldn't decide on a name when they were expecting Sandberg until they heard a television announcer introduce the New York Yankee's pitcher Ryne Duren. "We looked at each other and knew that would be the name if the baby was a boy," Sandberg's mother recalled in *Sports Illustrated*. His older brother, Del, was named after former major league slugger Del Ennis of the Philadelphia Phillies.

SCOREBOARD

1984 NATIONAL LEAGUE MOST
VALUABLE PLAYER.

TEN-TIME WINNER OF GOLD GLOVE
AWARD FOR FIELDING
EXCELLENCE.

BECAME FIRST SECOND BASEMAN
SINCE 1925 TO LEAD MAJOR
LEAGUES IN HOME RUNS
(WITH 40) IN 1990.

SMOOTH-FIELDING AND HARD-
HITTING SECOND BASEMAN WHO
MAY BE THE BEST OF ALL TIME.

"ALL-EVERYTHING." Sandberg's love for sports came from his dad. "My father loved baseball," Sandberg explained to *Sports Illustrated*. "He was a fan of all sports. We never had a lot of money, but he always had enough to buy me a glove and spikes." Sandberg was a star shortstop at North Central High School in Spokane, Washington, as well as an outstanding basketball and football player. "Ryne Sandberg was the first real three-sport star in high school: All-Everything in baseball, basketball, and football." Spokane resident Jerry Cain recalled in *Sports Illustrated*.

CHOOSES BASEBALL. Sandberg earned all-city honors in both baseball and basketball, was a first-team all-state selection in football, and was named to *Parade* magazine's high school all-America football team during his senior season of 1978. He signed to play quarterback at Washington State University, but changed his mind when he was picked by the Philadelphia Phillies in the 20th round of the 1978 draft. "I knew [baseball] would be easier on my body than football," he told *Boys' Life*. Sandberg signed with the Phillies and was given a $50,000 bonus.

Sandberg batted over .300 twice in his four seasons in the minor leagues. He made his major-league debut in 1981 when the Phillies called him up in September. He got his first big-league hit on September 27 and batted .167 in six at-bats with Philadelphia.

TRADED TO CUBS. The Phillies did not think Sandberg could hit in the major leagues and had a number of other young prospects from which to chose. Philadelphia traded Sandberg to the Chicago Cubs after the 1981 season, along with short-stop Larry Bowa, for shortstop Ivan DeJesus. The deal turned out to be a mistake for Philadelphia. "People ask me all the time," Hugh Alexander of the Phillies told *Sport*. "'Why did you trade Ryne Sandberg.' I always say, 'If I knew he was going to be this good, do you think I would have traded him?'"

Sandberg didn't have a position with the Cubs. They tried him at second base, third base, and the outfield. Chicago finally decided on third base and that is where Sandberg played in his rookie season of 1982. He got off to a slow start, going 1-32 at the plate at the beginning of the season, and the Cubs wondered if he would be able to hit. He calmed their fears by finishing with a solid .271 average and led the team with a franchise rookie record of 103 runs scored. He made only 11 errors at third base and was moved to second base late in the season.

NEW POSITION. During the off-season the Cubs acquired third baseman Ron Cey from the Los Angles Dodgers. The next season Sandberg was moved permanently to second base. He worked hard in spring training to learn his new position. The coaches hit thousands of ground balls to him and he worked on perfecting double plays. "I had to learn how to field the ball backhanded because my [high school] coach always stressed getting in front of the ball," Sandberg explained in *Boys' Life.*

In 1983 Sandberg became the first player in National League history to win a Gold Glove, awarded for fielding excellence, in his first season at a position. He led National League second basemen in all fielding categories. He batted .261, but had only eight home runs and 48 runs batted in (RBIs). When Jim Frey took over as Cubs manager in 1984 he instructed Sandberg to concentrate on hitting for more power. "Since I ran pretty well in my first couple of years in the league," Sandberg told *Sport,* "I was told to hit the ball and run.... So when [Frey] told me he wanted me to hit for more power, I was surprised." Frey worked with Sandberg, showing him how to hit the ball harder.

Ryne Sandberg

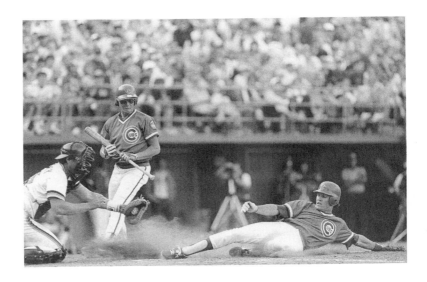

Ryne Sandberg steals home against the San Diego Padres in 1984.

SUPERSTAR

MVP. The hard work paid off in 1984. Sandberg batted .314 (fourth in the National League), had 200 hits (second in the National League), and led the league in triples (19) and runs scored (114). He showed his improved power by hitting 19 homers and driving in 84 runs. He committed only six errors all season and led National League second basemen in most defensive categories. Sandberg went 61 games during one stretch in the season without an error. On June 23 he drove in seven runs and hit two game-tying home runs in a 12-11 Cubs victory over the St. Louis Cardinals.

At season's end the Cubs had won a championship—the National League Eastern division title—for the first time since 1945. Chicago faced the Western division champion San Diego Padres in the National League Championship Series. The Cubs won the first two games of the best-of-five series and seemed in control. But San Diego came back to win Game Three. The Padres took Game Four when first baseman Steve Garvey hit a two-run homer in the ninth inning for a 7-5 win. San Diego topped off an amazing comeback by winning Game Five and the series. Sandberg batted .368 in the playoffs.

Sandberg won the National League Most Valuable Player award in 1984, beating out first baseman Keith Hernandez of the New York Mets and outfielder Tony Gwynn of the San Diego Padres. "It's a great feeling, there's no doubt about that," he said in the *New York Times,* reacting to the news. "When I heard about it, I got a real big thrill. It's one of the big moments of my career." He was the first Cub to win the MVP award since Ernie Banks (see box) won in 1958 and 1959.

LEAN YEARS. The Cubs could not repeat their success in 1985 and over the next three years were near the bottom of the Eastern division. In 1985 Sandberg became only the third player in major league history to hit more than 25 home runs and steal over 50 bases—he had 26 and 54—and scored 113 runs. He had unspectacular offensive years in 1986, 1987, and 1988, but was still the best defensive second baseman in baseball. Sandberg won the Gold Glove every season.

CLOSE AGAIN. Both Sandberg and the Cubs came to life in 1989. Sandberg batted .290, hit 30 home runs (fifth in the league), and scored a league-leading 104 times. In the season's final game he broke the single-season record of 89 consecutive errorless games by a second baseman. The Cubs were the surprise team of baseball and won the National League Eastern division title. But once again they failed to make it to the World Series, this time losing to the San Francisco Giants in the National League Championship Series, four games to one. Sandberg batted .400 in the series and had at least one hit in every playoff game during his career.

HOME RUN CHAMP. In 1990 Sandberg had one of the best all-around seasons by a second baseman. He batted .306 in 1993 and led the major leagues with 40 home runs and the National League with 116 runs scored. He also drove in 100 runs. He became the first second baseman to lead the major leagues in home runs since Hall-of-Famer Rogers Hornsby in 1925, and was the first second baseman to hit 30 or more home runs in

MR. CUB

During his 19-year career, Ernie Banks was the best player in the history of the Chicago Cubs. He batted .274, hit 512 home runs, and drove in 1,636 runs. Banks won the National League Most Valuable Player award in 1958 and 1959 and holds the major league record for most home runs in a season by a shortstop (47). Cub fans will always remember him as the ballplayer who said, "What a great day for baseball. Let's play two."

consecutive seasons. He also became the first player to slug 40 home runs and steal 50 bases in a season. (He stole 54 bases in 1985.) Sandberg's consecutive errorless-game streak was finally broken on May 17. He had reached 123 games—a major league record for any infielder other than a first baseman.

BIG MONEY. Sandberg made history again in 1991 by winning his ninth Gold Glove Award, more than any other second baseman. He batted .291, hit 26 home runs, drove in 100 runs, and scored 104 more. In March 1992 Sandberg signed a four-year, $28.4 million contract, making him the highest-paid player in baseball at the time. "My face will be sore today from the smile," he told a press conference after signing the contract. "It's more money than you'd like to spend," said Stanton Cook, the Cubs's chairman of the board, "but Ryne's a great athlete in great condition with a great history in Chicago."

Sandberg earned his money in 1992. He hit .304 with 26 home runs, 87 RBIs, and 100 runs scored (fourth in the National League). The Cubs continued to struggle, however, and suffered a blow when their best pitcher, **Greg Maddux** (see entry), decided to play for Atlanta. Sandberg suffered a broken hand in the Cubs's 1993 spring training opener when he was hit by a pitch thrown by Mike Jackson of the San Francisco Giants. He batted .309, his highest average since 1984, but hit only nine home runs. Sandberg dislocated a finger on his right hand sliding into home plate on September 13 and missed the rest of the season.

QUIET MAN. Sandberg is quiet on and off the field. "It's not like he doesn't say anything, but he's the same way off the field as he is on it," his teammate Doug Dascenzo told *Sport*. "He's quiet. He doesn't complain. He just does his job." Sandberg doesn't like to brag, despite his accomplishments. "He's still the best," shortstop Shawon Dunston observed in *Boys' Life*. "[But] he's not the kind of person to brag about it."

Sandberg tries to set a good example both on and off the field. "I am proud that he has been a very good role model for the rest of the country," his mother bragged to *Sports Illustrated*. "He lives an exemplary and moral life. People looked for skeletons in his closet, but they couldn't find any."

Many experts consider Sandberg to be the best second baseman in major league history. "I think [Sandberg's] one of baseball's all-time second basemen, and he's a future Hall-of-Famer. He has sure hands, excellent range, an accurate arm, hits with power and can steal a base. A Mr. Do-it-all-with-class," former major league second baseman Bobby Grich wrote in *Sport*.

OFF THE FIELD. Sandberg lives in Phoenix, Arizona, with his wife, Cindy, and their two children, Lindsey and Justin. His hobbies include hunting, fishing, hiking, golf, and music. In 1991 Sandberg donated $100 for each of his home runs, triples, doubles, singles, stolen bases, RBIs, and runs scored to the National Juvenile Diabetes/Danny Ray White Fund. His donation at the end of the season amounted to $42,900.

Sandberg has won ten Gold Glove Awards and has played in ten All-Star games. In 1993 he became the first major league second baseman to make nine All-Star starts and the first to make eight consecutive starts. His 240 career home runs are the fourth-most by a second baseman in major league history behind Joe Morgan (266), Rogers Hornsby (263), and Joe Gordon (246). Sandberg finds his success hard to believe. "I never dreamed of this," he admitted to *Sports Illustrated*. "Never. Not at all. I'm a lucky guy."

WHERE TO WRITE

C/O CHICAGO CUBS,

1060 W. ADDISON ST., CHICAGO, IL 60613.

BARRY SANDERS

1968—

Barry Sanders arrived in the National Football League (NFL) with high expectations. After a college football season in which he broke 13 National Collegiate Athletic Association (NCAA) records and won the Heisman Trophy (as the best player in college football), Sanders won the NFL's Rookie of the Year award. He won the NFL's rushing title in 1990 and has been named to the NFL All-Pro (all-star) team in his first five professional seasons.

During his career Sanders has made the exciting play his trademark. "I remember bracing myself to hit him," said Chicago Bears defensive end Trace Armstrong in the *Sporting News*. "He just stopped and turned, and he was gone. He's like a sports car. He can stop on a dime and go zero to 60 in seconds." Despite his success, Sanders realizes that football is just a game. "Pro football is my job, but I understand that," he told the *Philadelphia Daily News*. "I am at peace, and no one can place a price on that. Society has set up this false picture of what happiness is: How big your bank account is, what kind of car you drive, who your friends are. Gee, happiness is none of that."

GROWING UP

Barry Sanders was born July 16, 1968, in Wichita, Kansas. One of 11 children of William (Willie) and Shirley Sanders, Sanders learned early about hard work. His father owned his own roofing and carpentry company, and the three Sanders boys worked as his assistants as soon as they could handle tools. "All day long they would labor, with the hammers, tar, sweating in the hot summer sun," wrote Mitch Albom in the *Detroit Free Press*. "You did not complain in the Sanders family. Not unless you wanted a good whupping. Dad said 'Get in the car.' You got in the car. Dad said 'Get off that telephone and stop talking to girls.' You got off the telephone and stopped talking to girls. Money? Sanders was amazed that kids in school actually got an allowance 'just for being alive.' There were no allowances in the Sanders family." His mother insisted that he attend church and read the Bible regularly.

SCOREBOARD

AWARDED HEISMAN TROPHY, 1988, PRESENTED TO THE SEASON'S BEST COLLEGE FOOTBALL PLAYER.

BROKE 13 NCAA RECORDS IN HIS FINAL SEASON AT OKLAHOMA STATE UNIVERSITY (OSU).

NAMED NFL ROOKIE OF THE YEAR IN 1989.

LED NFL IN RUSHING IN 1990.

NAMED FIVE TIMES TO NFL ALL-PRO TEAM.

CONSIDERED ONE OF THE MOST EXCITING RUNNING BACKS IN NFL HISTORY.

LEARNS FROM MISTAKES. As a youth, Sanders got in his share of trouble. "I'm not perfect," he told *Sports Illustrated*. "When I was younger, people thought I was a bully. I got into fights and did a lot of wrong. My older brother Byron and I stole candy and got in a lot of fights at school. We'd throw rocks at cars." His brother Boyd, who overcame a rough childhood to become a minister, was a big influence on changing Sanders's life. To stay out of trouble, Sanders did his homework, helped with the roofing business, and stayed away from the drugs and alcohol his friends were involved with. "When my friends would be out drinking Friday and Saturday nights, me and my brother [Byron] would be running the stadium stairs," he told the *Sporting News*.

DECIDES ON FOOTBALL. Sanders was a good athlete, starring in both football and basketball. In his very first youth football

KEEP-AWAY

At five-feet-eight-inches tall, Sanders is considered small by NFL standards. Being small is an advantage for him, though, because it is hard for tacklers to grab, and sometimes even see, him. Sanders learned how to take advantage of being short when he was young. "We played a lot of keep-away, you know, when one guy gets the ball and everybody tries to tackle him," he told the *Chicago Tribune*. "Because I was smaller I had to learn real fast to avoid getting hit."

league game for the Beech Red Barons, he scored three touchdowns. His father was happy about his son's success, realizing that a sports scholarship was the best way for him to go to college. Barry liked basketball the best, but his dad pushed him toward football. "I told [Barry], 'There are just 12 spots for scholarships on a basketball team,'" his dad told the *Philadelphia Daily News*. "I said, 'There are more opportunities in football.'"

At Wichita's North High, Sanders did not play very often as a running back, because his coaches used him on defense instead. He was not given the starting tail-back position until there were only five games left in his senior season. He made the most of those five games, running for 1,417 yards—a city record. Because of his late start, however, Sanders wasn't highly sought after by college teams. Sanders chose Oklahoma State University, mainly because they had a quality business program and he wanted to earn his degree in that area.

STUDENT-ATHLETE. Sanders soon discovered that playing football and going to college classes was difficult. "I remember in my freshman year we [the football team] didn't have any days off," Sanders told the *Sporting News*. "I couldn't believe it and it never got better. They pretended [football] wasn't the main thing you were there for, but you were doing it 50 or 60 hours a week. I fell behind in my schoolwork." In addition to football and his schoolwork, Sanders also worked for minimum wage at a local supermarket.

BACK-UP. Sanders found it tough on the football field, too. During his first two seasons at Oklahoma State, he played behind **Thurman Thomas** (see entry), who now plays with the Buffalo Bills. In his first season (1986), Sanders returned punts and kickoffs, and rushed for 350 yards and two touchdowns. Getting more work in his second season (1987),

Sanders got more attention. He returned a kickoff 100 yards in the opening game and a punt 68 yards in the second game, both for touchdowns. By the end of the season, he and Thomas were sharing the tailback position, and Sanders ran for over 100 yards in three of the last four games.

SUPERSTAR

THE BEST. Sanders finally got the full-time starting tailback job as a junior, in 1988. That year Sanders set 13 NCAA records, including most rushing yards (2,628) and touchdowns (39) in a season. He averaged an amazing 7.6 yards per carry and 295.5 all-purpose yards (yards gained rushing, receiving, and returning kicks) per game, breaking a record set in 1937. Incredibly, Sanders rushed for over 300 yards in four different games. The Cowboys won nine games, losing only to long-time football powers Nebraska and Oklahoma. OSU topped off their season with a 62-14 rout of the University of Wyoming in the Holiday Bowl.

Barry Sanders

Sanders was named the College Football Player of the Year by *Sporting News*. During the season he was nominated for the most famous award in college football, the Heisman Trophy. He didn't campaign for the award, telling reporters that he hoped Rodney Peete of the University of Southern California would win. But Sanders was the runaway winner of the Heisman. In his acceptance speech, Barry thanked his blockers. A shy person, Sanders did not like the attention that came along with the award, and he turned down an invitation to have lunch at the White House, claiming he had studying to do.

TURNS PRO. Winning the Heisman Trophy made Sanders one of the most sought-after college players by professional teams. Sanders still had one year remaining at Oklahoma State, but his father talked him into turning professional. The decision was made easier when OSU was banned from television and bowl games by the NCAA for breaking various rules. The third player taken in the NFL draft, Sanders was chosen by the Detroit Lions. After holding out in a contract dispute for most of training camp, Sanders finally signed three days before the Lions's first game. He donated $210,000 of his signing bonus to his Baptist church in Wichita.

Sanders was an instant star for the Lions, gaining 1,470 yards (second in the league) in his first season and averaging 5.3 yards per carry. He broke team records for most yards rushing in a single season and most touchdowns (14). Sanders won the NFL's Rookie of the Year award and was named a starting running back for the National Football Conference (NFC) in the Pro Bowl, the NFL's all-star game. The Lions won six of their last seven games, but did not make the playoffs.

RUSHING LEADER. The Lions fell to six victories in 1990, but Sanders continued to shine. He won the NFL rushing title, with 1,304 yards, scored 16 touchdowns, and once again was an All-Pro. In 1991 the Lions made dramatic progress, winning 12 games and the NFC Central division title. Sanders ran for 1,563 yards, second in the league to **Emmitt Smith** (see entry) of the Dallas Cowboys, and led the league with 17 rushing touchdowns. The Lions won their first playoff game, against Smith and the Cowboys, 38-6. In the NFC championship game, the Lions lost 41-10 to the red-hot Washington Redskins, the eventual Super Bowl champions that season.

Hopes were high for the Lions entering the 1992 season, but injuries to members of the offensive line, Sanders's main blockers, hurt the team. Detroit dropped to five victories, even though Sanders had another great year, rushing for 1,352 yards. Heading towards his best season ever in 1993, Sanders suffered his first major injury, a knee problem that forced him to miss the final five games of the season. He still finished with 1,248 yards and the Lions won the Central division title, posting a 10-6 record. Sanders could have sat out the playoffs, to make sure his knee was completely healed. Instead, he played in the Lions first playoff game, against the Green Bay Packers, and rushed for 169 yards. It wasn't enough, though, as the Lions fell, 28-24.

FAITH. A devoted Christian, Sanders does not try to change other people's minds about religion, but lets his actions do the talking for him. "He doesn't wear his beliefs on his sleeve," said Lions Coach Wayne Fontes in *Sports Illustrated*. "Barry's not the type of guy who scores a TD and kneels down in front of everyone in the world. He's not for show, he's for real." Sanders holds church services on game days and weekly Bible study classes. He describes himself as an "average guy" who does not dance, smoke, or drink.

BIG CONTRACT. Sanders signed a new four-year, $17.2 million contract during the 1993 season making him the highest-paid running back in the NFL. He also stars in television commercials for Nike. Experts rank Sanders as one of the best running backs in the NFL, along with Emmitt Smith of the Dallas Cowboys and former college teammate Thurman Thomas of the Buffalo Bills. "He just has some incredible moves," Lions coach Wayne Fontes told the *Philadelphia Daily News*. "He runs into a pile of tacklers on the line, then you see his helmet come out and then some shoulder pads and then him." Sanders does not seek attention, however. "I feel uncomfortable being valued because of how well I play football," he told *Sporting News*. "It doesn't make any sense.... I don't have to talk about [it]. That's where athletes have problems off the field. People treat them differently and you start thinking you're better than everybody else. You're not."

ATHLETES FOR ABSTINENCE

Barry Sanders is a founding member of Athletes for Abstinence, along with basketball players A.C. Green of the Phoenix Suns and **David Robinson** (see entry) of the San Antonio Spurs, and football player Darrell Green of the Washington Redskins. The group has made a video called "It Ain't Worth It," and works to convince teenagers not to have sex before they are married.

WHERE TO WRITE

C/O DETROIT LIONS, PONTIAC SILVERDOME,

1200 FEATHERSTONE ROAD, BOX 4200, PONTIAC, MI 48057.

DEION SANDERS

1967—

"Kids on the street…look up to drug dealers…. I'm proving you can do it on the right side."—Deion Sanders

Deion Sanders, nicknamed "Prime Time" and "Neon Deion," made a name for himself with his flashy clothes, gold jewelry, and great athletic ability. The best defensive back in the National Football League (NFL) for the Atlanta Falcons and a solid major league outfielder with the Atlanta Braves, Sanders is out to prove that a player can be successful at two professional sports. Despite many obstacles, Sanders has always succeeded by doing things his way.

GROWING UP

Deion Luwynn Sanders was born August 9, 1967, in Fort Myers, Florida. He has little to say about his upbringing in a poor section of Fort Myers, except that athletics saved him from a life of crime. "It would've been easy for me to sell drugs," he told *Esquire.* "But I had to practice. My friends who didn't have practice, they went straight to the streets and never left."

"IDAS." Sanders began scoring touchdowns for the Pop Warner youth league team at the age of eight. Though he played football, basketball, and baseball in high school, basketball was his favorite. "Let me tell you something," Sanders said in

Esquire. "The best athletes in the world end up at home on the corner. Oh you bet they do. I call them Idas. 'If I'da done this, I'd be here today.' 'If I'da practiced a little harder ... I'd be a superstar.' They'll be standing on that corner till they die telling you all the things they woulda done. I see 'em all the time. Guys who were as fast as me when we were kids."

Though he tried to stay out of trouble, Sanders couldn't entirely escape the problems of his neighborhood. As a teenager he became friends with a drug dealer who convinced Sanders to stay away from drugs. To this day he does not drink, smoke, or do drugs. "See, in my hometown, [drug dealing] was the community job," Sanders told *Sports Illustrated.* "You graduated from high school to the streets and became a drug dealer. Kids from the streets ... look up to drug dealers [because of their cars and flashy jewelry]. But I'm showing them something else.... I'm proving you can do it on the right side."

PRIME TIME. Many colleges wanted Sanders, but he chose to attend Florida State University to play football. In high school he played quarterback, but in college switched to defensive back. Full of confidence, Sanders showed up on campus with a license plate on his car that read "Prime Time," and demanded that his own poster be sold at games. Throughout his career, Sanders has been known for "talking trash," or insulting the other team. Once during a halftime show at a game against the University of South Carolina, he shouted to the South Carolina fans (whose team was losing badly) that they should ask for their money back. Another time he prepared for a punt return by shouting at the Clemson Tigers's bench: "This one's going back [for a touchdown]!" He returned the punt 76 yards for a touchdown, before posing in the end zone.

At six feet tall and 185 pounds, Sanders was a quick and deadly opponent. During his career at Florida State he scored six touchdowns on punt and interception returns and was named an All-American two times as a defensive back. In his last season he led the country in punt return average (15.2 yards) and earned the Jim Thorpe Award as the best defensive back in the nation. He is best remembered at Florida State for being a member of the 1987 Fiesta Bowl championship team that beat Nebraska, 31-28. That year Florida State finished the season ranked second in the nation, behind the University of Miami.

PRO BASEBALL FIRST. Football was not the only sport in which Sanders excelled at Florida State. He also played baseball (helping Florida State to advance to the 1987 College World Series, where they finished fifth) and ran the 400-meters for the track team. In 1988 he signed with the New York Yankee organization to play professional baseball. In June of 1989 he was called up to the major league club to fill in for an injured outfielder. Although he had played less than 100 professional baseball games, he let everyone know that he felt he belonged in the big leagues. He told the media that baseball was, for him, a relief from the hard knocks of football. He played baseball as a rest from his real work—playing in the NFL. But his season with the Yankees didn't last long, as he batted only .234 in 47 at bats.

THEN FOOTBALL. Just before his major league baseball debut, Sanders was the fifth pick in the first round of the NFL draft by the Atlanta Falcons who offered him $400,000. He asked for $11 million. Fearing that he would stick with baseball, the Falcons increased their offer to $4.4 million, and Sanders signed. Only 24 hours after hitting a home run for the Yankees against the Seattle Mariners, Sanders said goodbye to baseball and headed to Atlanta for his first professional football game. Five minutes into his first game, he ran back a punt for a 68-yard touchdown. No player had ever before hit a home run and scored a touchdown in professional games in the same week.

As a rookie Sanders showed his ability to defend against the league's best receivers and had five pass interceptions. Showing his great athletic ability, he returned kickoffs and punts and even played briefly at wide receiver. Still, the Falcons finished the season at 3-13, their seventh straight losing season. When the football season ended, Sanders prepared to rejoin the Yankees in spring training. He played 57 games for the Yankees in 1990, batting .158 with three home runs and nine runs batted in (RBIs). Disappointed with his play, and wanting him to chose between baseball and

Deion Sanders

football, the Yankees released Sanders in 1990. Many people thought that was the end of his baseball career.

ALL-PRO. Before the 1990 NFL season, the Falcons hired a new coach, Jerry Glanville, who set up the Falcon's defense to take full advantage of Sanders's speed. The Falcons finished 5-11 in Glanville's first season, but Sanders returned two interceptions for touchdowns. In 1991 the team improved to 10-6 and made the playoffs. Sanders was a big reason for the turnaround, intercepting six passes (one which he returned for a touchdown), and running two kickoffs back for touchdowns. For the first time he was named to the NFL Pro Bowl (all-star game). The Falcons defeated the New Orleans Saints 27-20 in the first round of the playoffs, with Sanders intercepting a pass and returning it 31 yards. In the second round, the Falcons were defeated, 24-7, by the eventual Super Bowl champion Washington Redskins.

BECOMES A BRAVE. The danger of playing two sports became clear when **Bo Jackson** (see entry) injured his hip during the 1990 NFL season, ending his football career. Despite the risk, Sanders did not want to give up on baseball. The Atlanta Braves, aware of his baseball ability, signed him to a contract before the 1991 season which allowed him to play both sports.

He would stay with the Braves until football season began, and then join the Falcons. His first season with the Braves was disappointing. In 110 at bats he hit only .191 and was sent down to the minors in May. In the fall he was recalled by the Braves and a helicopter flew him from the Braves games to the Falcons practices. Because of his decision to play football, Sanders had to sit and watch as the Braves played in the 1991 World Series.

SUPERSTAR

REACHES GOAL. Entering the 1992 baseball season, Sanders set out to prove he could be a star in two sports. "I've accomplished my goal in that other thing [football]," he told *Sports Illustrated.* "I'm a good baseball player. But I can be a great baseball player. A star baseball player.... In baseball, it's going to be Prime Time's Year in '92." Sanders got his chance when Otis Nixon, the regular centerfielder for the Braves, was suspended for the first 18 games of the season for violating baseball's drug rules. Sanders responded by batting .426 in his first 13 games and .304 for the season, with 26 stolen bases and a major-league-leading 14 triples. More importantly to Braves fans, he stated, "I'm a full-time baseball player." When he was supposed to report to the Falcons, Sanders worked out an agreement to stay with the Braves, who were on their way to a second consecutive National League West division title. In the National League Championship Series, Sanders was the Braves forgotten man, batting only five times as Atlanta defeated the Pittsburgh Pirates, four games to three. Sanders was criticized when he flew to Miami to play against the Dolphins on the same day as Game Five of the series, even though he was back in time to play for the Braves. (In a now famous incident, Sanders poured water over the head of CBS baseball announcer Tim McCarver, who had criticized Sanders's decision.) Given a chance to play in the

World Series, Sanders batted .533 and scored four runs, but the Braves lost to the Toronto Blue Jays, four games to two.

FULL-TIME JOB. Despite being named to the Pro-Bowl for the second time, the 1992 football season was a disappointing one for Sanders, as the Falcons fell to 6-10. His 1993 baseball season was even worse. He left the Braves after the death of his father and stayed away due to an argument over his contract. Finally, he signed a three-year, $11 million deal and became a full-time baseball player with the Braves. As part of the deal, Sanders is not allowed to play football until baseball season is over. After a slow start, he raised his average to .276, playing behind the Atlanta outfield starting trio of Ron Gant, Otis Nixon, and Dave Justice. The Braves won their third straight National League West division title, finishing the season with the best record in the major leagues, 104-58. With Sanders hardly being used, the Braves lost to the Philadelphia Phillies, four games to two, in the National League Championship Series.

Nineteen ninety-three was a good football season for Sanders, even though the Falcons continued to struggle, finishing 6-10. Atlanta was 0-5, however, before Sanders began to play. He led the National Football Conference with seven interceptions and caught a pass from his own quarterback for a 70-yard touchdown. He was chosen for his third straight Pro Bowl appearance and his place as the best defensive back in the NFL was secured. Sanders became a football free-agent following the season.

Before the 1994 baseball season, Otis Nixon left the Braves to play for the Boston Red Sox, opening a starting outfield spot that Atlanta hoped Sanders would fill. Sanders was playing well and batting .286 when he was traded to the Cincinatti Reds for Roberto Kelly in May 1994. "It was a shock to me," Sanders said. "Cincinatti might have gotten a football and a baseball player." If Sanders can play well enough to be named to the baseball All-Star game, in his career he would join Bo Jackson as the only other player to participate in all-star games in two different professional sports.

OFF THE FIELD. Sanders lives in Alpharetta, Georgia, and has a daughter, Diondra. He is known throughout Atlanta for his charitable donations to children's hospitals and hopes to organize after-school sport programs to keep youngsters away from drugs. He is a spokesperson for Nike (for whom he did ads featuring "Deion Sanders Claus"), and is friends with rap star Hammer. When he is not on the field Sanders likes to fish. Though he is loud and proud on the field, he says he's not that way in real life. "People seem to take the way I perform on my job for the way I am in life," he told *Sports Illustrated*. "The truth is, I'm a very family and home-oriented person."

WHERE TO WRITE

C/O CINCINATTI REDS, 100 RIVERFRONT STADIUM, CINCINATTI, OH 45202

MONICA SELES

1973—

Monica Seles is a fantastic tennis player who hits the ball as hard as any woman in history. She is also famous for the grunts she makes when she swings that seem to make the ball go even faster. Seles is the number-one ranked woman tennis player in the world. She has won eight of tennis's Grand Slam tournaments—the Australian Open, French Open, Wimbledon, and U.S. Open. Unstoppable on the court, Seles suffered one of the most tragic injuries in sports history when she was attacked by a man with a knife during a tournament. Always a great competitor, the world of tennis awaits her return.

"With Monica, you don't really have an opening. You can't relax for one second with her."—tennis champion Martina Navratilova

GROWING UP

Monica Seles was born December 2, 1973, in Novi Sad, Yugoslavia. Her father, Karolj, was a cartoonist and film director, and her mother, Esther, was a computer programmer. Her brother, Zoltan, was also a tennis player, and Seles began playing at the age of six. Her dad taught her the unique style she uses today, hitting both her backhand and forehand with a two-handed grip. To encourage his daughter to hit the ball hard, Seles's dad drew cartoon characters on the balls for her to hit. His teaching style worked for Seles. "Because he used cartoons and lots of humor, I always enjoyed practicing," she told *World Tennis*. In addition to tennis, Seles was also a very good ice skater when she was young.

MOVES TO FLORIDA. With her dad as her coach, Seles won the Yugoslav 12-and-under girls championship when she was nine years old, and the European 12-and-under championship when she was 10. In 1985, when she was 12, she was named Yugoslavia's sportswoman of the year. Playing a tournament in Florida, Seles caught the attention of Nick Bollettieri, coach of many famous players, including **Andre Agassi** and **Jim Courier** (see entries). Bollettieri offered Seles a scholarship to play at his tennis academy in Bradenton, Florida, where she went to live at the age of 12. Her parents gave up their jobs to join her.

Seles developed her game at the academy, where the other girls refused to play against her, claiming she was too good. So Bollettieri had her practice with the boys, including Courier. "Nick ordered me to hit with Monica one day," Courier told *Sports Illustrated*. "First ball, *whap!*, she smacks a winner. Next, *whap!*, winner.... After fifteen minutes I walked off. I told Nick, never again." Seles was also a straight-A student.

TURNS PRO. Feeling that she was ready, Seles turned professional in February 1989. She reached the semifinals of her first professional tournament and defeated top-seeded Chris Evert to win her first title in her second tournament. (Evert got revenge at the U.S. Open, beating Seles, 6-0, 6-2.) Seles reached the semifinals of the French Open, where she lost in three sets to number-one ranked **Steffi Graf** (see entry). She ended her first year as a professional with a number-six ranking and was rising fast.

Seles became a star in 1990. She won the Italian Open, with a win over **Martina Navratilova** (see entry), and the

German Open, where she defeated Graf. Most importantly, she won her first grand slam title, the French Open, defeating Graf, 7-6, 6-4, in the final. "She hits the ball like she means it," Graf said of Seles. The victory made her the youngest player ever to win a Grand Slam final. Later in the year she became the youngest player to win the Virginia Slims Championships, a tournament considered the season's championship. (She would also win it the next two years.)

NUMBER ONE. From October 3, 1990, to March 18, 1992, Seles did not lose before the finals of any tournament she played (21 straight tournaments). Although Graf was still ranked number one, it seemed certain that Seles was ready to pass her. "Clearly, Seles looms as the single greatest threat to [Steffi] Graf," said *World Tennis*. "The lefty, with two-fisted strokes off both sides [backhand and forehand], overflows with confidence and a sense of limitless potential." She ended the year with a 54-6 record—second only to Graf—and won nine tournaments.

Monica Seles

Seles got more attention for her on-court grunting and her off-court giggles. The noises she made when hitting the ball were compared to the squawk of a goose and the oink of a pig. "I don't even realize I do it until I watch tape of myself on television," Seles admitted. Her laugh, often just giggling, was compared to that of the cartoon character, Woody Woodpecker. Seles was happy to win the French Open because: "I didn't want to go into the history books 20 years from now and have people read, 'She was a great grunter, a great giggler and had a lot of hair.'"

SUPERSTAR

TAKES OVER. Seles had a big year in 1991. She started the season by becoming the youngest player ever to win the Aus-

Monica Seles outfought Steffi Graf to win the 1992 French Open title.

tralian Open, and then successfully defended her French Open championship. In doing so, she became only the third player since 1969 to win the Australian and French Opens in the same year (Margaret Court and Steffi Graf are the other two). On March 11, Seles ended Graf's record streak as the number-one ranked woman player in the world (188 weeks) when she took over the top spot. She was the youngest player ever, male or female, to be the number-one ranked player in the world.

Despite her great play, Seles received the most attention from a tournament in which she didn't even play. She withdrew from Wimbledon only three days before the tournament was to start, claiming she had injured her legs. The media, which didn't seem to believe her story, spread rumors, some of them bizarre, about why Seles really missed the tournament. In the end, it was confirmed that she actually had injured her leg.

Seles continued her winning ways at the U.S. Open. In a great match, she defeated American (and fellow teenager) Jennifer Capriati, 6-3, 3-6, 7-6, in the semifinals. In the finals there was a 17-year, one-month age difference between Seles and her opponent, Navratilova—the biggest gap ever in a Grand Slam final. In a tough first set, Seles's youth and determination helped her win a close 7-6 decision. But Navratilova was no match for Seles in the second set, losing 6-1. Seles was the champion and the undisputed number-one player in the world.

KEEPS WINNING. In 1992 Seles won the Australian Open, defeating American Mary Joe Fernandez in the finals. In the French Open finals, Seles faced second-ranked Graf. The match was a classic, with both players at the top of their games. Seles won the first set 6-2, but Graf came back to win the second, 6-3. Leading 5-3 in the third set, Seles lost four match points and eventually the game. Graf then took the lead, twice being one game away from the title, at 6-5 and 7-6. Finally Seles, one of the fiercest competitors in tennis, won the third set and the match, 10-8. "That's the hardest I've ever had to work for a Grand Slam title," she said. "In a match like this when you are out there for so long and the last set is so close, in my opinion, both players deserve to win." With the victory, Seles became the first woman to win three straight French Open titles since Hilde Sperling won in 1935-37.

TO GRUNT OR NOT TO GRUNT. Returning to Wimbledon after her mysterious absence in 1991, Seles set out to prove she could play successfully on a grass surface. More important than her play, though, was a controversy about her grunting on court. In the semifinals, her opponent, Navratilova, complained that the grunting was distracting her. "It just gets louder and louder," Navratilova said. "You cannot hear the ball being hit." Seles defended herself, telling *Sports Illustrated* that: "It's part of my game. I hate it, I can't help it." Seles defeated Navratilova, 6-2, 6-7, 6-4, but was warned by the officials to tone down the grunting.

With her win over Navratilova, Seles advanced to the finals, where she faced Graf. She never had a chance, as Graf defeated her 6-2, 6-1. Seles was quiet during the finals, and it seemed to affect her game. "I didn't want to think about it [the grunting]," she told *Sports Illustrated*. "I just thought hopefully I can start [not grunting] somewhere, so I started here." This was the first, and so far only, time that Seles lost a Grand Slam final.

STAYS NUMBER ONE. Back in top form at the U.S. Open, Seles was hardly challenged, defeating Arantxa Sanchez Vicario from Spain, 6-3, 6-3, in the final, despite suffering from a cold and a sore throat. At the season-ending Virginia Slims Championship, she defeated Navratilova in a rare five-set

OOPS!

Wanting to do something a little crazy to relieve the pressure of playing in the French Open in 1992, Seles, a big fan of Madonna, decided to make a music video in Paris. "I think it's kind of good to take off and do something different," she told *Sports Illustrated*. "There's so much pressure in a Grand Slam tournament." Wanting to have a new look, Seles decided to have her hair done. Unfortunately, she didn't speak French. "Then things got a little confusing," she told *Sports Illustrated*. She wanted to have her hair darkened a little, instead she ended up with jet-black hair and a style she had a hard time explaining.

DOESN'T LOOK LIKE NUMBER-ONE?

Despite her success, Seles still has a hard time convincing people how good she is—until they see her play. "I'm different, I know," she told *Sports Illustrated.* "I don't look like a number-one player. People say to me, 'You don't look like an athlete. You look like a person.'" Her coach is her dad, Karolj, and he doesn't push his daughter too hard. "If I don't want to do it [practice], I don't," Seles told *Sports Illustrated.* "He's never said 'You've got to put in those four hours.'" Long-distance running is the only off-court training she does. On the court, few players can out-compete Seles, which has helped her win several close matches.

match (women usually only play best-of-three matches). "At her best," Navratilova told *Sports Illustrated,* "she's as good as anybody." Seles won ten tournaments in 1992 and lost only five matches all year. She also broke her own record for prize money earnings in one year.

TRAGEDY. In 1993 Seles started off hot, winning two out of the first four tournaments she played, including a big win over Graf in the finals of the Australian Open. On April 30, at a tournament in Hamburg, Germany, while she was sitting down between games, Seles was stabbed in the back, just below her left shoulder blade, by a 38-year-old unemployed German worker, Guenter Parche. The man claimed he was a fan of Graf and had attacked Seles because he wanted Graf to be the number-one player in the world again. Graf was terribly upset by the attack and was one of the first people to visit Seles in the hospital.

Seles has not played since the incident and has been greatly missed, even by the players she regularly beat. Because she wouldn't testify in court against her attacker, he received only probation and no jail sentence. Seles has appeared in public only a few times since the attack, once at the 1993 U.S. Open ceremonies honoring the late tennis great **Arthur Ashe** (see entry). Although she was expected to play at the 1994 Australian Open, Seles did not compete. "I've had a lot of time to think since that day [when she was attacked], and a lot of time to decide what my priorities are," Seles confessed to *Tennis* magazine. "So when I play tennis again, I have to play it for the right reason.... I only want to play because I love the game.... The only 'right' time for me to play again is when I see myself and think only this, Gosh, I'm happy again; this is fun."

OFF THE COURT. Seles lives in Sarasota, Florida. She is a spokesperson for Yonex racquets and Fila clothing and shoes. When not playing tennis, She likes to model clothes (she has appeared in *Vogue, Elle, Seventeen,* and on the cover of *Sports Illustrated* and *Shape*), act, swim, juggle, horseback ride, play basketball, and do aerobics. She also collects stuffed animals and her favorite flower is the rose. Seles hopes to attend college someday and also to become a U.S. citizen. Her home country, Yugoslavia, has split apart and is suffering through a civil war. Seles, who was born in what is now the country of Serbia, refuses to comment on the war in her homeland.

It is not certain when Seles will return to the professional tennis tour, but with 32 career titles—eight of them in Grand Slam tournaments—and $7.4 million in prize money, Seles has already established herself as one of the all-time best. Navratilova, one of her fiercest rivals, told the *New York Times:* "With Monica, you don't really have an opening. You can't relax for one second with her."

WHERE TO WRITE

C/O WOMEN'S TENNIS ASSOCIATION,

STOUFFER VINOY RESORT,

ONE FOURTH ST., N., ST. PETERSBURG, FL 33701.

EMMITT SMITH

1969—

"My talent came from God. What I add is desire. I have great desire."—Emmitt Smith

Emmitt Smith has always believed in setting goals. He wanted to be a high school football player and he became one of the best in history. When the experts said he was too small and too slow to play college or professional football, his goal was to prove them wrong. He did. Smith won All-America honors at the University of Florida and in 1993 became the first player ever to win the National Football League (NFL) regular-season and Super Bowl Most Valuable Player (MVP) awards. As the NFL rushing leader for three straight seasons with the Dallas Cowboys, Smith still sets his goals high: he wants to be the best running back of all time.

GROWING UP

Emmitt James Smith, III, was born May 15, 1969, in Pensacola, Florida, one of six children. His father, Emmitt Smith, Jr., was a bus driver who had been a high school basketball and football star. He spent his weekends playing minor league football with a local Florida team. The younger Smith, who says he got his athletic ability from his dad, was a football fan even as a baby. His mom, Mary, who worked in a bank, says the only way she could calm young Smith down was to turn on a televised game. She told *Sports Illustrated* that her son would be "just sort of rocking in his little swing, but watching everything" on the screen. His parents didn't push Emmitt into playing football. They didn't have to.

Gifted with great athletic ability from an early age, Smith spent hours playing backyard football with his friends and older cousins. *Sports Illustrated* reported that "Little Emmitt always played with older kids because of his athletic skills; he had the balance to walk forever on neighborhood fences and curbs without falling off." He joined his first organized football team when he was seven, the mini-mite division of the Salvation Army Optimists League, and stuck with it even when other kids began to lose interest. His mom provided him with religious training and was very strict in raising her sons. Smith never had time to get in trouble or join gangs because he was working too hard to stay in shape for football. When he was young, another of Smith's goals was to become an architect, a person who designs buildings.

HIGH SCHOOL STAR. The public high school nearest to the Smith home was Escambia High, a school whose football program had a long losing history. Before Smith arrived the Escambia Gators had not had a winning season in 21 years, but that soon changed. "All the other kids were acting like kids, fooling around, taking nothing seriously," Escambia coach Dwight Thomas told *Sports Illustrated*. "Then a boy in neat, pressed [ironed] clothes walks up to me and shakes my hand. 'Hi, Coach Thomas,' he said. 'I'm Emmitt.' I have three children, and I hope they can be like him. And I don't mean anything about athletics."

Smith made things easy for Thomas. "For four years we did three things, and won two state championships doing them," Thomas told *Sports Illustrated*. "Hand the ball to

SCOREBOARD

1993 NFL REGULAR-SEASON AND SUPER BOWL XXVII MOST VALUABLE PLAYER, BECOMING FIRST PLAYER IN HISTORY TO WIN BOTH AWARDS.

HAS WON NFL RUSHING TITLE THREE STRAIGHT YEARS (1991-93), ONLY THE FOURTH PLAYER TO ACCOMPLISH THIS FEAT.

NAMED TO NFL PRO BOWL (ALL-STAR) GAME FOUR TIMES (1990-93).

OVERCAME LACK OF SIZE AND SPEED TO BECOME THE TOP RUNNING BACK IN THE NFL.

Emmitt Smith

Emmitt, pitch the ball to Emmitt, throw the ball to Emmitt. It was no secret." Smith led Escambia to a four-year record of 42-7 while rushing for an unbelievable 8,804 yards and 106 touchdowns and setting a national high school record with 45 career 100-yard rushing games. By the end of his senior year, a season in which he averaged an amazing 16.2 yards per carry, Smith ranked second on the all-time high school yardage list and was named "National Player of the Year" by *Parade* magazine. Smith probably would have had even more yards but he often came out of the game when his team had a big lead. When he was pulled out, he sat on the bench and cheered for the other players. Thomas told *Sports Illustrated* that his star player was "unselfish, special, never complained about anything."

GREAT GATOR. After such a great high school career, it was surprising that top colleges in the country were not after Smith. Some scouts said he was too small (five-feet-nine inches and 209 pounds), others said he was too slow. One school that did want Smith was the University of Florida. In his very first game as a Florida freshman in 1987, against the heavily favored University of Alabama, Smith gained 224 yards on 39 carries (a University of Florida single-game rushing record), as the Gators won the game. During the 1987 college season, Smith became the only freshman to gain 1,000 yards in his first seven games. "[Smith] displayed a running style that defies easy description," reported *Sports Illustrated*. "He darted, slithered and followed his blockers, and squeezed yard after yard out of plays that didn't have any yards in them."

WHO'S TOO SMALL? By his junior year (1989) Smith had been named All-America and All-Southeast Conference three times. He had set 58 school records and had a career rushing mark of 3,928 yards and 37 touchdowns. In his junior year, in a game against New Mexico, he ran for 316 yards and was a finalist for the Heisman Trophy, given to the nation's best college football player (he lost to quarterback Andre Ware of the University of Houston). One question remained: could Smith take his success to the NFL? Again, many people said no, that he was too small or too slow. But Smith knew what he could do, and after his junior year he entered the NFL draft.

MISSING PIECE. One of the clubs interested in Smith was the Dallas Cowboys, who had just finished 1-15 under their new coach, Jimmy Johnson—who had coached against Smith when he was at the University of Miami. Dallas was rebuilding their team with young players and Smith was high on their list. "You had to be an idiot not to recognize the talent there," Dallas scout Joe Brodsky told *Sports Illustrated.* "What I did find out, though, was the kind of person [Smith] was: played in pain, never missed a workout ... an extra-good worker and not a complainer."

ROOKIE-OF-THE-YEAR. Dallas made a trade with the Pittsburgh Steelers to acquire the 17th pick in the first round of the draft in which they took Smith. Back home in Pensacola, Smith celebrated with his family and friends because the Cowboys had always been his favorite team. "When I came to the Cowboys, I was like a kid going into a toy store and having a chance to play with every toy," Smith told *Sports Illustrated for Kids.*

Unhappy with the contract offered him by Dallas, Smith missed training camp and didn't sign until the season was about to begin. Despite his late start, Smith was the starting running back in the Cowboys second game. By the end of the season he had gained 937 yards rushing and another 228 receiving and had scored 11 touchdowns. He was named NFL Offensive Rookie of the Year by the Associated Press and was selected to play in the Pro Bowl (all-star) game. (He would also make it the next three years.)

NFL LEADER. Smith exploded in his second year, leading the NFL in rushing with 1,563 yards and scoring 12 touchdowns. Just 22 at the time, Smith became the youngest player in NFL history to gain more than 1,500 yards rushing in a single sea-

Emmitt Smith (number 22) gains yardage during the Super Bowl against the Buffalo Bills.

son. The 1991 Cowboys finished the season with an 11-5 record and made the playoffs. Smith joined with quarterback **Troy Aikman** (see entry) and wide receivers Michael Irvin and Alvin Harper to give Dallas a high-powered offense. In the Cowboys first playoff game, a 17-13 victory over the Chicago Bears, Smith gained 105 yards against a team that had never in its long history allowed a running back to gain over 100 yards in a playoff game. The Cowboys lost their next game against the Detroit Lions, 38-6, but the team knew they were close to being a championship contender.

SUPERSTAR

SUPER BOWL CHAMPS. The Cowboys started out hot in 1992 and never cooled off. Smith became only the ninth player in NFL history to lead the league in rushing two seasons in a row, gaining a career best 1,713 yards, and led the league with 18 touchdowns. Dallas finished the year at 13-3 and won the National Football Conference (NFC) East division title. Smith gained 114 yards as Dallas defeated the Philadelphia Eagles, 34-10, in their first playoff game and gained 114 yards in the NFC championship game, won by Dallas against the San Francisco 49ers, 30-20. Smith and the Cowboys had earned the right to play in the Super Bowl.

In the Super Bowl the Cowboys faced the American Football Conference (AFC) champions, the Buffalo Bills, who were appearing in their third straight Super Bowl. But it was the Cowboys who seemed to own the game. Smith gained 108 yards, becoming the first Cowboy running back to gain over 100 yards in the Super Bowl, and Dallas romped over Buffalo, 52-17. Smith became the first player to lead the NFL in rushing and play on a Super Bowl championship team in the same season.

MVP. After their Super Bowl win, most people expected the Cowboys to repeat in 1993. But they ran into serious trouble early in the season when Smith, who felt like he deserved to be paid more money, refused to play until he got a new contract. The season began without him. Dallas played its first two games—and lost both—while Smith sat at home in Pensacola watching on television. Shortly after the second loss, Cowboys owner Jerry Jones realized how important Smith was to the team and gave in. Smith signed a four-year, $13.6 million deal—including a $4 million signing bonus—that made him the highest-paid running back in football history.

Smith quickly rejoined the Cowboys and helped to turn their season around. With Smith back in the saddle, the Cowboys were almost unbeatable, going 12-2 the rest of the regular season. Though he missed two games, Smith won his third straight NFL rushing title with 1,486 yards and led the NFL in total yards (rushing and receiving) with 1,700. In a season-ending showdown with the New York Giants for the NFC East division title, Smith showed how tough he really was. Despite a separated shoulder which was very painful, he gained 168 yards on 32 carries, leading the Cowboys to a 16-13 overtime victory. In recognition of his contribution to the Cowboys, Smith was named the NFL's Most Valuable Player.

SMITH ON SMITH

"I know I'm not the fastest guy around," Smith told *Sports Illustrated*. "And I know I'm not the strongest guy, either. It doesn't bother me at all. I see myself as being able to get the job done.... If you want to get through a hole bad enough, you'll get through it." Smith considers it a challenge when people doubt his abilities. "When someone says I can't do something, I try to prove that I can do it. If I can prove to myself I can do it, I've proved it to the world."

THREEPEAT!

When Emmitt Smith won the NFL rushing title for the third straight year in 1993, he became only the fourth player in league history to accomplish this feat. Only the legendary Cleveland Brown's hero Jim Brown won it more than three years straight (5) and he is the only player to have done it twice. Here is a list of this special group.

Player/ Team	Years
Steve Van Buren Philadelphia Eagles	1947-49
Jim Brown Cleveland Browns	1957-61 and 1963-65
Earl Campbell Houston Oilers	1978-80
Emmitt Smith Dallas Cowboys	1991-93

MVP II. Smith was still suffering from his shoulder injury when he entered the play-offs, and some thought he shouldn't play. He gained only 60 yards in the Cowboys's first-round 27-17 victory over the Green Bay Packers, but came back with 88 yards rushing and 85 yards and one touchdown receiving against the San Francisco 49ers in a 38-21 NFC championship game victory. Dallas once again met the AFC champion Buffalo Bills for the NFL title in the first-ever Super Bowl rematch.

Trailing 13-6 at halftime, Smith, according to the *Sporting News,* told his coaches that they had to "get the ball into my hands." They took his advice and Smith scored two touchdowns and gained 91 yards in the second half, leading the Cowboys to a 30-13 victory. For his heroics, Smith—who gained 132 yards rushing in the game—was given the Super Bowl MVP award, the first player ever to be the MVP in the regular season and the Super Bowl.

OFF THE FIELD. Smith lives in Irving, Texas, during the season, and returns to Pensacola during the off-season. He stays very close to his family, whose nickname for him is "Scoey" after comedian Scoey Mitchell. His brothers, Emil and Erik, both play college football. "I live for my family," Smith told *Sports Illustrated for Kids.* "I love the game of football, but I would never let it be bigger than my family." Always a good role model, Smith is determined to set a good example. "I always try to stand for something good," he told *Sport,* "which starts with projecting a clean image." Education is very important to Smith, and he is working in the off-season to finish his degree in therapeutic recreation.

Smith and his family run Emmitt, Inc., a company that sells sports merchandise. He also works to help keep kids off alcohol and drugs. He likes to play video games, collect model trains, listen to rhythm and blues music, and he plays basketball and golf. Smith has always set his goals high, and would like to break the all-time NFL rushing record of 16,726 yards held by former Chicago Bear great Walter Payton. He knows it won't be easy, but he feels that with hard work he can do anything. "The way I see it, my talent came from God," Smith told *Sports Illustrated*. "What I add is my desire. I have great desire."

WHERE TO WRITE

C/O DALLAS COWBOYS, COWBOYS CENTER, ONE COWBOYS PKWY., IRVING, TX 75063.

LYN ST. JAMES

1947-

> *"All the good things in my life have happened because of racing. It helped me develop an identity. I've learned a lot about myself, about how to stretch my limits."—Lyn St. James*

Lyn St. James is a rare athlete—a woman automobile racer. In her forties, she qualified for and drove in her first Indianapolis 500 in 1992. She became only the second woman in the 82-year history of the Memorial Day weekend race to qualify for the race and to complete the tough course, finishing eleventh in a starting field of 33 professional drivers. In addition to these auto racing accomplishments, St. James is also a writer-columnist, teacher, businesswoman, and piano player.

Throughout her career, St. James has been told what she can't do. As *Sports Illustrated* said: "At times her own crew members have made it clear that she would be more welcome in the garage if she fetched coffee rather than asked questions about chassis setup." And as St. James told the same magazine: "My entire career, it has been, 'Who's going to work with the girl driver?'... Many male drivers have told me, 'I couldn't do what you do.'"

GROWING UP

St. James was born Evelyn Cornwall on March 13, 1947. (Her last name is inspired by television actress Susan St. James.) An only child, she grew up in Willoughby, Ohio. Her father, Alfred, was a sheet-metal worker, from whom St. James gained an interest in machines. St. James's mother was crippled as a child and her only way of getting around was in a car. "A car gave my mother power and mobility," said St. James in *Sports Illustrated.* "She would talk about the car as if it were human."

St. James was educated at the Andrews School for Girls, an all-girls school near Cleveland, Ohio. When she was younger she was shy, but sports helped her become more outgoing. She played basketball, volleyball, tennis, and field hockey. Because there were no boys at Andrews, St. James went looking for them outside of school. In her youth she found her male friends were involved with drag racing.

In 1969 St. James traveled to the Indianapolis 500. This was the beginning of her interest in road machines and racing. It was a choice her mother didn't like. "My plan for Lyn was for her to get a good education and to be a nice lady," St. James's mom, Maxine Cornwall, told *Sports Illustrated.* "I didn't want her to be hard and fierce." St. James at first listened to her mother, attending the St. Louis Institute of Music and giving piano lessons.

STARTS RACING. After marrying John Carusso, who also loved racing, St. James and her husband began competing in local Sports Car Club of America (SCCA) races. In her first race, St. James spun out and wound up in a pond at Palm Beach International Raceway. She overcame this disappointment and won the 1976 and 1977 Florida Regional championships.

SUPERSTAR

SETS RECORDS. In her first professional season, St. James

SCOREBOARD

ROOKIE OF THE YEAR, INDIANAPOLIS 500, 1992

SECOND WOMAN DRIVER TO RACE IN INDIANAPOLIS 500, 1992

WON DAYTONA 24 HOURS MARATHON, 1990

BEAT PREVIOUS SPEED RECORD AT TALLADEGA SPEEDWAY, 1988

WON DAYTONA 24 HOURS MARATHON, 1987

FIRST WOMAN TO AVERAGE OVER 200 MILES PER HOUR ON AN OVAL TRACK, 1985

FIRST WOMAN TO WIN A NORTH AMERICAN PROFESSIONAL ROAD RACE, 1985

won the Top Woman Driver award in the International Motor Sports Association Kelly American Challenge series. In 1981 she was signed by Ford Motor Company to be a part of its motorsports program. According to St. James, she spent two years telephoning and writing Ford asking for the position. "I read an article in *Car and Driver* called 'Ford and Feminism,'" she said. "I started writing to Ford, sending race results, trying to convince them I should race for them."

St. James traveled around the country acting as a products spokesperson for Ford as well as racing for them. Although it took five years for her to win her first race, at Elkhart Lake, Wisconsin, since then she has achieved many firsts. She was the first woman to average more than 200 miles per hour on an oval track, at Alabama's Talladega Superspeedway in 1985 and later set a second speed record there in 1988. She was the first woman to win a North American professional road race driving solo at Watkins Glen, New York in 1985. And she won, along with her male teammates, in the GTO class of the famed Daytona 24 Hours marathon in 1987 and 1990.

WRITER. In addition to writing a book, *Lyn St. James' Car Owner's Manual,* the always busy St. James also wrote a weekly column in the *Detroit Free Press* in which she answered readers' questions. She guided owners, particularly women, in buying new cars or helping them figure out why their cars weren't working the way they thought they should. In addition to her writing, St. James finds time to train for racing. She works out with a personal trainer on a exercise program that includes weightlifting and aerobics.

EQUAL RIGHTS. A longtime supporter of greater opportunities for women in sports, St. James has been involved with the Women's Sports Foundation for the last ten years and served as its president in 1990. The following year she was named director of consumer relations for the Car Care Council, a trade group that addresses safety and maintenance concerns on behalf of car and truck owners. She has been a guest at the White House five times.

KEEPS TRYING. In 1991 Ford cut back on their support for road racing, and St. James was one of the drivers to be dropped. Instead of giving up her dream, she worked to build up her confidence. "Whenever I get to a low point," she told *Sports Illustrated,* "I go back to the basics. I ask myself, 'Why am I doing this?' It comes down to passion. I love racing. I truly know that ... [racing] is absolutely necessary in my life." St. James never stopped working to get what she wanted. "Speed costs money," said Leo Mehl, director of worldwide racing for Goodyear, to *Sports Illustrated.* "To get to this level, Lyn had to improve not only her driving skills but also her business skills. I've watched her yelling and pounding to get what she wants. Some of the men supplying the equipment didn't take her seriously. She could have easily given up."

After 16 years of trying, St. James was finally able to convince J. C. Penny, Agency Rent-A-Car, Goodyear, and Danskin to sponsor her million-dollar car in the Indianapolis 500 in 1992. She found out only weeks before qualifying that she was set to race at the famous "Brickyard" in Speedway,

MAX

St. James suffered a tragedy in 1976 when her Irish setter Max was run over at a racetrack. "I wanted to go home," St. James told *Sports Illustrated.* "I kept asking John, 'How can you pull yourself together to race?' He said, 'Crying won't bring Max back. If you can't race, pull into the pits, but I'm not going home until the end of the day.' Well, I drove the pace lap past the spot where Max was killed, took the green flag [starting the race] and ran the entire race.... If you put your mind to something, you can override whatever you might feel emotionally."

JANET GUTHRIE

The first woman driver to race in the Indianapolis 500 was Janet Guthrie. Guthrie was dismissed as a publicity seeker and many said that women were too weak to drive race cars. In 1976 Guthrie qualified for the race, but the owner of her car withdrew his support at the last minute. In 1977 and 1978 she did qualify for the race, going only 27 laps in 1977 and finishing ninth in 1978. Through her efforts she proved that women could be capable race car drivers.

Indiana. Becoming only the second female driver in the race, St. James finished eleventh and earned Rookie of the Year honors, the first woman to gain that honor.

In 1993 St. James was able to raise the $3 to $5 million necessary to run an Indy car program for an entire year. Sponsors hope she will be effective in attracting women to auto racing and to their products. "These companies are major hitters," St. James told *Sports Illustrated*. "This can't just be a racing thing: 'O.K., you put your name on my car, would you like tickets to the race?' It must be, 'How can we help improve your business?'" St. James qualified for the 1993 Indianapolis 500, and finished twenty-fifth because her engine stopped running.

THE FUTURE. In February 1993 St. James married Roger Lessman, a man whose hobby is trying to break the land speed record on the Bonneville Salt Flats in Utah. St. James and Lessman have been working on a car she will drive in an attempt to set a new record. Throughout her career St. James has tried to stretch her limits, both as a woman and a race car driver. As St. James told *Sports Illustrated*: "All the good things in my life have happened because of racing. It helped me develop an identity. I've learned a lot about myself, about how to stretch my limits."

WHERE TO WRITE

C/O DAYTONA BEACH INTERNATIONAL SPEEDWAY,

2570 INTERNATIONAL SPEEDWAY,

SUITE H, DAYTONA BEACH, FL 32114

FRANK THOMAS

1968—

Frank Thomas of the Chicago White Sox is a big man at six-feet-four inches and 240 pounds. Because his size enables him to smash the baseball and hurt opposing pitchers' statistics with his hitting, Thomas has earned the nickname "The Big Hurt." In 1993 he hurt American League pitching badly enough to become only the tenth player in major league history to be the unanimous choice as Most Valuable Player. He has become a great player through hard work and a desire to learn all he can about hitting. Only 26 years old, Thomas should be hurting major league pitching for many years to come.

"I don't want to be just a good hitter. I want to be great."—Frank Thomas

GROWING UP

Frank Edward Thomas, Jr., was born May 27, 1968, in Columbus, Georgia, the youngest of five children. His father, Frank, Sr., worked for the city and was a deacon at the local Baptist Church. His mother, Charlie Mae, worked in a fabric factory. Thomas grew up in a poor neighborhood and, in order to keep their children out of trouble, his parents were very strict. "Sometimes I would get really mad at my mom and dad [for being so strict]," Thomas told *Sports Illustrated for Kids*. "But now that I'm older, I understand that they just loved me. They raised me right." It was also tough being the youngest child in the family. "I hung out with my older brother and his friends," Thomas recalled in *Sports Illustrated,* "and I got pushed around a lot until I started pushing back."

SPORTS FANATIC. As a youngster, Thomas spent most of his free time playing sports at the Boys Club. His dad loved sports, but says he never pushed his son. "I'm not bragging," Frank, Sr., told *Sports Illustrated,* "but Frank did so well in all sports. And he loved them all. I never crammed them down his throat. I never had to worry about him. It didn't matter what time of day or night it was, I knew Frank was at the Boys Club or the playground, somewhere with a ball in his hands." Thomas and his dad are still close, though Frank, Sr., does not get to see many of his son's games in person because he doesn't like to fly. "He's made me prouder than a father could be," his dad told *Sports Illustrated.*

Big for his age, Frank was playing football with 12-year-olds when he was nine. One of his first football coaches, Chester Murray, told *Sports Illustrated:* "[I told his dad] This kid will be a professional athlete. I don't know in what sport. But he will be a professional athlete." In baseball Thomas was already a feared hitter. "Kids would throw the ball behind him, over the backstop, all over the place," his dad told *Sports Illustrated.* "They'd do anything to avoid pitching to him."

PLAYS THREE SPORTS. At Columbus High School Thomas was a multi-sport star, playing baseball, basketball, and football. As a basketball forward, he had a great jump shot and reminded many of **Charles Barkley** (see entry). In football he played tight end and was the team place kicker—making all 15 of his extra point attempts. In baseball, he led his team to the state championship two years in a row, hit .440 as a senior, and was named to the all-state team.

NOT DRAFTED. When he graduated from high school in 1986, Thomas was not drafted by any major league baseball team, though 888 other players were drafted. "It was a ridiculously bad job of scouting," said Auburn baseball coach Hal Baird to *Sport*. "Once everyone saw how good he turned out, the scouts all started to say, 'Well, we thought he wanted to play football.' If some pro team had just offered him something—anything—I think he'd have signed to play baseball right out of high school." Thomas was disappointed that he wasn't drafted. "I couldn't believe it when the phone never rang that day." Thomas told *Sport*. "I couldn't believe no one would take a chance on me. I basically played college football because football was my only choice. But I was grateful for a football scholarship. And, looking back, it was probably a blessing that it happened that way."

Frank Thomas

Thomas accepted a scholarship to play football at Auburn University in Alabama. Auburn was the top-ranked team in the country, and Thomas knew that to be successful he would have to train hard. "Playing football for Auburn was a whole new world for me," Thomas said in *Sport*. "I had always thought I was working hard. But there, I learned what hard work means." The hard work in football also made Thomas a more powerful hitter in baseball. The first pitch he hit in batting practice almost knocked the shortstop down. "And I'll never forget it," said his coach, Hal Baird to *Sport*. "I said, 'I think we just found our number 4 hitter.'" Thomas hit .359, led the team in runs batted in, hit a school record 21 home runs his first year at Auburn, and was named to the All-Southeastern Conference (SEC) team. Many of his home runs were incredibly long drives.

QUITS FOOTBALL. Thomas played only one year of football at Auburn, catching three passes for 45 yards. "I could have made it to the NFL [National Football League], but I wouldn't have been a star," he told *Sports Illustrated for Kids*. His coaches disagreed, saying that had he played football, Smith could have been an NFL star tight end. The decision to drop football, however, wasn't too hard. "Too many of my friends in college football go down with injuries, guys with unbelievable talent," Thomas told *Sport*. "One day, you might get torn knee ligaments that you could never rebuild. Or a broken neck—I saw a couple unbelievable broken necks. So I switched after one season."

Thomas admits he tried too hard during his second baseball season. "My second year in college, I decided that I was going to be the most feared hitter in baseball," he told *Sports Illustrated for Kids*. "I swung [too] hard ... and struck out 20 out of 30 times at bat." Thomas learned a lesson from all those strikeouts. "Being a good power hitter has a lot to do with [strategy]," he told *Sports Illustrated for Kids*. "I try to be patient and hope the pitcher makes a mistake. When he does, I'll make the most of it." Thomas is a very patient hitter, swinging only at pitches he knows he can hit hard. "If there's a ball I can't sting like I want to, I leave it alone."

After being cut from the 1988 U.S. Olympic baseball team, Thomas returned to Auburn to prove he should have made the team. He led the SEC in batting average (.403) and RBIs (83), hit 18 home runs in his junior year (1989) and was named the SEC's Most Valuable Player. Major league teams began to take notice. Thomas was chosen by the Chicago White Sox as their seventh pick in the 1989 draft. Though he was impressive during spring training in 1990, the White Sox sent him down to their minor league team in Birmingham, Alabama. Disappointed, Thomas talked to his dad about his problems. "He was hurt," Frank, Sr., told *Sports Illustrated*. "Really hurt. But he was going up there [to Birmingham] dedicated to working hard and being ready."

JOINS SOX. Thomas proved the White Sox had made a mistake, becoming the minor league player of the year, batting

.323 with 18 home runs. He was finally called up to the White Sox on August 2, 1990. He batted .330, with seven homers and 31 runs batted in (RBIs) in only 60 games and has been a starter at first base ever since. Thomas had a great season in 1991, batting .318, hitting 32 home runs (fifth in the American League), driving in 109 runs (fifth in the American League), and walking an American League-leading 138 times. He finished third in the voting for the American League's Most Valuable Player. It was also during the 1991 season that White Sox radio broadcaster Ken Harrelson gave him his nickname, "The Big Hurt," because of how hard he hit the ball.

PATIENT HITTER. In 1992 Thomas had another great year, batting .323 (third in the American League) with 115 RBIs (second in the American League) and 198 runs scored (second in the American League). He also tied for the American League lead in walks (128) and doubles (46). But many fans were disappointed with his total of 24 home runs. Because of his size and power, many people expected him to hit more home runs. But Thomas, unlike most power hitters, does not always swing for the fences. He just tries to make contact with the ball and let his natural power lead to home runs. "I don't get into the home run game like most people do," he told *Sport*. "I don't care anything about that."

SUPERSTAR

MVP. Thomas took his game to another level in 1993. He finished the season with a .317 average, hit a team-record 41 home runs, and finished second in the major leagues with 128 RBIs. He became the first player to have more than 100 RBIs and 100 walks in each of his first three full-time seasons since Babe Ruth in 1920-23, and he became only the fifth player in major league history to bat over .300 with 20 home runs and 100 RBI, 100 runs scored, and 100 walks in three consecutive seasons. (The other four players are all in the Hall of Fame— Jimmie Foxx, Lou Gehrig, Babe Ruth, and Ted Williams.) In addition to his offensive statistics, Thomas improved his defense at first base, an area of weakness in his first two seasons.

The White Sox won the American League West division—their first title since 1983—and at the end of the season Thomas became only the tenth player in major league history to be a unanimous choice for the Most Valuable Player award. Unfortunately for Chicago, Thomas injured his left shoulder when he ran into a post while chasing a foul ball near the end of the regular season. He entered the playoffs still hurting, but pulled off a great American League Championship Series against the Toronto Blue Jays. He batted .353 with one home run and three RBIs, but the White Sox fell in six games to the eventual World Series champion Blue Jays. Thomas was disappointed, but knows that winning a championship is not easy. "I'm the kind of guy who would rather win a championship than get MVP," he told *Sport*. "I'm the kind of guy who understands there are no shortcuts to success."

OFF THE FIELD. Thomas lives in Burr Ridge, Illinois, with his wife, Elise, and their son, Sterling. Although he often looks mean when he's playing, Thomas is really friendly and very polite. Always good to his fans, he signs a lot of autographs. His favorite movie is "Mr. Baseball," mainly because of his sma'' .ole in the film. He is a spokesperson for Reebok athletic equipment and founded the Frank Thomas Charitable Foundation in 1993 to aid the underprivileged. He is also the White Sox's spokesperson for the "Give School a Major League Effort" program. Thomas credits his outstanding hand-eye coordination to ping-pong, a game he plays to help make him a better hitter.

Thomas tries not to get a big head about his success. He wrote the letters DBTH on masking tape and stuck it on his locker. "It [DBTH] stands for Don't Believe the Hype," he told *Sports Illustrated for Kids*. The words come from one of his favorite rap songs.

"I have a gift for hitting," Thomas told *Sport*. "But it's a lot of hard work too." He intends to continue to work hard because he sets his goals high. "Not many guys in this game have ever been able to hit for average, for power, and drive in runs," Thomas told *Sport*. "I'd like to combine all those things. I'd like to do things that no one has ever done before. I don't want to be just a good hitter. I want to be great."

WHERE TO WRITE

C/O CHICAGO WHITE SOX,
333 W. 35TH ST., CHICAGO, IL 60616.

FRANK AND BO SHOW

In 1993 Thomas was joined on the White Sox by **Bo Jackson** (see entry) who had also played baseball and football at Auburn University (before Thomas attended the school). The two became friends. "I think it's because we have so much in common," Jackson told *Sports Illustrated for Kids*. "We grew up in the same part of the country [Jackson is from Alabama], went to the same school, played the same sports. And now, Frank's locker is just one down from mine." "We give each other a hard time," Thomas told *Sport*. "Bo is the greatest all-around athlete I've ever seen. But I'm probably better at some things in baseball, like hitting." The White Sox decided not to keep Jackson after the 1992 season and he signed to play with the California Angels.

ISIAH THOMAS

1961—

Isiah Thomas is one of the best "little men" to play in the National Basketball Association (NBA). Twice he led the Detroit Pistons to NBA Championships and he has been an NBA All-Star 11 times in 12 seasons. Thomas survived a tough childhood in a Chicago ghetto and, with the help of a strong mother and a loving family, he reached the top of his sport.

GROWING UP

Isiah Lord Thomas III was born April 30, 1961, in Chicago, Illinois. He grew up in a ghetto on Chicago's West Side, the youngest of seven boys and two girls born to Mary and Isiah Thomas II. "He was well behaved, but spoiled," his mother told *Sports Illustrated*. "He's still like that, spoiled rotten—by me and his brothers. They try to put the blame on me, and I can't say I didn't treat him special. He was the baby. He got special attention."

DAD LEAVES. Thomas's father was a plant supervisor who pushed his children to read, barred them from watching anything but educational television, and taught them to stick together and protect one another. He lost his job when Thomas was a baby and took a job as a janitor, but didn't make enough money to support his family. Eventually, he and his wife separated. Mary Thomas worked in the cafeteria and ran the youth center at Our Lady of Sorrows school to support her family.

"MEET ME AT THE COURT." Thomas played basketball at Gladys Park, next to Chicago's Eisenhower Expressway. "Go anywhere on the West Side and say, 'Meet me at the court,' and they'd know what you were talking about," he explained in *Sports Illustrated*. "That's where I really learned to play.... You could always get a game there. Any time of day, any time of night."

HARD TIMES. When Isiah was 12 the Thomas family moved when the gangs again became a problem. "Those were probably the worst times as a kid," Thomas recalled in *Sports Illustrated*. "Everything broke down in the house once we bought it." Thomas slept in the closet between his brothers' and sisters' rooms, or on the ironing board in the hall. The family lived on food donated by the church where his mother worked. Thomas began to steal his classmates' lunches and was thrown out of one school for slapping a girl across the face.

LAST HOPE. Thomas's childhood idol was his brother, Larry, who was nine years older. Larry had become a drug dealer and was involved in prostitution. Thomas saw crime as the only way out of poverty. "I'd go in and try on Larry's clothes. I'd walk like him, talk like him," Thomas told *Sports Illustrated*. "I knew how to hustle at an early age." When Larry realized what was happening he talked to his younger brother. He told Thomas that he was the family's last hope to make it in professional sports. The first three children with real athletic talent had already failed. The oldest, Lord Henry, had become a heroin addict. The second, Gregory, struggled with alcohol. And Larry, a college star, suffered an ankle injury during a professional tryout.

TOUGH MOM

Mary Thomas was very strict with her children and insisted they be home before the streetlights came on. There was little that she would not do to protect her children from the gangs that controlled the streets of Chicago's West Side. Once the members of a gang known as the Vice Lords knocked on the Thomas family's door. They wanted the children to join their gang. Mary Thomas came to the door with a shotgun. "If you don't get off my porch," she told them, according to *Sports Illustrated.* "I'll blow you across the expressway." They never returned and the gangs did not bother the Thomas children for several years after the incident.

Isiah was the most talented of the Thomas children. When he was three, he was performing halftime shows at his brothers' basketball games. His brothers worked with Thomas to help improve his game and convinced the basketball coach at St. Joseph High School, Gene Pingatore, to give Isiah financial aid so he could enroll. The school was in the suburbs and Thomas traveled three hours each day, took three buses each way and arrived home long after dark. He struggled to keep his grades up and had to learn how to play organized basketball. Thomas led St. Joseph to a second-place finish in the state high school championship tournament in his junior year, and by his senior year was one of the top high school players in the country.

GOES TO INDIANA. Thomas's family wanted him to attend DePaul University in Chicago, but he chose to go to Indiana University of the Big-Ten Conference, one of the few schools that did not offer him illegal financial payments. "All [Indiana coach] Bobby Knight promised was he'd try to get Isiah a good education and give him a good opportunity to get better in basketball," Mary Thomas told the *New York Times.*

Thomas was All-Big Ten his freshman year, and was an All-American as a sophomore. He led Indiana to the Final Four of the National Collegiate Athletic Association (NCAA) basketball tournament in his sophomore year. There they defeated Louisiana State University, 67-49, in the semifinals. Indiana won the national championship by defeating the University of North Carolina in the final game, 63-50. Thomas, who scored 25 points in the championship game, was named the tournament's Most Valuable Player.

Thomas had a hard time getting along with Hoosier coach Bobby Knight, who is known for his tough discipline and strict rules. On the advice of his friend **Earvin "Magic" Johnson** (see entry), Thomas decided to turn professional after his sophomore year. "There was a lot to consider," he admitted in the *New York Times*. "I know I'm a role model for a lot of people back in the ghetto. Not too many of us get the chance to get out, to go to college. If I quit school, what effect would that have on them?"

JOINS PISTONS. Thomas was the second selection in the 1981 NBA draft, behind his friend Mark Aguirre of DePaul University. He went to the Detroit Pistons, who were a struggling team when Thomas arrived. Detroit had won only 37 of their 164 games the previous two seasons. Thomas was considered the team's savior. Though he was only 19 years old, he did not give in to the pressure. "It doesn't bother me," Thomas told the *Boston Globe*. "I can't play basketball or live the way they want me to. So I have to set my own goals and objectives." One of the first things Thomas did after signing his contract was buy his mother a house in the suburbs.

Isiah Thomas

Thomas was an instant success in his rookie season (1981-82). He averaged 17 points per game, led his team in assists and steals, and was named to the NBA Eastern Conference All-Star team. He improved his second season, averaging 22.9 points and 7.8 assists per game. In the 1983-84 season Thomas finished third in the NBA with an average of 11.1 assists per game and finished second in the league in steals (2.49 per game). He was named the Most Valuable Player in the All-Star game after scoring 21 points and passing for 15 assists.

The Pistons made the playoffs in 1983-84 for the first time in Thomas's career. They faced the New York Knicks in the first round and Thomas put on one of the greatest performances in NBA history. He scored a remarkable 16 points in the last 94 seconds of the fourth quarter to singlehandedly send a game against the Knicks into overtime. The Pistons eventually lost the game and the series to the Knicks.

RECORD BREAKER. Thomas made history during the 1984-85 season when he broke the NBA single-season assist record with 1,123, an average of 13.1 per game. The Pistons defeated the New Jersey Nets in the first round of the playoffs, but lost to the Boston Celtics in the Eastern Conference semifinals. Thomas finished second in the NBA in assists with 10.8 per game in the 1985-86 season and was the MVP of the All-Star game for the second time.

TEAM PLAYER. The inability of the Pistons to contend for the NBA Championship bothered Thomas. In 1985 he briefly considered retiring or asking the Pistons to trade him to a better team. But the Piston's fortunes began to change when Chuck Daly was hired as coach. Daly abandoned the fast-breaking offensive style that Thomas was used to and encouraged the team to play tough defense. The change meant that Thomas would have to sacrifice his personal statistics for the team's goal. He was up to the challenge.

The Pistons improved under Daly's guidance and Thomas's leadership. In the 1987 playoffs Detroit came within seconds of eliminating the defending champions, the Boston Celtics. But in what should have been Thomas's finest moment, he made a major mistake. With Detroit leading by a point with five seconds left in Game Five of the Eastern Conference finals, Celtics star **Larry Bird** (see entry) stole Thomas's sloppy inbound pass and set up a layup that cost the Pistons the game and, as it turned out, the series. Five days later the Pistons lost Game Seven and Boston went to the finals.

SO CLOSE. Thomas viewed the 1987-88 season as an opportunity to make his dream of winning an NBA championship come true. He had a typically solid season, averaging 19.5 points per game. The Pistons won 54 regular season games and the franchise's first Central division title. Detroit defeated the Washington Bullets, Chicago Bulls, and Celtics in the playoffs to reach the NBA finals for the first time in franchise history. Before the first game against the defending champions, the Los Angeles Lakers, Thomas told the *Los Angeles Times:* "I'm not on a mission or anything. This is really for peace of mind. Seven years I've waited for a chance to win the championship."

Thomas and his friend Earvin "Magic" Johnson kissed each other on the cheek as the players came on the floor to start Game One, then did everything they could to win. Thomas's play in the series was spectacular. He injured his back in Game Two and severely sprained his ankle in Game Six, but still averaged 19.7 points per game during the seven-game series, including a phenomenal performance in Game Six, in which he scored 43 points—including an NBA record 25 points in one quarter. In the end, it wasn't enough. The Lakers won the series, four games to three. But Thomas's effort was regarded as heroic. "He was out of this world," wrote *Los Angeles Times* columnist Mike Downey.

SUPERSTAR

BAD BOYS. Thomas and the Pistons would not be denied in the 1988-89 season. With tough players like forward Rick Mahorn and center Bill Laimbeer, the team became known as the "Bad Boys," because of their physical, and some claimed dirty, style of play. Midway through the season the Pistons made a major trade, sending high-scoring forward Adrian Dantley to the Dallas Mavericks for forward Mark Aguirre, Thomas's boyhood friend. The Pistons earned the best regular season record in the NBA with 65 wins.

Detroit returned to the NBA finals and again faced the Lakers, a team seeking its third straight championship. This season the Lakers were the team that was hurt by injuries. Starting guards Byron Scott and Johnson suffered hamstring injuries, and the Lakers were no match for the determined Pistons. Thomas won his championship ring with a 4-0 sweep of Los Angeles. "We did everything we had to," an overjoyed Thomas told the *Detroit Free Press* after the victory. "It [the championship] was everything I had ever wanted."

REPEAT. The Pistons were determined to repeat as NBA champions in the 1989-90 season. They returned to the NBA

MIGHTY MITE

At six-feet-one inch and 185 pounds, Thomas is one of the smallest men to be a dominant player in the NBA. He is very quick and has the ability to make great passes and shots against much taller opponents and was third on the all-time NBA career assist list with 8,662 at the end of the 1992-93 season. He has frequently been injured during his career, but has shown an impressive ability to play while he is hurt. He knows what it takes to win and has often sacrificed his own fame to help the Pistons be successful. He has been a goodwill ambassador for the NBA and is one of the game's most popular players.

finals for the third consecutive season. Detroit faced **Clyde Drexler** (see entry) and the Portland Trail Blazers in the finals. The teams split the first two games in Detroit. The Pistons swept the final three games in Portland—where they had not won for 17 years—to win the series and repeat as NBA champion. Thomas was the unanimous choice as the series' Most Valuable Player. He averaged 27.6 points per game and played great defense on Trail Blazers guard Terry Porter.

DISAPPOINTMENT. The following four seasons were difficult for the Pistons. Thomas struggled to overcome injuries and the team fell out of title contention. Detroit was swept by **Michael Jordan** (see entry) and the Chicago Bulls in the 1991 Eastern Conference finals, falling short in their attempt to "threepeat." In 1992 Thomas was disappointed when he was not chosen to be a member of the U.S. Olympic basketball "Dream Team." The decision was especially painful because he was scheduled to play in the 1980 Olympics until the United States decided not to participate because of the Soviet Union's invasion of Afghanistan. The Pistons missed the playoffs in 1992-93 for the first time since the 1983-84 season.

LOOKS TO FUTURE. Thomas considered leaving the Pistons at the beginning of the 1993-94 season. The New York Knicks were interested in acquiring Thomas to help lead their team to the NBA finals. But he decided to stay in Detroit after negotiating a new contract. Though his greatest honor came when it was announced that he would be a member of "Dream Team II" (the U.S. Olympic basketball team that will compete in the 1996 Olympics in Atlanta, Georgia), a late 1993-94 season injury to his achilles tendon will make it impossible for him to participate.

THOMAS RETIRED FROM THE SPORT. In May 1994 it was announced that Thomas would become vice-president and part-owner of the NBA's new expansion franchise, the Toronto Raptors.

OFF THE COURT. Thomas lives in Bloomfield Hills, Michigan, with his wife, Lynn, and their son, Joshua, and has installed his own indoor basketball court in his home. Thomas, who promised his mother he would get his college degree when he turned professional, returned to Indiana and earned a bachelor's degree in criminal justice. He is active in many community service activities and makes anti-drug commercials and speeches. The movie *A Mother's Courage* told the story of Thomas's mother's struggle to raise her children. Thomas admitted to the *Chicago Tribune* that he would like to be considered one of the best guards in history. "When I'm retired, I'd like for people to be comparing [great guards] to Isiah."

WHERE TO WRITE

C/O DETROIT PISTONS, PALACE OF AUBURN HILLS,

TWO CHAMPIONSHIP DR., AUBURN HILLS, MI 48326.

THURMAN THOMAS

1966—

At five-feet-ten-inches tall, 198 pounds, Thurman Thomas is one of the smallest players in the National Football League (NFL). The Buffalo Bills running back is also one of the best. Thomas led the league in total yards from scrimmage (yards gained rushing and receiving) for four consecutive seasons (1989-92), breaking the record held by Hall-of-Famer Jim Brown. Voted the league's Most Valuable Player in 1991, Thomas led the Bills to an NFL record, four straight Super Bowl appearances. Unfortunately, Buffalo also set an NFL record by losing all four Super Bowls, becoming the first team in the history of the four major professional sports (baseball, basketball, football, and hockey) to lose the championship final four years in a row.

GROWING UP

Thomas was born May 16, 1966, in Houston, Texas. An only child, he moved to nearby Missouri City before the seventh grade. His parents were divorced when he was four. Both parents remarried, and Thomas stayed close to both his parents and stepparents. "I grew up with two mommas and two dads," he told the *Houston Post*. "But I was an only child. I always had a lot of time by myself. I used to sit and think a lot."

EARLY TRAINING. Thomas learned to play football at Missouri City Junior High School. It was clear from the start that he had great talent. "Once you see him play, you believe he can do anything and you know he believes he can do anything, too," his high school coach, Neal Quillin, told the *Houston Post*. "My impression was that he always had a lot of self-confidence."

Texas high school football is considered to be among the best in the nation. "In Texas, football was it," Thomas told the *Houston Post*. "You start with football and the other sports fall behind it. We've had a lot of good players come out of Texas—[former NFL running backs] Earl Campbell and Eric Dickerson. If I had played high school football anywhere else in the nation, I don't think I would have had the success I've had."

After Coach Quillin put Thomas into Willowridge High's starting lineup as a sophomore in 1982, he led Willowridge to two state championship games and one state title. In three seasons of high school play, Thomas rushed for 3,918 yards and 48 touchdowns. He was named a *Parade* magazine All-American and Texas Player of the Year by the Houston Touchdown Club. Although he was an all-star running back in high school, most local colleges were interested in Thomas as a defensive back. So he left Texas for Oklahoma State University. As a freshman tailback, he led the team with 543 rushing yards and was named Most Valuable Player in the Cowboys's 1984 Gator Bowl victory over South Carolina.

COLLEGE CAREER. As a sophomore, Thomas emerged as one of the nation's premier runners, gaining 1,650 yards and scoring 15 touchdowns. He finished tenth in the voting for the Heisman Trophy, college football's top award. During this season Thomas earned the nickname "The Thurmanator." Then,

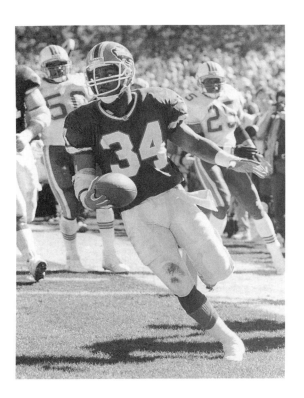

Thurman Thomas

in the summer between his sophomore and junior years, injury struck. Thomas tore a ligament in his knee during a pickup basketball game. He required surgery and missed the first few games of the 1986 season. When he returned, he gained 714 yards, but was still nervous about the injury. "I really didn't know what to expect out of it," he told the *Wichita Eagle-Beacon*. "I was afraid that something else was gonna happen to it, that the injury was gonna get worse." As a senior, Thomas returned to All-American form, rushing for 1,613 yards. He finished his college career as the second-best runner in Big Eight Conference history.

TURNING PRO. Most experts expected Thomas would be picked in the first round of the 1988 NFL draft. So did Thomas. But many pro clubs still had doubts about his knee. Instead of being a first-round pick, Thomas was drafted 40th overall, in the second round. The Bills, in fact, were worried about drafting Thomas even that high after he failed a physical exam. "If the knee didn't hold up, we decided we'd reconstruct it, bring him back the next year and see if he could do it then," Bills's team physician Richard Weiss told *Sports Illustrated*.

As a rookie in 1988, Thomas rushed for 881 yards on 207 carries, despite missing two games with a sore leg. The next year, the Bills's offense improved dramatically after Buffalo coach Marv Levy installed a brand new "no-huddle" offense. This type of offense moved quickly between plays to keep opposing teams off-balance.

SUPERSTAR

LEAGUE LEADER. Used both as a runner and receiver in 1989, Thomas scored 12 touchdowns and led the NFL with 1,913 total yards from the line of scrimmage. This would be the first of four consecutive years in which he led the league in this category, a feat that broke the NFL record. Teammate James Lofton told the *Houston Post* that Thomas was the best player he had seen during his 14-year NFL career. "I'm talking about backs who create something from nothing, who are out there scratching and clawing for everything they can get and that's what Thurman does so well," Lofton continued. "He just doesn't accept a 2-yard gain."

> ## TOTAL YARDS
>
> In football, the line of scrimmage is the spot at which the ball rests when a play begins. Total yards from the line of scrimmage for a running back include yards gained rushing (running with the ball after a handoff or pitchout) and receiving (catching passes).

RESPECT. Thomas has often complained about being overshadowed by teammates Jim Kelly and other top NFL runners such as **Barry Sanders** (see entry) of the Detroit Lions and **Emmitt Smith** (see entry) of the Dallas Cowboys. "People talk about Barry as being the best running back," Thomas told the *Washington Post*. "Then they say that I am the best all-around. The difference with me is that I catch the ball downfield and block, and do a lot of other things that Barry doesn't do. Barry is a great runner. But that's all he is."

TOO SHORT? Being 5-feet-10-inches tall, Thomas has often been told that he is too small to be a successful NFL running back. "It always kind of bothered me people saying, 'Well, you're too small to do this, you're too small to do that,'" he told the *Pioneer Press*. "'Don't even try it. You can't do it. You can't dunk a basketball. Or you can't run over a guy that weighs 220 pounds when you only weigh 130.' [Thomas actually weighs 198 pounds.]Things like that have always motivated me toward doing something that I know I can do when other people say I can't do it."

SUPER BOWL. In 1990 Thomas and the Bills got their share of national attention. The team went 13-3 in the regular season and beat the Los Angeles Raiders in the American Football Conference (AFC) championship game (51-3) to get to their first Super Bowl ever. Thomas turned in another sensational season, rushing for 1,297 yards (second in the NFL) and catching 49 passes for an additional 532 yards.

WHO'S BEST

Use the following chart—listing the career statistics for Thomas, Barry Sanders, and Emmitt Smith—to decide who is the best running back in the NFL.

	B. Sanders	E. Smith	T. Thomas
Seasons	5	4	6
Rushing Yards	6,789	5,699	7,631
Receiving Yards	1,499	1,235	3,053
Total Yards	8,288	6,934	10,684

His best game of the season came in Super Bowl XXV against the New York Giants. Thomas showed off to a worldwide audience, carrying the ball 15 times for 135 yards and a touchdown. In addition, he caught five passes for 55 yards. He surely would have been the game's Most Valuable Player, except that the Bills missed a field goal with four seconds left and lost the game, 20-19.

"At first, I didn't give the [MVP] award much thought," said Thomas describing his disappointment after the game to *Newsday*. "The loss was all that mattered. But every time a friend or someone in my family said, 'You should have been MVP,' it lingered on me for a long time. I thought 'I should have been MVP.'" Thomas showed up at training camp in 1991 with a message written on the tape wrapping his shoes. The message said Super Bowl XXVI, MVP. And he vowed to get back to the Super Bowl to prove his point.

SUPER RETURN. The Bills did get back to the Super Bowl. They went 13-3 during the 1991 regular season and beat the Denver Broncos in the AFC title game. During the season, Thomas improved his own performance. He rushed for 1,407 yards and caught 62 passes for 631 yards, becoming only the 11th player in NFL history to exceed 2,000 total yards in a season. At season's end, Thomas was voted the NFL's Most Valuable Player by a panel of sportswriters, and he was also named to the Pro Bowl (the NFL's all-star game).

Once again, however, the Bills lost the Super Bowl. The Washington Redskins defeated Buffalo, 37-24, and Thomas had a horrible day. He gained just 13 yards in 10 carries and never seemed to get warmed up. To make matters worse, Thomas misplaced his helmet moments before the game began. He missed the first two plays and received very tough criticism. "God, that stuff hurt," Thomas said to *Sports Illus-*

trated. "To be remembered for losing my helmet in the Super Bowl? I've accomplished too much for that. People always remember the worst times."

THREE TIMES NOT A CHARM. Individually, 1992 was Thomas's best season. He once again led the NFL in total yards gained from scrimmage (2,113) and set a personal best in yards rushing (1,487). The Bills lost their AFC Eastern division title, but they did make the playoffs as a "wild card" team. In their first playoff game, against the Houston Oilers, Buffalo overcame a 35-3 third quarter Houston lead to win, 41-38. They then defeated the Pittsburgh Steelers and the Miami Dolphins to reach their third straight Super Bowl. Slowed by ankle and shoulder injuries, Thomas suffered with his teammates as the Dallas Cowboys embarrassed the Bills, 52-17, in Super Bowl XXVII.

RECORD SETTING LOSS. In 1993, the Bills again proved they were the best team in the American Football Conference. Buffalo won the AFC East crown with a 12-4 record, and Thomas had another excellent season. He led the AFC with 1,315 yards rushing and 1,702 total yards. (Thomas did not lead the NFL in total yards for the first time in five seasons, finishing second to Emmitt Smith.) With playoff wins over the Los Angeles Raiders and the Kansas City Chiefs, the Bills earned themselves an NFL-record, fourth consecutive trip to the Super Bowl. For the first time in Super Bowl history, the game featured a rematch, as the Bills opponent was the defending champion Dallas Cowboys. The result was the same as the year before, as Buffalo, hurt by two fumbles by Thomas, lost to Dallas, 30-13. With the defeat, the Bills tied the Minnesota Vikings with four Super Bowl losses and set a major professional sport (baseball, basketball, football, and hockey) record by losing in the championship final for four straight years.

COMMUNITY INVOLVEMENT. In addition to his on-field success, Thomas is also active in his community. He donated the $30,000 he was awarded as the Miller Lite Player of the Year in 1991 to the United Negro College Fund and Buffalo-area chapters of the YMCA and the Special Olympics. Thomas also has donated money to Oklahoma State University, partly to repay his college scholarship. In 1992, Thomas established the Thurman Thomas Foundation, which provides inner-city youth with scholarships to a local community college. Thomas donates five dollars to the scholarship fund for every yard he gains.

FAMILY MAN. Thomas has two children—Olivia and Angelica. "The girls bring out different emotions in me," he told *Sports Illustrated*. "Angelica is the first to greet me at the door at the end of the day. Just hearing her say 'Dah-dee' touches me. Patti [his girlfriend] and the kids are a stabilizing force in my life."

Thomas has overcome many difficulties to become one of the best players in the NFL. "I have a good grip on who I am," Thomas told *Sports Illustrated*. "I know I can't completely change my image, and I realize that not everyone is going to like me. What's important is to be true to myself, to my football talent and to my teammates. I'll stay focused straight ahead, driven by my goal of being the best running back who has ever played the game. I won't let anything stop me. I want to be known as the best ever. That's my goal. Then I'll enjoy the game."

WHERE TO WRITE

C/O BUFFALO BILLS,
ONE BILLS DR., ORCHARD PARK, NY 14127.

ALBERTO TOMBA

1966—

Alpine Skiing is a dangerous sport. A split-second decision can mean the difference between winning a race and disaster. Alberto Tomba has achieved what no other skier has by risking everything, including his life. He is the only Alpine skier to win gold medals at consecutive Olympic Games and is one of only three skiers to win five Olympic Alpine skiing medals. Tomba is the most popular skier in the world. His athletic ability and controversial personality have earned him the nickname "La Bomba."

GROWING UP

Alberto Tomba was born December 19, 1966, in San Lazzaro di Savenna, Italy. His father, Franco, was a textile manufacturer and clothier, and his mother, Maria, was a housewife. He grew up in Bologna, a wealthy community near the Apennines Mountains with many fancy shops and expensive restaurants. His father owned Minarelli, an exclusive men's clothing shop. "From the time he was a baby, Alberto was always looking to have fun," his mother remembered in *Sports Illustrated*. "God forbid if he had been any different. He was splendid and adorable because of it."

"I don't think about the competition. I only go. That's it.— Alberto Tomba

STARTS SKIING. Tomba grew up on an estate outside of Bologna. On the grounds was a hill about 50 yards high and 300 yards long. On cold winter nights, young Alberto and his brother Marco would leave a faucet running over the hill and by morning it would be a short ski slope. In the summer Tomba ran the ski course in his tennis shoes. He began formal ski training at the age of six. His father, a former competitive skier, made no secret of the fact that he wanted one of his sons to be a skiing champion.

WORRYING MOM. Tomba's brother Marco seemed to be the better skier, so Alberto was advised to concentrate on soccer. "My father really didn't believe in me," Tomba admitted in *Sports Illustrated*. "He thought I would never become a champion. It made me mad. It motivated me." Tomba's mother was afraid her son would injure himself and insisted that he stay out of the super-fast downhill races. Tomba concentrated on the slalom and giant slalom because they required the least speed. (The giant slalom course is about twice as long as the course used for the slalom, and the gates placed along the course are spaced farther apart. Skiers go faster in the giant slalom than they do in the slalom, but still must make sharp turns around the gates. A skier must complete two runs in each event. The best combined time in the two runs wins the event.) Even today Tomba's mother watches his races only on replays, after she knows he is safe.

When he was 18 years old, Tomba made the Italian World Cup team in time for the 1985-86 season. He was still immature and overweight, but his natural talent enabled him to be the 15th-best skier in the world. In 1986-87 he moved up to 13th place. He won his first medal, a bronze, in the giant slalom at the 1987 World Cup Games in Switzerland. Tomba also gained attention for his unusual behavior, spending some of his spare time at the world championship event washing cars to earn extra money.

THE BEAST. During the summer of 1987 Tomba dieted and lost 13 pounds. He also worked on new skiing techniques that enabled him to make smaller turns around the gates on a slalom skiing course and ski in a straighter line down the mountain. Tomba had an advantage because he was strong enough to knock the gates over without being thrown off his skis. The training and dedication worked. Tomba took the skiing world by storm in 1987-88, winning seven World Cup races, the most ever by an Italian skier, and finishing second in the overall World Cup standings. He also earned a reputation for bragging about his victories. Tomba crossed the finish line at one competition screaming, *"Sono una bestia!"* ("I am a beast!"). When he won the World Cup giant slalom title, he shouted, "I am the new messiah of skiing!"

Alberto Tomba

SUPERSTAR

OLYMPIC DOUBLE. Entering the 1988 Olympics in Calgary, Alberta, Canada, Tomba was the world's most exciting skier. He was not the favorite, however. Most experts expected Sweden's Ingemar Stenmark or Switzerland's Pirmin Zurbriggen to win the gold medals in Alpine skiing. Tomba fell in his first race, the super giant slalom, but the accident didn't shake his confidence. "The giant slalom and slalom are my own races, the titles I can't miss," he said. "My resurrection is near."

Tomba surprised the experts by winning the slalom and giant slalom. He built up such a big lead in the first of two giant slalom runs that he could coast in his second trip down the mountain and still win by a full second—a long time in skiing. He finished third in the first run of the slalom behind

Stenmark, then skied an amazing second run to overcome Stenmark and win the gold. Afterward, Tomba told the *Philadelphia Inquirer,* "I really lack the words to compliment myself today." Stenmark also congratulated Tomba. "Today, there is only Tomba," he said to the *Washington Post.* "He's way above everyone, the best overall and maybe the best slalom skier ever."

Tomba's strategy was simple. "I don't think about the competition," he told *Sports Illustrated.* "I only go. That's it. And the results, they come.... To be a good racer today you must be brainless, or be able to turn off the brain." After his Olympic victories, Tomba became a superstar in Italy, earning close to $3 million in commercial endorsements. He met with Italian president Francesco Cossiga and Pope John Paul II, and his father bought him a new Ferrari. Tomba made headlines at the Olympics when he asked figure skater **Katarina Witt** (see entry) out on a date. "If she [Witt] doesn't win a gold medal, I will give her one of mine," he told a press conference. (Witt did not respond to his offer.) His personality earned him the nickname, *La Bomba,* which means the bomb.

LETDOWN. The three seasons following the Olympics were not very successful for Tomba. He didn't concentrate on his training and spent most of his time going out, eating, and having fun. "After the Olympics, I admit I was partying too much, not training hard, going all over the place," he told *Skiing.* Tomba broke his collarbone in 1989 and many wondered if he would ever regain his Olympic form. The lowest point for Tomba came at the 1989 World Championships. He finished sixth in the super giant slalom, seventh in the giant slalom, and failed to finish the slalom.

Tomba's father took over at this point. He hired Gustavo Thoeni, the greatest skier in Italian history, to be his son's private coach. The change seemed to work and Tomba listened to Thoeni, a former Olympic gold medal winner. He began to take his training more seriously and lost 15 pounds. "Alberto

Alberto Tomba winning the men's giant slalom at the 1988 Winter Olympics in Calgary, Alberta, Canada.

has worked harder this season than he ever has in his life." Armando Trovati, a friend of Tomba, revealed to the *New York Times*. "He knows if he doesn't ski well this year, he'll return to being a nobody.... He loves the attention ... and he knows that he has to win to have it." The new program showed results during the 1990-91 season. Tomba won six World Cup races—two more than any other man—and won the giant slalom World Cup title.

"ALBERTO-VILLE" OLYMPICS. Tomba was still not back on top. He did not win a medal at the 1991 World Championships, but vowed that he would not disappoint anyone at the 1992 Winter Olympics in Albertville, France. "The Olympics mean more to me, because they happen only every four years," he told *Sports Illustrated*. Tomba trained hard and tried to give up his activities outside of skiing. "I am still outgoing, but not while I'm training," he told the *Los Angeles Times*. "When I used to train with the [Italian] team, my attitude was different. I was able to go all out in skiing and have fun, too. Then things became more difficult for me, and I matured. But I still like to have fun—outside skiing."

An estimated 23,000 adoring Italian fans, called "Tomba-maniacs," followed him to the Albertville games. Tomba made headlines when he arrived at the top of the mountain for practice runs by helicopter. "I will win," he predicted in the *Washington Post.* "After the Games, they will have to change the name of this town to Alberto-ville."

WINS GIANT SLALOM. Tomba backed up his boasts. He won the Olympic gold medal in the men's giant slalom, beating silver medalist Marc Girardelli of Luxembourg by .32 seconds, which is considered a wide margin in skiing. "From the top, I could see thousands of people along the course," Tomba said in *Time,* describing the scene. "I felt their emotion. They were yelling, 'Hop! Hop!' pushing me through gate after gate. Many thought I couldn't do it—but here I am." Tomba fell to his knees when he realized he had won, then celebrated with his fans in the crowd. "I fought to win," he explained to *Time.* "I gave the best of myself."

Tomba became the first skier to win gold medals in consecutive Olympics and tied the all-time record with three Alpine skiing gold medals. He fell short of his goal of defending both of his 1988 gold medals. Tomba finished second to Christian Finne Jagge of Norway in the slalom. "I just wanted to ski close," he told the *Detroit Free Press.* "After three gold medals, I'm very happy with my silver medal."

OLYMPICS NUMBER III. Tomba returned to the Olympics in 1994 in Lillehammer, Norway. Kjetil Andre Aamodt was the World Cup champion in the giant slalom, but Tomba was the skier everyone wanted to see. He disappointed his fans in the giant slalom when he missed a gate on his second run and was disqualified. But even if he'd made the gate, Tomba's time would not have been fast enough to win the race. "I'm aware that Italian fans had a lot of expectations," he told *USA Today* after the giant slalom, "but I go for all or nothing in the Olympics, and today it was nothing ... better this [being disqualified] than finishing seventh or eighth."

Tomba had a slow first run in the slalom and seemed to be too far behind Thomas Stangassinger to possibly catch up. He made an amazing comeback but finished .05 of a second behind Stangassinger. "Magic Alberto," he exclaimed in *USA Today.* "It was a magical recovery." Tomba failed in his attempt to be the first Alpine skier to win gold medals at three consecutive Olympics, but became the first skier to win medals of any kind in three consecutive games. He also tied the record for most Olympic Alpine skiing medals won—five. "I am moved, although I should be used to these kinds of emotions," Tomba said after the race.

OFF THE SLOPES. Tomba is a bachelor and lives in Italy. He has told reporters that he would like to be an actor. "I would like to go to Hollywood some time and make films," Tomba told the *Los Angeles Times*. "And I have already talked to Sylvester Stallone about this. I think I would be good in adventure pictures, playing action roles, something like Rambo." Tomba has already made his mark on skiing. As Phil Hersch wrote in the *Chicago Tribune:* "No alpine skier is or has ever been like Alberto Tomba."

TOMBA ON TOMBA

Tomba has won 31 World Cup races during his career, but many experts say he would have won more had he taken his training more seriously. He often frustrates his coaches by arriving late to practice and not staying on his diet. But Tomba refuses to change. "I'm considered the clown of my team because I cannot be serious for two minutes," he confessed to *Sports Illustrated.* "I'm afraid if I become more serious I will stop winning ... I want every day to be a holiday.... This is my character and I cannot change."

REGGIE WHITE

1961—

For almost a decade Reggie White has dominated the National Football League (NFL) as one of its most ferocious defensive players. White has struck terror into many an offense with his strength, speed, stamina, and ability to make the big play. Curiously enough, White's gift for reeking havoc begins and ends on the football field. The rest of his time is spent doing charity work inspired by his deep Christian faith. In 1993 White became the highest-paid defensive player in football history when he signed a four-year, $17 million contract with the Green Bay Packers. Green Bay was one of a half dozen teams that bid for White's services when he became a free-agent (able to sign with any team) after the 1992-93 football season.

GROWING UP

As a child White lived in Chattanooga, Tennessee, where he was raised by his mother and his grandparents. The family was deeply religious, and they attended the local Baptist church regularly; White was inspired by the ministers and teachers he met there. White found his ties to Christianity growing stronger during his youth. His mother, Thelma Collier, told

Sports Illustrated that when White was 12 years old he announced that he wanted to be two things: a football player and a minister.

DISCOVERS FOOTBALL. Football was a welcome escape for White, who was teased and bothered by bullies as a youth. "When I was a child, I was always bigger than the other kids," White told *Sports Illustrated*. "Kids used to call me Bigfoot or Land of the Giant. They'd tease me and run away. Around seventh grade, I found something I was good at. I could play football, and I could use my size and achieve success by playing within the rules. I remember telling my mother that someday I would be a professional football player and I'd take care of her for the rest of her life."

COLLEGE CAREER. White's strength and size indeed seemed to be God-given. He never lifted weights or worked out, but he was always in shape. At Howard High School in Chattanooga he played both football and basketball, earning All-America honors in football and All-State honors in basketball. Many colleges tried to sign him, but he chose to stay near home. He enrolled at the University of Tennessee, whose team, the Volunteers, was glad to have him.

At Tennessee, White was a talented and determined athlete who spent his Sundays preaching sermons in churches all over the state. As a senior in 1983, he was an All-American and one of four finalists for the Lombardi award, given annually to the outstanding college lineman (he did not win). During his years with the Volunteers, White earned the nickname "Minister of Defense." The name followed him into his professional career, which began in 1984.

TURNING PRO. After graduating from college White signed a five-year, $4 million contract with the Memphis Showboats, one of the teams in the new United States Football League (USFL). The USFL was a rival league competing with the bet-

Reggie White

ter established NFL. When it became clear that the new league would not survive, White moved to the Philadelphia Eagles of the NFL. With his wife, Sara—whom he had met in church—he ventured north to join the Eagles.

JOINS EAGLES. White took a salary cut in Philadelphia. The Eagles signed him to a four-year, $1.85 million deal, because at the time White was still an unproven professional. That didn't last long. He joined the Eagles after the 1985 season had begun, missing the first few games. When he finally did start, he made ten tackles and two-and-a-half sacks (tackling the quarterback for a loss of yards)in his very first game. By season's end he had turned in 13 sacks in as many games, and was named NFC Defensive Rookie of the Year.

COMMUNITY INVOLVEMENT. The citizens of Philadelphia soon discovered that they had won the services of more than just a star athlete. "I believe that I've been blessed with physical ability in order to gain a platform to preach the gospel," White told *Sports Illustrated*. "A lot of people look at athletes as role models, and to be successful as an athlete, I've got to do what I do, hard but fair.... I try to live a certain way, and maybe that'll have some kind of effect. I think God has allowed me to have an impact on a few people's lives."

White spent countless hours of his spare time preaching on street corners in Philadelphia's troubled inner-city neighborhoods. He gave money to dozens of Christian outreach organizations and spoke as a member of the Fellowship of Christian Athletes. And he led by example. In the rough-and-tumble world of professional football, none of his opponents or teammates could ever recall hearing him curse or seeing him fight.

SUPERSTAR

NEW COACH. White became a star in 1986 with the arrival of Buddy Ryan as the Eagles's head coach. Ryan had made a name for himself as a defensive coordinator (assistant coach in charge of running the defense) with the Minnesota Vikings and Chicago Bears. Ryan quickly recognized White's potential and built the defense around him. Opponents tried to double- and triple-team White, but he was still able to reach the quarterback. In his first season with Ryan as his coach, White sacked the quarterback 18 times in 16 games. He was named to the Pro Bowl (the NFL all-star game) and won Most Valuable Player recognition during the game with four quarterback sacks. This was the first of seven straight appearances in the Pro Bowl for White.

UNION LEADER. In 1987 White led the league with an NFC record of 21 sacks. He would certainly have broken the all-time record if the season had not been shortened to 12 games by a players' strike. The strike saw White emerge as a team leader. As one of the player-elected union representatives, White worked hard to keep his fellow Eagles united. Owners fought the strike by using "replacement" players, less-talented players used to continue the season until the regulars gave in to the owners' demands. Under White's leadership, the Eagles remained one of the most united teams in opposing the owners. The hard feelings between White and the Eagles's management probably began to develop during this strike season, and grew as the years passed.

EAGLES MAKE PLAYOFFS. White's continued excellence on the field, however, kept the Eagles from trading their star player. In 1988 he led the NFL in sacks for the second straight year with 18, and the Eagles won the NFC Eastern division title before losing 20-12 to the Chicago Bears in the first round of the playoffs. In 1989, the Eagles won 11 games, but finished second in the Eastern division to the New York Giants. White had an off season, recording only 11 sacks, and the Eagles lost 21-7 to the Los Angeles Rams in the first round of the playoffs. The Eagles bounced back from a 1-3 start in 1990 to win ten games and once again qualify for the playoffs. White had

REGGIE WHITE VS. BRUCE SMITH

During his career, Reggie White has been considered the best defensive end in the National Football Conference. The best defensive end in the American Football Conference during the same time has been Bruce Smith of the Buffalo Bills. The chart below compares the two players' sack records:

Year	Smith	White
1985	6	13
1986	15	18
1987	12	21
1988	11	18
1989	13	11
1990	19	14
1991	1	15
1992	14	14
Totals:	91	124

14 sacks during the regular season, but the Eagles lost again in the first round of the playoffs, this time 20-6 to the Washington Redskins. Coach Buddy Ryan, criticized by the teams owners for not being able to win in the playoffs, was fired.

CONFLICTS WITH OWNERS. In 1989 White signed a four-year, $6.1 million contract that made him the highest-paid defensive player in the NFL at the time. The deal came at the end of angry arguments between White and the Eagles's ownership and management. The problem became worse when Philadelphia fired Buddy Ryan. Although he continued to play at the top of his game for new coach Rich Kotite, White was convinced that the Eagles's ownership was not willing to do what was necessary to build a winning team.

The Eagles failed to make the playoffs in 1991, but in 1992 they won 11 games and were once again in the run for the Super Bowl. In the first round of the playoffs, they defeated the New Orleans Saints 36-20, scoring 26 unanswered points in the fourth quarter. Their season ended the next game, however, when the eventual Super Bowl champions, the Dallas Cowboys, defeated them 34-0. The end of the season also marked the end of White's career in Philadelphia.

FREE AGENT. In 1992, White became part of a lawsuit against the NFL. The players in the lawsuit claimed that it was illegal for the NFL to restrict the ability of players to play for any team of their choice. On March 1, 1993, the NFL and the NFL Players Association (the players' union) reached an agreement that brought free-agency to the NFL. White quickly became the most sought-after free agent and began looking for a new team. In every city that White visited he was greeted by team owners, management, and players. He was also met by ordinary citizens who had heard about his community work and his strong belief in Christianity. During his visits, White noted that in 16 years as a football player (high school, college, and in the pros) he had never been in a top championship game, and he wanted especially to go to a Super Bowl.

SIGNS WITH GREEN BAY. White finally signed with the Green Bay Packers in 1993. The Packers's offer was the largest financially, $17 million over four years. The new contract once again made White the highest-paid defensive player in NFL history. The investment paid off for the Packers as White, after a slow start, ended up tied for the NFC lead in sacks with 13. The Packers finished the season 9-7, making the playoffs for the first time since 1982. They defeated the Detroit Lions, 28-24, in the first round of the playoffs, but lost in the next round to the defending Super Bowl champions, the Dallas Cowboys, 27-17.

Since he is past age 30—an old man by NFL standards—White will almost certainly end his playing career in Green Bay. White's other career—carrying the gospel of Christ to those in need—will last his entire life. He plans a ghetto ministry in Wisconsin while he plays for the Packers. He and his wife have built Hope Place, a shelter for unwed mothers, on property near their home in rural Tennessee. White has continued his missionary work among teenaged gang members, abused children, and young women who are pregnant. Hope Place alone has received more than a half-million dollars from White, who also gives a good portion of his NFL income to several Baptist churches. "The Bible says, 'Faith without works is dead,'" White told the *Philadelphia Daily News.* "That is just another way of saying: 'Put your money where your mouth is.'" White backs up his words, on the field and off.

PHILADELPHIA ON REGGIE WHITE

White is "a man who made a giant impact ... a symbol of hope, for the Eagles and for the city in general," wrote *Philadelphia Daily News* correspondent Ray Didinger when it became official that White was leaving. "White is more than just a superb football player. He is an ordained Baptist minister whose tireless work in the community touched thousands of lives. He is a man who always wore his heart on his extra-long sleeve."

WHERE TO WRITE

C/O GREEN BAY PACKERS,

P.O. BOX 10628, GREEN BAY, WI 54307.

DAVE WINFIELD

1951—

When Dave Winfield left the University of Minnesota, he was drafted by professional baseball, basketball, and football teams. He chose to sign with the San Diego Padres and began one of the greatest careers in major league history. A 12-time All-Star, Winfield has earned some impressive lifetime statistics. He is one of only 19 players to have over 3,000 hits, and in 1992 when the Toronto Blue Jays won the World Series championship, Winfield delivered the game-winning hit. In addition to his playing highlights, he has helped kids through his Winfield Foundation, making him a hero on and off the field.

GROWING UP

David Mark Winfield was born October 3, 1951, in St. Paul, Minnesota. His father, Frank, worked as a waiter on passenger trains. When Winfield was three, his parents separated. His mother took a job in the St. Paul public school system and, along with his grandmother, raised him and his older brother Steve alone. Winfield and his brother were close and depended quite a bit on each other. "Considering that we grew up in a broken home, we had a happy childhood because of the love and affection our mother gave us," Winfield told *Sport* magazine.

FATHER FIGURE. The Winfield brothers played at the Oxford Playground, where they met playground director, Bill Peterson, who became a father figure to the two young boys. Peterson encouraged them to play basketball and baseball. "Bill Peterson was a white man in the black community, but he gave more to that community than anyone I know," Winfield said. "To me, at different times, he was coach, friend, father, all rolled into one."

Winfield, who now stands six-feet-six inches tall, was small as a teenager and did not try out for the varsity baseball team at St. Paul's Central High School until he was a junior. Like many teenagers, Winfield had a growth spurt, and soon caught up with his schoolmates. During his senior year, he was All-City and All-State in both baseball and basketball. His talent attracted baseball scouts, and when he graduated from high school Winfield was offered a contract with the Boston Red Sox. Because he'd heard that African American players had a hard time in many of the small minor-league baseball cities, Winfield decided to go to college instead.

STAR PITCHER? The University of Minnesota offered Winfield a scholarship that allowed him to attend school and still live at home. As a college sophomore he was a starting pitcher for the Golden Gophers, winning eight of 11 games. When he hurt his arm the following year, he moved to the outfield. By his junior year Winfield was playing both baseball and basketball. In his senior year the Gophers won the Big Ten Conference basketball and baseball championships. Winfield was a reserve player in basketball, but a star in baseball. Returning to the pitcher's mound, he had a 13-1 pitching record and hit .385. He was named the Most Valuable Player (MVP) in the National Collegiate Athletic Association (NCAA) College

SCOREBOARD

IN 1993 BECAME 19TH PLAYER TO HAVE OVER 3,000 HITS IN THE MAJOR LEAGUES (3,014).

ONE OF ONLY FIVE PLAYERS TO HAVE OVER 3,000 HITS *and* 400 HOME RUNS. AMONG ALL-TIME LEADERS IN MANY DIFFERENT CATEGORIES.

12-TIME ALL-STAR AND SEVEN-TIME GOLD GLOVE AWARD WINNER FOR FIELDING EXCELLENCE.

ONE OF THE BEST ALL-AROUND PLAYERS IN MAJOR LEAGUE HISTORY.

Dave Winfield

World Series and was named an All-American.

CHOOSES BASEBALL. When he finished with college, Winfield had a tough decision to make. In 1973 he was drafted in three major sports: baseball (by the San Diego Padres), basketball (by the Atlanta Hawks of the National Basketball Association and the Utah Stars of the American Basketball Association), and football (by the Minnesota Vikings). Winfield was surprised to be drafted by the Vikings, since he never played football in college, but the football coaches recognized a great athlete when they saw one. "Kids don't realize that I was Bo [Jackson] long before Bo came along," he once said. Winfield chose baseball and the Padres, who brought him directly to the major league club.

SUPERSTAR

"SINK OR SWIM." A franchise that was struggling to win, the Padres told Winfield to forget about pitching. He became a full-time outfielder. The first few months in San Diego were tough. "I was thrown into a sink-or-swim situation," he told *Sports Illustrated.* "I learned to swim the hard way." Winfield had a solid rookie season with San Diego, batting a respectable .265, with 20 home runs and 75 runs batted in (RBIs). Over the next two seasons Winfield proved a good, but not great, player, often struggling with long slumps. That changed in 1977 when he was named to his first All-Star game and batted .275 with 25 homers and 92 RBIs, while scoring 104 runs. He followed that performance with his two best seasons so far, 1978 and 1979. In 1978 Winfield raised his average to .308 (fifth in the National League), hit 24 home runs, and had 97 RBIs. In 1979, Winfield had his first monster season, again batting .308, hitting 34 home runs (third in the National League), and driving in 118 runs to lead the National League. He also won his first Gold Glove Award for fielding excellence in 1979.

BECOMES A YANKEE. Following the 1980 season, Winfield became a free agent, which let him sign a contract with any team he chose. Tired of playing on losing teams in San Diego, he jumped at the chance to play with the New York Yankees—an annual baseball powerhouse. In his first season (1981) the Yankees reached the World Series, where they faced the Los Angeles Dodgers. Winfield was thrilled to be in the Series, but wasn't happy with his performance. He had only one hit in 22 at bats and the Yankees lost four games to two.

WINFIELD VS. "THE BOSS." After the series, Yankees owner George Steinbrenner, known as "The Boss," criticized Winfield, saying he didn't play well in big games. Part of Winfield's contract called for Steinbrenner to contribute money to the Winfield Foundation, an organization which helps underprivileged children. As the feud between Steinbrenner and Winfield got worse, Steinbrenner stopped making the contributions to the foundation. Winfield took him to court, forcing him to pay the money owed. Steinbrenner was suspended from baseball for several seasons, partly for hiring a private detective to spy on Winfield. During Winfield's nine seasons with the Yankees, the two men argued constantly and still dislike each other.

YANKEE SEASONS. Though the Yankee owner did not like Winfield, the fans did. Beginning in 1982, Winfield drove in over 100 runs in six of the next seven seasons and hit over 25 home runs in five. In 1982 he hit 37 home runs (third in the American League) and had 106 runs batted in. His 116 RBIs in 1983 were the third highest total in the American League and his 32 home runs placed fourth. In 1984 Winfield decided

BIG MISTAKE

Winfield got in trouble after his freshman year at Minnesota. He was arrested for stealing a snowblower from a Minneapolis store, and was taken to jail. The experience changed his life. "My mother came to the jail and there were tears in her eyes," Winfield told *Sport.* "I pledged [promised] to my mother that I would never do anything like that again, ever. I was lucky. They let me go. But I was on probation the rest of my time in college. I feel that shame burning through me again, just telling the story.... But I do it so that kids can know what a terrible feeling it is to do something so stupid and wrong and how awful it is to hurt someone who has loved you and cared for you."

to prove he could hit for a high batting average. In a close race, he lost the American League batting title to his teammate, Don Mattingly, who batted .343 to Winfield's .340. Despite his consistently excellent play, Winfield could not get the Yankees back to the World Series, even though they had only one losing record in Winfield's seasons with the team.

In 1988, his last season with the Yankees, Winfield batted .322 (fourth in the American League), hit 25 home runs, and had 107 RBIs (fifth in the American League). But because of his problems with Steinbrenner and other off-the-field scandals, Winfield was unhappy and wanted to leave New York. He published his autobiography, *Winfield: A Player's Life,* a book that criticized Steinbrenner and some of his teammates. Right before the 1989 season, Winfield suffered the first major injury of his athletic career, undergoing back surgery and missing the entire season. When he returned to the field in 1990, Winfield got his wish and was traded to the California Angels 20 games into the season. In California he led the Angels in runs batted in (78), finished second in home runs (21), and batted .290 after the All-Star break. The *Sporting News* named him "Comeback Player of the Year," an award given to the player who best overcomes an injury.

DREAM COME TRUE. In 1992 Winfield was once again a free agent. Even though he was 40, many teams still wanted him. Winfield chose the Toronto Blue Jays because he felt they had the best chance to accomplish his one unfinished goal—winning a World Series. Toronto had been a contender for several years, but always came up short in the big games. Winfield's leadership helped change that. He batted .290, hit 26 home runs, and had 108 RBIs (becoming the oldest player ever to have more than 100 RBIs in a season), playing full-time as a designated hitter (a player who does not play the field and bats instead of the pitcher). He was named the American League Designated Hitter of the Year. The Blue Jays won 96 games and the American League East division.

For only the second time in his 19-year career, Winfield would be in the playoffs. Determined to improve on his performance in the 1981 World Series, he helped lead the Blue

Jays to a four-games-to-two victory in the American League Championship Series over the Oakland Athletics. He hit two home runs (becoming the oldest player ever to hit a home run in the playoffs) and had three RBIs in the series. In the World Series the Blue Jays played the Atlanta Braves, who returned to the series for the second straight year. Once again Winfield struggled, batting only .223. But in Game Six, with the game and the Series on the line, Winfield came through with one of the biggest hits of his career, an eleventh-inning double into the left field corner that drove in two runs. The Blue Jays won Game Six 4-3, and with it, their first World Series, four games to two. Winfield finally had his championship.

3000 HIT CLUB. In 1993 Winfield started his 20th season in his home town. During the off season following their World Series victory, the Blue Jays decided not to sign him to a new contract. But the Minnesota Twins were happy to sign Winfield, who entered the season with 2,866 hits and had a chance to reach the important 3,000 mark (a level only 17 players had reached before). In September 1993, Winfield ripped a single to left field off Oakland A's relief pitcher Dennis Eckersley for his 3,000th hit.

Winfield finished the 1993 season with 3,014 hits (16th all-time), 453 home runs (17th all-time), and 1,786 RBIs (14th all-time). In addition to his hitting feats, he has won seven Gold Glove Awards for fielding excellence. During his career Winfield has had eight 100-RBI seasons, has had hits off almost 700 different pitchers, and has played through the terms of six presidents. A certain Hall-of-Fame inductee after he retires, Winfield has proven that he deserves the honor of being one of baseball's all-time great players.

OFF THE FIELD. Winfield enjoys photography and fishing and owns several Burger King restaurants. He continues to help

3,000 HITS AND 400 HOMERS

Only five players in major league history have ever had 3,000 hits and 400 home runs. The following chart lists these players and their hit and home run totals.

Player	Hits	Home Runs
Hank Aaron	3,771	755
Stan Musial	3,630	475
Carl Yastremski	3,419	452
Willie Mays	3,283	660
Dave Winfield	3,014	453

kids through the Winfield Foundation, which gives away base-ball tickets, food, college scholarships, and toys. "The reason I do this ... is that I never got where I am by myself. I had a lot of people helping me. Now I want to return that favor and help the kids." Even though he is in his early forties, Winfield doesn't plan to retire anytime soon, as he told *Sports Illustrated:* "I've seen a lot of phenomenal players—and my career is far from over."

WHERE TO WRITE

C/O MINNESOTA TWINS, 501 CHICAGO AVE., S.,
MINNEAPOLIS, MN 55415.

KATARINA WITT

1966—

Representing her native country of East Germany (now part of the reunited German nation), figure skater Katarina Witt won two straight Olympic figure skating gold medals, in 1984 and 1988—the first woman since 1936 to do so. She also won five world championships, four of them in a row, breaking the record of three in a row (held by American legend Peggy Fleming), and six European championships. The beautiful and graceful Witt charmed skating fans throughout the world. Following a successful professional career, Witt returned to the Olympics in 1994 after being out of competition for six years. In Lillehammer, Norway, she proved that winners don't always finish in first place.

GROWING UP

Katarina Witt was born in December 1965 in Karl-Marx-Stadt, East Germany. Her father, Manfred, was a plant director, and her mother, Kathe, was a physical therapist. Witt's training as a world-class ice skater began when she was five years old at the Kuechwald rink in her local neighborhood. She begged her parents for skating lessons, and they gave in. In East Germany the government controlled the national sports organizations

"I'm a performer."—Katarina Witt

and decided which children would be placed in programs to develop their skills. The local sports and education experts saw enough talent in the young Witt by the time she was ten years old to have her work with Coach Jutta Mueller. Mueller's students have won 48 medals in international competition, nearly half of them gold. Mueller was described by *Sports Illustrated* as East Germany's "most famous, fearsome skating coach."

TOUGH TRAINING. Witt spent more time with Mueller than her parents. "In many ways, I am closer to Jutta than anyone," she told *Maclean's* magazine. "There has never been much time for anything other than skating." Six-hour practice sessions, under Mueller's close supervision, were not unusual for Witt. She left the house at seven each morning and did not return until dinnertime. But her training did not end on the ice. Witt ran, worked on a trampoline, attended dance lessons, and completed all of her schoolwork. Mueller also worked on Witt's appearance, deciding how she wore her hair and makeup, and what costumes were appropriate for competition.

Certain things were strictly forbidden in Mueller's training program. For example, Witt was not allowed to eat ice cream because Mueller feared she would gain too much weight. The young skater could not go out dancing with her friends and boyfriends were out of the question, even though Witt received love letters from thousands of men who claimed to be in love with her. Although she often fought with Mueller, Witt tried to follow the rules.

STAR SYSTEM. Being a star skater provided Witt with many things that skaters in other countries did not have. Her coaching, ballet instruction, and ice rink rental were all paid for by the government—costs that add up to more than $1 million for a skater in the United States. She also received privileges other citizens of her country did not. In East Germany there was a ten-year waiting list for an apartment, twelve years for a car. Witt had a house as well as a car. She was also allowed to travel throughout the world, while most East Germans were not allowed to leave the country.

OLYMPIC CHAMPION. Witt had her first success in international competition in 1980 when she was fourteen, finishing tenth in the world championships. She won her first of six consecutive European championships in 1982, and finished second in the world championships. She became a star in the world of figure skating at the 1984 Winter Olympics in Sarajevo, Yugoslavia. Her main competition was Rosalind Summers of the United States. Never strong in that part of the competition where skaters traced figures in the ice with their skates, Witt excelled in free skating, where she was able to use her beauty, grace, and bubbly personality to their fullest. She won the gold medal in Sarajevo, in one of the best figure skating performances of all time.

Katarina Witt

RIVALRY. While one Olympic championship might be enough for some skaters, Witt decided to continue competing. She won the European championship in 1984 and 1985 and the world championship in 1985. "It was a golden performance, a hard— perhaps impossible—act to follow," reported *Sports Illustrated* after her 1985 world championship win. She was the overwhelming favorite to win the 1986 world championship, but was upset by Debbie Thomas of the United States, the first black person ever to win a world figure skating championship.

This began a fierce rivalry between the two skaters that lasted through the 1988 Olympics. Thomas was more athletic, jumped higher, and attempted more difficult moves during her routine. Witt's strengths were her style and artistic ability. "When you are on the ice and the audience is with you and you can hear the music and express the music, it is so much more than a sport," she told the *Chicago Tribune.* The rivalry turned into a battle between East and West—the United States and communist countries.

SUPERSTAR

SECOND GOLD. Witt defeated Thomas in the 1987 world championships. "I trained harder than I ever have," Witt said. She won the 1988 European championships for the sixth time, breaking the record of the legendary Sonje Henie of Norway (see box). Entering the 1988 Winter Olympics in Calgary, Alberta, Canada, Witt was favored to win the figure skating competition. Over 15,000 spectators saw Thomas and Witt compete in what came to be known as "Dueling Carmens" because both skaters were using the music to the same opera. As Carmen, Witt dressed in a frilly black and red costume, with her hair pulled back and held by a Spanish-style fan. At the end of her program, still playing Carmen, Witt pretended to be stabbed and fell to the ice. The performance was greeted with a standing ovation and Witt easily won her second gold medal. The victory made her the first to win women's singles figure skating gold medals in consecutive Olympics since Henie won her third straight in 1936.

TURNS PRO. In 1988 Witt won her final world championship and began to skate professionally. She teamed up with 1988 Olympic male gold medalist **Brian Boitano** (see entry) of the United States. The two had become friends during the 1988 "Tour of World Figure Skating Champions" and made a television special, *Canvas of Ice.* Witt and Boitano continued to work together and won an Emmy award for their performance in *Carmen on Ice.* Finally, the champions decided to start their own touring ice show called *Katarina Witt and Brian Boitano—Skating.*

DEFENDS SYSTEM. Witt was a member of the Socialist Unity Party, the ruling group in East Germany, to which only a limited number of people could belong. She was criticized for supporting communism in East Germany, especially after the Berlin Wall was torn down in 1989 and Germany was reunified. Witt defended herself to the *Christian Science Monitor* by saying: "There is no way I could have achieved this success in another country." She also told *Maclean's* magazine that "Some North Americans criticize the way we work, but over here [in the United States], few people could afford the training I have been given. Here [in East Germany], all you need is talent and desire." Some people have accused Witt of being a spy for the East German secret police, the Stasi, a charge she has denied. Still, fans in Germany began to boo when she competed, feeling that she represented a terrible past they wanted to forget.

When Witt turned professional she had to receive permission from the leaders of East Germany to perform in ice shows, and had to pay the government most of what she earned. Witt was an announcer during the 1992 Olympics and was spokesperson for Diet Coke. But she missed competing, and in 1993, when it was announced that professional skaters would be allowed to participate in the 1994 Olympics (before this only amateur, or unpaid, skaters could participate), Witt decided to make a comeback. Reuniting with Mueller, she set out to train for her return.

RETURNS TO OLYMPICS. Figure skating had changed dramatically since Witt's last competition. Skaters were performing more difficult jumps—never one of Witt's strengths. "Skating should be more than skate-jump, skate-jump, skate-jump," she told *Newsweek*. "I am fighting for a balance between athleticism and artistry." In the 1994 European championships Witt fell during a relatively easy jump, a mistake that caused her to finish eighth in the competition, barely qualifying for the

SONJA HENIE

Sonja Henie of Norway holds the record for figure skating gold medals with three. She won the gold in the 1928, 1932, and 1936 Olympics and skated in the 1924 Olympics when she was just 11 years old. Henie also won 10 world championships and 1,400 prizes in all. When she retired from competition she signed a movie contract with 20th–Century Fox and made 11 movies, most of which featured her skating. Henie became a U.S. citizen in 1941 and died in 1969.

Olympics. "I felt like I wanted to quit," Witt told *USA Today.* "But then I remembered the reason I started all of this in the first place. If I quit, I would never know if I could make it or not."

Entering the 1994 Games Witt's chances were doubtful. Many experts felt that if she did not attempt the difficult jumps she would not defeat her younger opponents. Their opinion didn't seem to bother Witt. As she told *USA Today:* "I think the Olympics are going to be fun. I'll probably be the only person there who won't care what happens, because I don't care." Witt skated a flawless short program, but the lack of difficult jumps placed her in sixth place. In her long program she brought the crowd out of their seats, skating to the music "Where Have All the Flowers Gone." Earlier Witt announced that she was dedicating her performance to the memory of the 1984 Sarajevo Winter Olympics and to peace in war-torn Bosnia-Herzegovina. Though she made mistakes, finishing seventh in the competition, Witt succeeded in her goal and touched the hearts of everyone who watched her skate.

OFF THE ICE. Despite Mueller's watchful eye, Witt has been romantically linked with several boyfriends. Some people have said Witt has become famous not because of her skating but because of her beauty. When asked if she likes all the attention, she told *Current Biography:* "I like it. Yes, I like it very much. Which young woman doesn't like it?" Witt owns an expensive wardrobe, but especially likes blue jeans and sweatshirts. She hopes to someday become an actress and likes to dance to Madonna and Michael Jackson's music. Her older brother, Axel, a former soccer player, is married to Anett Potzsch, winner of the 1980 Olympic gold medal for figure skating. Witt plans to continue skating professionally and entertaining audiences because, as she explained to *Newsweek,* "I'm a performer."

WHERE TO WRITE

C/O NATIONAL OLYMPIC COMMITTEE OF GERMANY, POST-FACH 71 02 63, 60492 FRANKFURT-AM-MAIN, GERMANY

KRISTI YAMAGUCHI

1971-

Only five-feet tall and 93 pounds, Kristi Yamaguchi was a giant in 1992 when she won what many consider the biggest prize of the Olympic Winter Games in Albertville, France—the gold medal in women's figure skating. She put on a spectacular, near-perfect performance that reminded experts of earlier champions—Peggy Fleming, Dorothy Hamill, and **Katarina Witt** (see entry). According to *Sports Illustrated,* Yamaguchi "lands her jumps so softly it seems as if she is skating in her slippers." Even though she's small, she's still tough. "She has character. She has guts," Witt told *Newsday.* "You have to have guts to win the Olympics."

"When I'm skating, I just feel like I can express myself. I feel free."—Kristi Yamaguchi

GROWING UP

Kristi Tsuya Yamaguchi was born July 12, 1971, in Hayward, California. Although Yamaguchi was born and raised in California, fans and reporters often think she is a native of Japan. "Not long ago, a photographer said to me 'You speak nice English,'" Yamaguchi told the *Miami Herald.* "I said, 'I should. I'm a fourth-generation Japanese-American. I don't even speak Japanese except for a few words.'"

WOMEN'S SINGLES CHAMPION,
OLYMPIC WINTER GAMES 1992

WOMEN'S SINGLES CHAMPION
U.S. FIGURE SKATING
CHAMPIONSHIPS 1992

WOMEN'S SINGLES CHAMPION,
WORLD FIGURE SKATING
CHAMPIONSHIPS 1991

CHAMPION, PAIRS FIGURE
SKATING, U.S. FIGURE SKATING
CHAMPIONSHIPS 1990

CHAMPION, PAIRS FIGURE
SKATING, U.S. FIGURE SKATING
CHAMPIONSHIPS 1989

OVERCOMES DISABILITY. Jim Yamaguchi, her father, is a dentist. Carole Yamaguchi, her mother, is a medical secretary. Yamaguchi was born with a foot problem—both feet pointed inward—that her mother said may have made her a better skater. Until she was a little over one year old, she wore tiny plaster casts on her feet. Inside each cast was a metal bar that forced her feet into the correct position. "She learned how to walk in those casts," her mom told the *San Jose Mercury News*. She also wore corrective shoes until she was about five. "It was in part because of that that I wanted her to get involved in things involving her legs and feet, like dancing and skating," her mother continued. "That, and the fact that she really liked skating."

"My grandfather didn't talk much about World War II, but he let me know how proud he was to see me make it as an Asian-American representing the United States," Yamaguchi told the *Chicago Tribune* in 1992. "My parents let us know how fortunate we are now. Otherwise, they really don't look back on [being in the camps] too much. It was just a time of a lot of fear in the country."

BEGINS SKATING. Yamaguchi fell in love with skating when she was four, watching American Dorothy Hamill win a gold medal in the 1976 Olympics. "She's part of the reason why I'm in the sport right now," Yamaguchi told the *St. Paul Pioneer Press*. "I had my Dorothy doll and I took it with me everywhere." Sixteen years after watching Hamill for the first time, Yamaguchi told the *Mercury News*: "I loved the music and the pink costumes and the way they [figure skaters] seemed to float around on the ice like little dolls. It's all I ever wanted to be."

At the age of six (1975), she took her first skating lesson at the Southland Mall in Hayward, California. From the start she took skating seriously. "When I look back on it, I worked incredibly hard for a little kid," Yamaguchi told the *Mercury News*. "I would not get off the ice until I did some particular move right or until I did something a certain number of times. From the time I was six, I kept bugging my mom, 'Let's go skating, let's go skating.'"

Yamaguchi went to lessons six days a week, starting at 5 a.m. and—from the time she was 11—lasting five hours. After school, Yamaguchi took dance lessons or learned how to skate with a partner. She had a private tutor until her junior year in high school. Attending school for half the day, she did the rest of her work on her own. She never went out with friends on Friday nights because she had to be up so early on Saturday to practice. She never dated and did not go to high school football games. Although her mom was her manager among other duties, she never pushed Kristi. "It wasn't like I pushed her or her father pushed her," Carole Yamaguchi told the *Mercury News*. "Kristi was the one who wanted to do this."

INTERMENT CAMPS

Both of Yamaguchi's parents were among the 12,000 Japanese-Americans who spent time in interment (detention) camps during World War II because the U.S. government feared they might help Japan, a country the United States was fighting at that time. Jim Yamaguchi was four when his family was taken from its California ranch and sent to a relocation camp in Arizona. For three years, he lived behind a fence. Carole Yamaguchi was born in a Colorado camp, even while her father, George Doi, was fighting in Europe with the U.S. army.

PARTNERSHIP. In 1982, when Yamaguchi was 11, her coach, Jim Hulick, had her team up with 13-year-old Rudy Galindo (Galindo later changed the spelling of his first name to Rudi to match Kristi). They were a good match: both were small and not very strong. But both were good technical skaters and had style on the ice. "We were both little jumpers," Yamaguchi told *USA Today*. "From the beginning, we always seemed in synch [worked well together]."

The two young skaters worked together every day. By 1986 they won a bronze medal (for third place) in the pairs competition at the World Junior Figure Skating Championship. The next year they won the gold medal in the same competition. In January of 1988 Yamaguchi and Galindo competed against adult skaters for the first time. They finished fifth at the

Kristi Yamaguchi

national championships in Denver, Colorado. One year later, when Yamaguchi was 17 and Galindo 20, they won the national championships in Baltimore, Maryland. A month after that they finished fifth at the world championships in Paris, France, and most experts felt that they would be a strong pair at the 1992 Winter Olympic Games.

ON HER OWN. In 1989, however, Hulick, who had coached the pair for seven years, died of cancer. "That took something out of the partnership," Galindo told the *Los Angeles Times*. "Jim was very much part of the glue holding us together." The pair continued to work together, winning their second straight national title in 1990 and once again placing fifth in the world championships. Then Yamaguchi decided to give up pairs skating and concentrate on becoming a single skater. "I started as a single skater and did pairs just for fun," she told the *Detroit Free Press*. "It was clear to me that if I was going to make great improvements in one or the other, I had to drop one. It's just really too tough trying to do both."

Splitting with Galindo allowed Yamaguchi to focus on singles. She moved to Canada full time to train with her coach, Christy Kjarsgaard Ness. "Since Kristi quit pairs," Ness told the *Los Angeles Times,* "she has taken up off-ice training daily and it's helped." Yamaguchi worked to perfect her own style. Not having the athletic ability of some others, her grace and choreography [the planning of her routine] were the best in the sport. And no one was better in pure skating ability. "Kristi's very much a complete skater now," Ness told *Newsday* in 1992.

Her first success as a singles skater came at the 1989 U.S. Figure Skating Championships in Baltimore, Maryland. She won the pairs competition with Galindo, and finished second in the women's singles. She would also finish second the next two years. "I began to worry that there was this plateau [level] I just couldn't reach," she told the *Mercury News*. "I didn't always want to be second best. I wanted to be the champion. But I always seemed to make a little mistake that kept me from the top."

In 1991 her career got a boost when compulsory figures were dropped from most competitions. Compulsory figures require a skater to trace figures on the ice and spend endless hours in practice. This elimination helped artistic skaters like Yamaguchi. At the 1991 world Championships in Munich, Germany, Yamaguchi broke her string of second-place finishes by winning the championship. In doing so Yamaguchi earned her first perfect 6.0 mark for the artistic parts of her performance.

Winning the world championship made Yamaguchi the favorite for the 1992 Winter Olympic Games, and she also won her first U.S. title in January 1992 in Orlando, Florida. In Albertville, France, Yamaguchi's Olympic short program, skated to the music of *Madame Butterfly,* was nearly perfect. When her two main competitors, Midori Ito of Japan and Tonya Harding of the United States, fell during their short programs, Yamaguchi was solidly in first place.

Two nights later, moments before her long program, Yamaguchi met her idol, Dorothy Hamill, who told her to relax. Despite a fall, Yamaguchi's long program held the crowd spellbound. Her scores left other skaters little chance to overcome her lead. "Consistency is what separates Kristi from the others," men's silver medalist Paul Wylie of the United States told the *Detroit Free Press*. "I don't think she's had a bad performance in her life. She's so calm under pressure. It would have shocked me to see her anywhere but first." When the final results were added up, Yamaguchi was the winner.

SHORT AND LONG PROGRAMS

Olympic singles figure skating competitions are made up of two programs, the short, or original, program, and the long, or freestyle, program. In the short programs, worth one-third of the total score, a skater must complete, in two minutes and forty seconds, eight required moves (jumps, spins, and footwork combinations) in a program set to music. In the long program, the skaters can execute moves of their choice in a set time limit (four-and-a-half minutes for men and four minutes for women) in a program set to music. The wider range of moves in the long program allows skaters to be much more artistic and individual. In each program, a skater is given two sets of marks, one for technical skill and the other for the artistry and style of the program.

ROLE MODEL. Yamaguchi's stardom has made her a hero to many Asian-Americans. Even before the Olympics she had been honored by the San Francisco Asian Chamber of Commerce, the National Chinese Women's Business Association, the Pan Asian National Chamber of Commerce, the Japanese-American Citizens League, and the Taiwanese-American Citizens League.

THE FUTURE. "I'm a little surprised everything happened to me so fast," Yamaguchi told the *Detroit Free Press* about her Olympic win. "I've dreamed of it ever since I was a little girl and first put a pair of skates on. To think that it came true.... Wow!" The only remaining question after the Olympics was whether Yamaguchi would return for the 1994 Olympic Winter Games in Lillehammer, Norway. In the end, Yamaguchi decided not to return. She now skates professionally in exhibitions and ice shows and acts as spokesperson for several different products. Describing her sport, Yamaguchi told the *San Jose Mercury News,* "When I'm skating, I just feel like I can express myself. I feel free."

WHERE TO WRITE

C/O U.S. FIGURE SKATING ASSOCIATION,

20 FIRST ST., COLORADO SPRINGS, CO 80906.

STEVE YOUNG

1961—

Steve Young once said that he's had one of the strangest careers in National Football League (NFL) history. It's hard to argue with him. Who else could have been named the NFL's Most Valuable Player, as Young was in 1992, and still not be sure he was going to be the starting quarterback the next year? The problem was that the quarterback he replaced was the legendary **Joe Montana** (see entry), who had led Young's team, the San Francisco 49ers, to four Super Bowl championships. Overcoming many obstacles, Young has earned his place as the best quarterback in the NFL by never quitting, a lesson he learned from his father.

GROWING UP

Jon Steven Young was born October 11, 1961, in Salt Lake City, Utah. He is the great-great-great-grandson of Brigham Young, one of the founders of the Church of Latter Day Saints (Mormons) and the first governor of the territory of Utah. The oldest of five children, Steve has three brothers and one sister. His father, LaGrande "Grit" Young, was a lawyer and former Brigham Young University football player. "He was the kind of guy that when I'd wake up Saturday mornings at, say, nine

"A winning attitude will see you through the bad times."—Steve Young

o'clock and was supposed to mow the lawn, the lawn mower would be going. He would want me to come sprinting out so he could say, 'I can't wait all day.' My dad wanted you to do everything perfectly. And he wanted to keep you humble.''

NEVER QUIT. When Young was a child his hero was Roger Staubach, the Hall-of-Fame quarterback of the Dallas Cowboys. A great all-around athlete, in high school Young was the captain of the football, basketball, and baseball teams. Though he went to high school in Greenwich, Connecticut, where his family had moved, when it came time for college, Young was drawn back to Utah. He signed to play at Brigham Young University, named for his great-great-great-grandfather, and known for producing great quarterbacks. After a tough first season, one in which coaches thought about moving him to defensive back, Young thought about giving up on football. But his father told him not to come home if he quit, so Young stuck it out and says it was the best advice he ever received.

It turned out to be the right decision. By his senior year (1983) Young was the Cougars's starting quarterback. He led Brigham Young to an 11-1 record, including a victory over Missouri in the Holiday Bowl. He passed for 3,902 yards and 33 touchdowns in the Cougars's high-powered offense and led the National Collegiate Athletic Association (NCAA) in total offense (passing and running yards combined). He was named to many All-American teams and finished second in the voting for the Heisman Trophy, given annually to the nation's best college football player. (University of Nebraska running back Mike Rozier won the award.)

BIG CONTRACT. Young was the object of a bidding war when he left Brigham Young and had the opportunity to be a professional quarterback. The Cincinnati Bengals of the NFL made him the first player picked in the 1984 draft, but he was also highly sought by the Los Angeles Express of the United States

Football League (USFL). The two teams kept pushing up Young's price until, finally, he signed with the Express for what was, at the time, the biggest contract in the history of sports—over $60 million in 44 years. Unfortunately for Young, the USFL went out of business after his second year in the league.

During his two seasons in the USFL, Young showed he had what it took to be a professional quarterback. He passed for 4,102 yards and 16 touchdowns and ran for 883 more yards. Even with Young's success, the team was losing money and it was clear that the USFL wouldn't last. Young paid the USFL $1.2 million to release him, then signed with the Tampa Bay Buccaneers of the NFL in 1985. The Buccaneers were a poor team that last had a winning record in 1981. Young spent most of his first season in Tampa Bay warming the bench and watching veteran quarterback Steve DeBerg. At the end of the season the Buccaneers were tied for the NFL's worst record at 2-14.

TAMPA BAY BLUES. Young became the starting quarterback for Tampa Bay in 1986, but the team finished with an identical 2-14 record. He passed for 2,382 yards and ran for 425 more, but threw for only eight touchdowns. These two seasons were frustrating for Young because the team was so bad and the coaches didn't seem to know how to take advantage of his many skills. The best offensive coach in the NFL was Bill Walsh of the San Francisco 49ers. Under his coaching Joe Montana had become a superstar and the 49ers had won two Super Bowls. Walsh saw potential in Young and set out to sign him with the 49ers as insurance, in case Montana was injured. In April 1987 Tampa Bay traded Young to San Francisco for $1 million and two draft picks.

BIG-TIME BACK-UP. With Montana the starting quarterback, Young knew he would be the back-up. In his first four seasons

QUARTERBACK U's

In recent years two colleges have been known for producing great quarterbacks, Brigham Young University and the University of Miami. Young, Jim McMahon (who led the Chicago Bears to victory in Super Bowl XX and is currently with the Minnesota Vikings), and Ty Detmer (the 1990 Heisman Trophy winner, now with the Green Bay Packers), all played at Brigham Young. Former Miami Hurricane players include **Jim Kelly** (see entry), who has quarterbacked the Buffalo Bills to four-straight Super Bowls, Bernie Kosar of the Dallas Cowboys, Vinnie Testaverde, 1986 Heisman Trophy winner now with the Cleveland Browns, and Gino Torretta, the 1992 Heisman Trophy winner.

Steve Young

with the 49ers, Young started only 10 games. Though he didn't play much, Young was happy to be with a winning team. In Super Bowl XXIV he came into the game with the 49ers well ahead, and had his first championship game experience. But it was getting harder for Young to sit on the bench. "I really felt ready," he told *Sports Illustrated for Kids.* "It was hard for me to come to the stadium on Sundays and never get into the game." Feeling that Young was a threat to his job, Montana did not get along well with his back-up. But Young proved his outstanding sportsmanship as *Sports Illustrated* noted: "Young will not criticize Montana, as painful as the star's treatment of him must have been."

STARTING QB. Before the 1991 season Montana suffered a torn tendon in his throwing arm elbow. This was Young's chance to make his mark, and he took advantage of the opportunity. In 11 games Young threw for 2,517 yards, 17 touchdowns, and was the NFL's top-rated quarterback. In addition he ran for 415 yards. The 49ers stumbled, however, starting 4-6 before putting together a six-game winning streak to finish at 10-6. Young was 5-5 in games he started and missed six weeks with a knee injury. The 49ers missed the playoffs for the first time since 1982, and Young took most of the blame. Critics said that he wasn't as good as Montana, that he didn't play well in tough situations, and that he ran too much. Young took all the criticism without getting angry. He just became more determined to improve.

SUPERSTAR

MVP. Young entered the 1992 season as the starting quarterback for the 49ers because Montana had still not recovered from his injuries. In order to play better on the field, Young realized, he had to improve his mental attitude. He explained his problem to *Street and Smith's Pro Football:* "When you take the job of quarterback with this team, there's a lot of history and a lot of expectations that go along with it. I used to try to do everything possible all at once, sometimes on every play."

For Young 1992 was a dream season. He threw for 3,465 yards (tops in the National Football Conference) and an NFL best 25 touchdown passes, with only seven of his passes intercepted, 268 of his 402 passes were completed for an NFL-leading 66.7 completion percentage, and he ran for 537 yards. At the end of the season Young was the NFL's top-rated passer for the second straight year and was named to the Pro-Bowl (all-star game) for the first time. In addition to his statistics, Young improved as a team leader. When the pressure was on, he played his best, and developed the ability to know when to run and when to pass. The 49ers finished 14-2, far and away the best record in the NFL, and Young was voted the league's Most Valuable Player.

UNITED STATES FOOTBALL LEAGUE

The United States Football League (USFL) was formed to compete with the older NFL and played in the spring and summer, after the NFL season had ended. Trying to make their teams as good as they could be, the owners of USFL teams spent a lot of money to sign college and NFL star players. Current NFL stars who started out in the USFL include Steve Young, Bobby Herbert of the Atlanta Falcons, Jim Kelly of the Buffalo Bills, Herschel Walker of the Philadelphia Eagles, and **Reggie White** (see entry) of the Green Bay Packers. Unable to earn enough money to pay the big salaries they had promised to these stars, the USFL went out of business in 1985.

Even though Young was the MVP, when Montana said he was healthy near the end of the season many 49ers fans wanted him to replace Young as the starting quarterback in the team's playoff games. Montana played the second half of the 49ers's last game of the season, throwing for 126 yards and two touchdowns against the Detroit Lions. In the 49ers's first playoff game, however, Young was the starting quarterback in a 20-13 victory over the Washington Redskins. He passed for 227 yards, but fumbled four times. In the NFC Championship game, Young passed for 313 yards and one touchdown and ran for another score, but he also threw two interceptions in a 30-20 loss to the Dallas Cowboys.

MONTANA TRADED. After the 1992 season the 49ers were forced to make a decision between their two quarterbacks.

Young was a free agent and could sign with any team. But he wouldn't sign with the 49ers if he was going to be Montana's back-up. Montana wanted to be the starting quarterback, and many fans in San Francisco thought he could lead the 49ers to the Super Bowl as he'd done four times before. Finally the 49ers made a decision and traded Montana to the Kansas City Chiefs in the spring of 1993. The 49ers were Young's team.

No longer having to look over his shoulder at Montana, Young had an excellent season in 1993. For the third straight year Young was the top-rated quarterback in the NFL. He led the NFC with 4,023 yards passing and led the NFL with 29 touchdowns. He completed 68 percent of his passes and ran for 407 more yards. The 49ers started strong, but slumped at the end of the season to finish 10-6. In their first playoff game, against the New York Giants, the San Francisco offense exploded, scoring 44 points in a 44-3 victory. Young threw for 226 yards on 17 of 22 passes. For the second year in a row, however, the 49ers fell one game short of the Super Bowl, losing 38-21 in the NFC Championship game to the Dallas Cowboys.

OFF THE FIELD. Young is a bachelor and lives in Palo Alto, California during the season and in Park City, Utah, when not playing football. He received a law degree from Brigham Young in 1993 and signed a five-year, $26.75 million contract with the 49ers. Young contributes to many charities, including sports programs in the San Francisco public schools and aid to Navajo Indian tribes. When not playing football, Young likes to watch golf on television, ski, and go to the movies. Even though Montana is gone and Young is the man in San Francisco, he knows he won't be seen as a successful quarterback to 49ers fans until he leads his team to a Super Bowl championship. "A winning attitude will see you through the bad times," Young told *Sports Illustrated for Kids*. "Enjoy the down times and fighting through them."

WHERE TO WRITE

C/O SAN FRANCISCO 49ERS,

4949 CENTENNIAL BLVD., SANTA CLARA, CA 95054.

Further Reading

The sources used to compile the entries are included in this list.

ATHLETE

JIM ABBOTT

Gutman, Bill. *Star Pitcher*. Brookfield, Conn.: Millbrook Press, 1992.

Hollander, Zander, ed. *Complete Handbook of Baseball: 1990*. New York: Signet, 1990.

Johnson, Rick L. *Jim Abbott: Beating the Odds*. Minneapolis: Dillon Press, 1991.

Reiser, Howard. *Jim Abbott: All American Pitcher*. Chicago: Children's Press, 1993.

Savage, Jeff. *Sports Great Jim Abbott*. Hillside, N.J.: Enslow Publishers, 1993.

Sporting News, July 19, 1993.

Sports Illustrated, May 25, 1987.

White, Ellen Emerson. *Jim Abbott: Against All Odds*. New York: Scholastic, Inc., 1990.

ANDRE AGASSI

Collins, Bud, and Zander Hollander, eds. *Bud Collins' Modern Encyclopedia of Tennis*. 2nd ed. Detroit: Visible Ink Press, 1994.

New York Times Magazine, October 30, 1988.

Newsweek, September 12, 1988.

Sports Illustrated, March 13, 1989; July 12, 1993.

Tennis, February, 1993.

TROY AIKMAN

Hollander, Zander, ed. *Complete Handbook of Pro Football: 1993.* New York: Signet, 1993.

Sport, January 1991; July 1993.

Sporting News, February 8, 1993.

Sports Illustrated, November 14, 1988; August 21, 1989; February 15, 1993.

ROBERTO ALOMAR

New York Times, October 11, 1993.

Sport, March 1991.

Sports Illustrated, March 28, 1988; June 8, 1992; November 1, 1993.

ARTHUR ASHE

Ashe, Arthur. *Arthur Ashe: Portrait in Motion.* Boston: Houghton Mifflin, 1975.

Ashe, Arthur. *Days of Grace: A Memoir.* New York: Alfred A. Knopf, 1993.

Ashe, Arthur. *A Hard Road to Glory.* 3 vols. New York: Warner Books, 1988.

Ashe, Arthur. *Off the Court.* New York: New American Library, 1981.

Collins, Bud, and Zander Hollander, eds. *Bud Collins' Modern Encyclopedia of Tennis.* 2nd ed. Detroit: Visible Ink Press, 1994.

Chicago Tribune, November 28, 1988.

McPhee, John A. *Levels of the Game.* New York: Farrar, Straus & Giroux, 1969.

Robinson, Louie. *Arthur Ashe: Tennis Champion.* Garden City, N.Y.: Doubleday, 1967.

Sports Illustrated, December 21, 1992.

OKSANA BAIUL

Detroit Free Press, February 24, 1994.

The Olympic Factbook: A Spectator's Guide to the Winter Games. Detroit: Visible Ink Press, 1994.

People, December 6, 1993.

Sporting News, February 14, 1994; March 7, 1994.

Sports Illustrated, March 22, 1993; February 7, 1994.

Sports Illustrated for Kids, February 1994.

CHARLES BARKLEY

Barkley, Charles. *Outrageous!: The Fine Life and Flagrant Good Times of Basketball's Irresistible Force.* New York: Simon and Schuster, 1992.

Barkley, Charles, and Rick Reilly. *Sir Charles: The Wit and Wisdom of Charles Barkley.* New York: Warner Books, 1994.

Chicago Tribune, February 15, 1987; February 1, 1988.

Esquire, March 1992.

Los Angeles Times, May 8, 1985; February 22, 1987; January 10, 1988; January 17, 1988.

Macnow, Glen. *Sports Great Charles Barkley.* Hillside, N.J.: Enslow Publishers, 1992.

New York Times Magazine, March 17, 1991.

People, April 27, 1987.

Philadelphia Daily News, May 13, 1986; May 14, 1986; May 15, 1986; December 22, 1987.

Sporting News, January 18, 1988; February 22, 1988.

Sports Illustrated, March 12, 1984; March 24, 1986; January 11, 1988; August 10, 1992; November 9, 1992; March 8, 1993; April 12, 1993; May 3, 1993; June 7, 1993; June 14, 1993.

Washington Post, April 23, 1984; February 2, 1987.

LARRY BIRD

Bird, Larry. *Bird on Basketball: How-to Strategies From the Great Celtics' Champion.* Reading, Mass.: Addison-Wesley Publishing Co., 1985.

Bird, Larry, and Bob Ryan. *Drive: The Story of My Life.* 1st ed. New York: Bantam, 1990

Burchard, Marshall. *Sports Hero Larry Bird.* New York: G.P. Putnam's Sons, 1982.

Burchard, S. H. *Larry Bird.* San Diego: Harcourt Brace Jovanovich, 1983. Doubleday, 1989.

Italia, Robert. *Larry Bird.* Edina, Minn.: Abdo & Daughters, 1992.

Kavanagh, Jack. *Sports Great Larry Bird.* Hillside, N.J.: Enslow Publishers, 1992.

Krugel, Mitchell. *Magic and the Bird.* New York: St. Martin's Press, 1989.

Levine, Lee Daniel. *Larry Bird: The Making of an American Sports Legend.* New York: McGraw-Hill, 1988.

New Yorker, March 24, 1986.

Rosenthal, Bert. *Larry Bird: Cool Man on the Court.* Chicago: Children's Press, 1988.

Schron, Bob. *The Bird Era: A History of the Boston Celtics, 1978-1988.* Boston: Quinlan Press, 1988.

Sport, June 1993.

Sports Illustrated, January 23, 1978; February 5, 1979; April 2, 1979; October 15, 1979; November 9, 1981; March 21, 1988; December 11, 1989; March 23, 1992; December 14, 1992; February 15, 1993.

BONNIE BLAIR

Maclean's, February 1988.

The Olympic Factbook: A Spectator's Guide to the Winter Games. Detroit: Visible Ink Press, 1994.

People, February 15, 1988.

Sporting News, March 7, 1994.

Sports Illustrated, January 27, 1988; March 7, 1988; January 15, 1990; February 17, 1992; February 24, 1992.

TYRONE "MUGGSY" BOGUES

Hollander, Zander, ed. *Complete Handbook of Pro Basketball: 1994.* New York: Signet, 1994.

Sporting News, November 8, 1993.

Sports Illustrated, February 16, 1987; April 12, 1993.

BRIAN BOITANO

Newsweek, February 29, 1988.

The Olympic Factbook: A Spectator's Guide to the Winter Games. Detroit: Visible Ink Press, 1994.

Sporting News, February 14, 1994.

Sports Illustrated, February 16, 1987; January 27, 1988.

Sports Illustrated for Kids, February 1994.

Washington Post, February 12, 1988.

BARRY BONDS

San Francisco Examiner, October 8, 1990.

Sports Illustrated, June 25, 1990; October 11, 1993.

RIDDICK BOWE

Los Angeles Times, November 12, 1992; November 15, 1992; November 29, 1992; December 21, 1992.

Sports Illustrated, December 10, 1992; March 11, 1991; August 19, 1991; July 27, 1992; November 23, 1992; November 30, 1992.

MICHAEL CHANG

Collins, Bud, and Zander Hollander, eds. *Bud Collins' Modern Encyclopedia of Tennis.* 2nd ed. Detroit: Visible Ink Press, 1994.

Sports Illustrated, June 19, 1988; October 17, 1988.

Tennis, April 1994.

ROGER CLEMENS

Clemens, Roger. *Rocket Man: The Roger Clemens Story.* Lexington, Mass.: S. Greene Press, 1987.

Clemens, Roger, and Peter Gammons. *Rocket Man.* New York: Penguin Books, 1987.

Devaney, John. *Sports Great Roger Clemens.* Hillside, N.J.: Enslow Publishers, 1990.

Los Angeles Times, October 11, 1990; October 12, 1990.

Newsday, May 22, 1988.

Providence Journal, February 12, 1991.

Sport, May 1993.

Sports Illustrated, June 6, 1988; October 1, 1990; November 26, 1990; February 11, 1991.

JIM COURIER

Collins, Bud, and Zander Hollander, eds. *Bud Collins' Modern Encyclopedia of Tennis.* 2nd ed. Detroit: Visible Ink Press, 1994.

New York Times, February 3, 1992.

Sports Illustrated, June 17, 1991; February 24, 1992.

Tennis Illustrated, September 1991.

Tennis Week, December 24, 1992.

CLYDE DREXLER

Los Angeles Times, June 2, 1992.

Oregonian, May 27, 1992.

Philadelphia Inquirer, June 2, 1992.

Sporting News, May 18, 1992.

Sports Illustrated, June 11, 1990; January 27, 1992; May 11, 1992.

Sports Illustrated for Kids, February 1993.

LENNY DYKSTRA

Philadelphia Daily News, June 21, 1989; June 15, 1991; July 2, 1991.

Philadelphia Inquirer, May 20, 1990; June 15, 1991; September 8, 1991; February 21, 1993.

Philadelphia Inquirer Magazine, October 1, 1989.

Sports Illustrated, June 4, 1990; May 11, 1992.

JOHN ELWAY

Akron Beacon Journal, January 22, 1987.

Boston Globe, January 24, 1987; January 30, 1988; January 25, 1990.

Fox, Larry. *Sports Great John Elway.* Hillside, N.J.: Enslow Publishers, 1990.

Los Angeles Daily News, December 3, 1989.

Orlando Sentinel, January 28, 1990.

Sport, November 1993.

Sporting News, October 20, 1986.

Sports Illustrated, November 10, 1986; January 19, 1987; January 26, 1987; February 8, 1988; November 6, 1989; January 29, 1990; July 27, 1992; August 2, 1993.

JANET EVANS

Chicago Tribune, August 18, 1988; August 28, 1988; September 19, 1988; September 23, 1988.

New York Times Magazine, July 12, 1992.

The Olympics Factbook: A Spectator's Guide to the Winter and Summer Games. Detroit: Visible Ink Press, 1992.

St. Louis Post-Dispatch, August 7, 1988; September 21, 1988; September 23, 1988; October 16, 1988.

PATRICK EWING

Ebony, February 1986.

Kavanagh, Jack. *Sports Great Patrick Ewing.* Hillside, N.J.: Enslow Publishers, 1992.

Newsday, October 9, 1988.

Sports Illustrated, September 19, 1988; October 3, 1988; October 10, 1988.

Time, March 14, 1983; July 8, 1985; July 29, 1985.

NICK FALDO

Golf, June 1990; September 1990; February 1991; September 1992; October 1992.

People, August 17, 1992.

Sports Illustrated, July 10, 1989; April 16, 1990; July 30, 1990; August 20, 1990; April 8, 1991; July 27, 1992; July 26, 1993.

CECIL FIELDER

Boston Globe, April 5, 1991.

Detroit Free Press, May 12, 1990; September 25, 1990; October 4, 1990; October 5, 1990; December 26, 1990.

Philadelphia Daily News, September 18, 1991.

Philadelphia Inquirer, August 31, 1990; July 28, 1991.

EMERSON FITTIPALDI

Fittipaldi, Emerson. *Flying on the Ground.* London, England: W. Kimber, 1973.

Motor Trend, January 1990.

New York Times Magazine, October 15, 1989.

Sports Illustrated, June 5, 1989; May 28, 1990; June 7, 1993.

GEORGE FOREMAN

Boston Globe, March 11, 1987.

Jet, May 6, 1991; April 27, 1992; June 28, 1993.

Sport, May 1991.

Sports Illustrated, October 8, 1984; July 17, 1989; January 29, 1990; June 25, 1990; March 25, 1991; April 20, 1992.

JUAN GONZALEZ

Detroit Free Press, September 17, 1993.

Sport, May 1992; May 1993.

Sporting News, April 5, 1993.

Sports Illustrated, July 23, 1990; April 1, 1991; April 5, 1993; July 26, 1993.

Washington Post, August 23, 1993.

STEFFI GRAF

Collins, Bud, and Zander Hollander, eds. *Bud Collins' Modern Encyclopedia of Tennis.* 2nd ed.

Detroit: Visible Ink Press, 1994.

Sports Illustrated, March 16, 1987; June 15, 1987; July 11, 1988; March 27, 1989; June 19, 1989; July 17, 1989; September 18, 1989; February 5, 1990; April 23, 1990; July 15, 1991; September 16, 1991; June 15, 1992; July 13, 1992; June 14, 1993; July 12, 1993; September 20, 1993.

Tennis, October 1984; July 1986; August 1986; September 1986.

WAYNE GRETZKY

Gretzky, Wayne. *Gretzky: An Autobiography.* 1st ed. New York: HarperCollins Publishers, 1990.

Hanks, Stephen. *Wayne Gretzky.* New York: St. Martin's Press, 1990.

Hollander, Zander, ed. *The Complete Encyclopedia of Hockey.* 4th ed. Detroit: Visible Ink Press, 1993.

Los Angeles Herald Examiner, September 17, 1988.

Maclean's, October 5, 1992.

Raber, Thomas R. *Wayne Gretzky: Hockey Great.* Minneapolis: Lerner Publications Co., 1991.

Sporting News, November 9, 1992; May 24, 1993; November 29, 1993; April 4, 1994.

Sports Illustrated for Kids, November 1993.

KEN GRIFFEY, JR.

Gutman, Bill. *Ken Griffey, Sr., and Ken Griffey, Jr.: Father and Son Teammates.* Brookfield, Conn.: Millbrook Press, 1993.

Jet, April 6, 1992.

People, July 17, 1989.

Sport, March 1991.

Sports Illustrated, May 16, 1988; May 7, 1990; August 9, 1993.

Sports Illustrated for Kids, April 1993.

FLORENCE GRIFFITH JOYNER

Aaseng, Nathan. *Florence Griffith Joyner: Dazzling Olympian.* Minneapolis: Lerner Publications Co., 1989.

Chicago Tribune, July 22, 1988.

New York Times Magazine, July 21, 1993.

Newsday, July 24, 1988; September 7, 1988; September 30, 1988.

Newsweek, August 1, 1988.

The Olympics Factbook: A Spectator's Guide to the Winter and Summer Games. Detroit: Visible Ink Press, 1992.

Sporting News, October 10, 1988; October 17, 1988; February 23, 1989.

EVANDER HOLYFIELD

Boston Globe, December 9, 1988; October 24, 1990.

Chicago Tribune, May 4, 1990; April 18, 1991.

Current Biography, August 1993.

People, November 16, 1992.

Philadelphia Daily News, July 27, 1989.

Philadelphia Inquirer, October 9, 1990.

Sporting News, November 15, 1993.

Sports Illustrated, July 5, 1993.

BRETT HULL

Goldstein, Margaret J. *Brett Hull: Hockey's Top Gun.* Minneapolis: Lerner Publications Co., 1992.

Hollander, Zander, ed. *The Complete Encyclopedia of Hockey.* 4th ed. Detroit: Visible Ink Press, 1993.

Los Angeles Times, November 2, 1989; March 31, 1991.

People, April 9, 1990.

Sporting News, January 21, 1991.

Sports Illustrated, December 23, 1985; December 25, 1990; February 4, 1991; March 18, 1991.

St. Louis Post-Dispatch, March 8, 1988; February 7, 1989; January 20, 1990; June 23, 1990; October 4, 1990; January 20, 1991.

MIGUEL INDURÁIN

Abt, Sam. *Champion: Bicycle Racing in the Age of Induráin.* San Francisco: Bicycle Books, Inc., 1993.

Bicycling, July 1992; September/October 1992; July 1993.

Economist, August 1, 1992.

Sports Illustrated, August 3, 1992; August 2, 1993.

BO JACKSON

Devaney, John. *Bo Jackson: A Star for All Seasons.* New York:

Walker and Co., 1992.

Gutman, Bill. *Bo Jackson: A Biography*. New York: Pocket Books, 1991.

Jackson, Bo. *Bo Knows Bo: The Autobiography of a Ballplayer*. 1st ed. New York: Doubleday, 1990.

Johnson, Rick L. *Bo Jackson: Baseball/Football Superstar*. 1st ed. New York: Maxwell Macmillan International, 1991.

New York Times, December 29, 1984; May 19, 1985; November 4, 1985; December 2, 1985; December 7, 1985; December 8, 1985; June 22, 1986.

Rolfe, John. *Bo Jackson.* New York: Warner Juvenile Books, 1991.

Sports Illustrated, October 3, 1983; September 5, 1984; May 13, 1985; December 2, 1985; March 31, 1986; July 14, 1986; June 12, 1989; March 1, 1993; April 19, 1993.

USA Today, June 24, 1986.

DAN JANSEN

The Olympic Factbook: A Spectator's Guide to the Winter Games. Detroit: Visible Ink Press, 1994.

People, January 14, 1992.

Rolling Stone, February 20, 1992.

Sporting News, March 2, 1992; February 14, 1994; February 28, 1994.

Sports Illustrated, February 24, 1992; December 20, 1993; February 21, 1994; February 28, 1994.

Sports Illustrated for Kids, February 1994.

Time, February 24, 1992.

USA Today, March 1, 1994.

EARVIN "MAGIC" JOHNSON

Chicago Tribune, February 1, 1980.

Detroit Free Press, May 11, 1986.

Greenberg, Keith Elliott. *Magic Johnson: Champion With a Cause.* Minneapolis: Lerner Publications Co., 1992.

Gutman, Bill. *Magic Johnson: Hero On and Off Court.* Brookfield, Conn.: Millbrook Press, 1992.

Haskins, James. *Sports Great Magic Johnson.* Hillside, N.J.: Enslow Publishers, 1992.

Johnson, Earvin. *Magic.* New York: Viking Press, 1983.

Johnson, Earvin. *My Life.* New York: Random House, 1992.

Johnson, Rick L. *Magic Johnson: Basketball's Smiling Superstar.* 1st ed. New York: Dillon Press., 1992.

Krugel, Mitchell. *Magic and the Bird.* 1st ed. New York: St. Martin's Press, 1989.

Levin, Rich. *Magic Johnson: Court Magician.* Chicago: Children's Press, 1981.

Los Angeles Times, May 18, 1987.

Morgan, Bill. *The Magic: Earvin Johnson.* New York: Scholastic, Inc., 1992.

People, November 25, 1991; December 30, 1991.

Sports Illustrated, May 13, 1985; June 29, 1987; November 18,

1991; January 20, 1992; February 17, 1992; October 11, 1993.

Strauss, Larry. *Magic Man.* Los Angeles: Lowell House Juvenile, 1992.

Washington Post, May 31, 1984.

LARRY JOHNSON

Peninsula Times Tribune, January 10, 1990.

Philadelphia Inquirer, March 20, 1991.

San Jose Mercury News, March 22, 1990.

Washington Post, April 5, 1990.

MICHAEL JORDAN

Aaseng, Nathan. *Sports Great Michael Jordan.* Hillside, N.J.: Enslow Publishers, 1992.

Charlotte Observer, January 10, 1990; June 27, 1991; October 31, 1991; October 13, 1992; November 6, 1992; February 20, 1993; February 21, 1993.

Columbia State, June 30, 1991; January 11, 1992.

Ebony, March 1985; June 1987.

Greene, Bob. *Hang Time: Days and Dreams With Michael Jordan.* 1st ed. New York: Doubleday, 1992.

Gutman, Bill. *Michael Jordan: Basketball Champ.* Brookfield, Conn.: Millbrook Press, 1992.

Herbert, Mike. *The Bulls' Air Power.* Chicago: Children's Press, 1987.

Jordan, Michael. *Rare Air: Michael on Michael.* 1st ed. San Francisco: Collins Publishers, 1993.

Krugel, Mitchell. *Jordan.* New York: St. Martin's Press, 1992.

Naughton, Jim. *Taking to the Air: The Rise of Michael Jordan.* New York: Warner Books, 1992.

New York Times Magazine, November 9, 1986.

Newsweek, August 23, 1993; October 18, 1993.

People, March 19, 1984.

Raber, Thomas R. *Skywalker.* Minneapolis: Lerner Publications Co., 1992.

Sakamoto, Bob. *Michael "Air" Jordan.* Lincolnwood, Ill.: Publications International, 1991.

Sporting News, October 18, 1993.

Sports Illustrated, November 28, 1983; April 30, 1984; October 1, 1984; December 10, 1984; January 21, 1985; May 13, 1985; March 24, 1986; November 17, 1986.

JACKIE JOYNER-KERSEE

Chicago Tribune, September 25, 1988.

Cohen, Neil. *Jackie Joyner-Kersee.* 1st ed. Boston: Little, Brown, and Co., 1992.

Los Angeles Times, August 8, 1992.

The Olympics Factbook: A Spectator's Guide to the Winter and Summer Games. Detroit: Visible Ink Press, 1992.

Sports Illustrated, April 27, 1987; September 14, 1987; October 10, 1988.

JIM KELLY

Boston Globe, December 29, 1988; January 23, 1991; January 27, 1991.

Buffalo News, September 7, 1989; December 30, 1989; March 24, 1990; May 10, 1990; May 13, 1990; January 27, 1991.

Detroit Free Press, January 31, 1994.

Kelly, Jim. *Armed and Dangerous.* 1st ed. New York: Doubleday, 1992.

Philadelphia Inquirer, January 5, 1990.

Sports Illustrated, July 21, 1986; September 15, 1986; September 10, 1990; January 28, 1991.

St. Louis Post-Dispatch, January 25, 1991.

Washington Post, November 1, 1987.

JULIE KRONE

Callahan, Dorothy M. *Julie Krone: A Winning Jockey.* Minneapolis: Dillon Press, 1990.

New York Times Magazine, July 25, 1993.

Newsweek, December 28, 1987.

People, May 2, 1988.

Sports Illustrated, June 14, 1993.

Sports Illustrated for Kids, September 1993.

MARIO LEMIEUX

Cox, Ted. *Mario Lemieux (Super Mario).* Chicago: Children's Press, 1993.

Detroit Free Press, June 3, 1984; June 10, 1984; September 24, 1984; October 31, 1984.

Gutman, Bill. *Mario Lemieux: Wizard with a Puck.* Brookfield, Conn.: Millbrook Press, 1992.

Hollander, Zander, ed. *The Complete Encyclopedia of Hockey.* 4th ed. Detroit: Visible Ink Press, 1993.

Maclean's, February 20, 1989; May 1, 1989; April 26, 1993.

Montreal Gazette, November 12, 1983.

Sporting News, May 16, 1988; June 8, 1992; November 22, 1993.

Sports Illustrated, February 6, 1989; November 27, 1989; June 8, 1992; November 16, 1992; April 19, 1993; January 25, 1993.

Sports Illustrated for Kids, December 1993.

CARL LEWIS

Coffey, Wayne R. *Carl Lewis.* 1st ed. Woodbridge, Conn.: Blackbirch Press, 1993.

Inside Sports, August 1984.

Lewis, Carl. *Inside Track: My Professional Life in Amateur Track.* New York: Simon and Schuster, 1990.

New York Times Magazine, June 19, 1992.

The Olympics Factbook: A Spectator's Guide to the Winter and Summer Games. Detroit: Visible Ink Press, 1992.

Philadelphia Daily News, July 26, 1984; August 2, 1984; January 25, 1985; July 23, 1985; June 3, 1988; June 25, 1992; August 7, 1992.

Washington Post, July 22, 1984.

ERIC LINDROS

Boston Globe, March 22, 1991.

Chicago Tribune, June 23, 1991.

Detroit Free Press, September 10, 1991; September 27, 1991.

Hollander, Zander, ed. *The Complete Encyclopedia of Hockey.* 4th ed. Detroit: Visible Ink Press, 1993.

Lindros, Eric, and Randy Starkman. *Fire on Ice.* Toronto, Ontario, Canada: HarperCollins Publishers, 1991.

Philadelphia Inquirer, February 9, 1990; March 3, 1991; June 22, 1991.

San Francisco Examiner, June 23, 1991.

Sporting News, December 27, 1993.

Sports Illustrated, April 1, 1991; September 23, 1991.

St. Paul Pioneer Press, February 10, 1991.

Toronto Globe and Mail, September 10, 1991.

NANCY LOPEZ

Atlanta Journal, December 10, 1992; November 4, 1993.

Golf, May 1990.

New York Times Magazine, July 2, 1978.

Sports Illustrated, August 4, 1986; February 9, 1987; May 29, 1989.

GREG MADDUX

Baseball Digest, March 1994.

Detroit Free Press, April 15, 1994.

New York Times, November 12, 1992; December 10, 1992; November 4, 1993.

Sport, May 1993.

Sports Illustrated, April 5, 1993.

KARL MALONE

Inside Sports, October 1989.

Sporting News, January 16, 1984.

Sports Illustrated, January 14, 1985; November 7, 1988.

Sports Illustrated for Kids, June 1993.

DIEGO MARADONA

New York Times, May 27, 1990.

People, June 18, 1990.

Washington Post, March 6, 1994.

DAN MARINO

Inside Sports, September 1982.

Marino, Dan. *Marino!* Chicago: Contemporary Books, 1986.

New York Times, November 4, 1984.

Rubin, Bob. *Dan Marino: Wonder Boy Quarterback.* Chicago: Children's Press, 1985.

Sports Illustrated, September 1, 1982; December 24, 1984.

MARK MESSIER

Hollander, Zander, ed. *The Com-*

plete Encyclopedia of Hockey. 4th ed. Detroit: Visible Ink Press, 1993.

New York Daily News, November 18, 1991; November 20, 1991.

Newsday, October 3, 1991; October 13, 1991; December 12, 1991; April 12, 1992; May 10, 1992.

St. Louis Pioneer Press, December 29, 1991; April 19, 1992.

Sports Illustrated, May 9, 1988; March 16, 1992.

USA Today, November 30, 1989.

Washington Post, May 9, 1990; May 10, 1990; February 27, 1992.

SHANNON MILLER

Current Health, May 1993.

Dallas Morning News, September 30, 1993.

Sporting News, July 20, 1992.

Sports Illustrated, August 10, 1992; December 14, 1992; August 26, 1993.

Sports Illustrated for Kids, July 1993.

Time, July 27, 1992.

TOMMY MOE

New York Times, February 14, 1994.

The Olympic Factbook: A Spectator's Guide to the Winter Games. Detroit: Visible Ink Press, 1994.

Rolling Stone, February 20, 1992.

Sporting News, February 21, 1994.

Sports Illustrated, February 21,
1994; February 28, 1994.

Time, February 28, 1994.

U.S. News & World Report, February 28, 1994.

JOE MONTANA

Boston Globe, January 20, 1989; January 21, 1989; January 23, 1989.

Kavanagh, Jack. *Sports Great Joe Montana.* Hillside, N.J.: Enslow Publishers, 1992.

Montana, Joe. *Audibles: My Life in Football.* 1st ed. New York: W. Morrow, 1986.

Raber, Thomas R. *Joe Montana, Comeback Quarterback.* Minneapolis: Lerner Publications Co., 1989.

San Jose Mercury News, July 18, 1985; October 13, 1986; November 9, 1986; January 19, 1989; January 23, 1989.

Sporting News, December 20, 1993; January 24, 1994.

Sports Illustrated, December 21, 1981; January 25, 1982; September 4, 1985; November 17, 1986; August 15, 1988.

WARREN MOON

Houston Post, December 25, 1987; March 13, 1988; November 13, 1988; April 8, 1989; July 29, 1989.

Los Angeles Times, November 18, 1989; November 3, 1990.

Rocky Mountain News, November 18, 1990.

Seattle Times, December 2, 1990.

Sports Illustrated, November 5, 1990; December 24, 1990; September 27, 1993.

Sports Illustrated for Kids, December 1993.

St. Louis Post-Dispatch, October 28, 1990.

MARTINA NAVRATILOVA

Collins, Bud, and Zander Hollander, eds. *Bud Collins' Modern Encyclopedia of Tennis.* 2nd ed. Detroit: Visible Ink Press, 1994.

Navratilova, Martina. *Martina.* 1st ed. New York: Knopf, 1985.

New York Times Magazine, June 19, 1977.

Sport, March 1976.

Sports Illustrated, February 24, 1975; September 21, 1987.

HAKEEM OLAJUWON

Chicago Tribune, May 22, 1986.

Ebony, March 1984.

People, December 5, 1983; December 17, 1984.

Sport, April 1988.

Sporting News, May 24, 1993.

Sports Illustrated for Kids, September 1993.

SHAQUILLE O'NEAL

Atlanta Constitution, February 8, 1991; May 30, 1991.

Cox, Ted. *Shaquille O'Neal: Shaq Attack.* Chicago: Children's Press, 1993.

Hollander, Zander, ed. *Complete Handbook of Pro Basketball: 1993.* New York: Visible Ink Press, 1993.

Houston Post, November 5, 1989.

O'Neal, Shaquille, and Jack McCallum. *Shaq Attack.* New York: Hyperion Press, 1993.

Orlando Sentinel, February 24, 1991.

Philadelphia Daily News, February 12, 1991.

Rocky Mountain News, March 2, 1991.

Sporting News, November 29, 1993.

Sports Illustrated, January 21, 1991; May 25, 1992; November 30, 1992.

SCOTTIE PIPPEN

Chicago Tribune, May 24, 1991; June 17, 1991.

Hollander, Zander, ed. *Complete Handbook of Pro Basketball: 1994.* New York: Signet, 1994.

New York Times, October 27, 1991.

Reiser, Howard. *Scottie Pippen: Prince of the Court.* Chicago: Children's Press, 1993.

Sports Illustrated, November 30, 1987; June 14, 1993.

KIRBY PUCKETT

Aaseng, Nathan. *Sports Great Kirby Puckett.* Hillside, N.J.: Enslow Publishers, 1993.

Bauleke, Ann. *Kirby Puckett: Fan Favorite.* Minneapolis: Lerner Publications Co., 1993.

Esquire, April 1992.

Hollander, Zander, ed. *Complete Handbook of Baseball: 1988*. New York: Signet, 1988.

Puckett, Kirby. *Be the Best You Can Be*. Minneapolis: Waldman House, 1993.

Puckett, Kirby. *I Love This Game!: My Life and Baseball*. 1st ed. New York: HarperCollins Publishers, 1993.

Sports Illustrated, July 23, 1984; May 12, 1986; June 15, 1987; April 6, 1992.

JERRY RICE

Dickey, Glenn. *Sports Great Jerry Rice*. Hillside, N.J.: Enslow Publishers, 1993.

Evans, J. Edward. *Jerry Rice: Touchdown Talent*. Minneapolis: Lerner Publications Co., 1993.

Los Angeles Times, December 13, 1987.

Newsday, January 28, 1990.

San Jose Mercury News, September 2, 1988.

Sporting News, February 22, 1990; December 20, 1993.

CAL RIPKEN, JR.

Baseball Digest, June 1983; March 1986.

Macnow, Glen. *Sports Great Cal Ripken, Jr.* Hillside, N.J.: Enslow Publishers, 1993.

Sport, May 1992.

Sporting News, July 22, 1991; April 26, 1993.

Sports Illustrated, September 12, 1983; April 2, 1984; July 23,

1984; June 18, 1990; July 29, 1991; June 28, 1993.

Thornley, Stew. *Cal Ripken, Jr.: Oriole Ironman*. Minneapolis: Lerner Publications Co., 1992.

DAVID ROBINSON

Aaseng, Nathan. *Sports Great David Robinson*. Hillside, N.J.: Enslow Publishers, 1992.

Charlotte Observer, September 28, 1988; December 26, 1989.

Chicago Tribune, June 29, 1987; August 13, 1989; November 19, 1989.

Gentleman's Quarterly, February 1991.

Gutman, Bill. *David Robinson: NBA Super Center*. Brookfield, Conn.: Millbrook Press, 1993.

Los Angeles Times, May 18, 1987; September 24, 1987; December 3, 1987; May 21, 1988; September 30, 1988; August 27, 1989; May 15, 1990.

Miller, Dawn M. *David Robinson: Backboard Admiral*. Minneapolis: Lerner Publications Co., 1991.

Rolfe, John. *David Robinson*. 1st ed. Boston: Little, Brown, and Co., 1991.

Savage, Jim. *The Force: David Robinson, the NBA's Newest Sky high Sensation*. New York: Dell, 1992.

Washington Post, March 20, 1986; October 15, 1986; November 22, 1986; August 19, 1988; October 7, 1988; May 15, 1990; December 7, 1991.

NOLAN RYAN

Lace, William W. *Sports Great Nolan Ryan.* Hillside, N.J.: Enslow Publishers, 1993.

Philadelphia Daily News, June 8, 1989.

Rappoport, Ken. *Nolan Ryan— The Ryan Express.* 1st ed. New York: New York: Maxwell Macmillan International, 1992.

Reiser, Howard. *Nolan Ryan: Strikeout King.* Chicago: Children's Press, 1993.

Rolfe, John. *Nolan Ryan.* 1st ed. Boston: Little, Brown and Co., 1992.

Ryan, Nolan. *Miracle Man: Nolan Ryan, The Autobiography.* Dallas: Word Publishers, 1992.

Sports Illustrated, September 29, 1986; May 1, 1989; May 13, 1991; October 4, 1993.

PETE SAMPRAS

Collins, Bud, and Zander Hollander, eds. *Bud Collins' Modern Encyclopedia of Tennis.* 2nd ed. Detroit: Visible Ink Press, 1994.

New York Times, May 6, 1991.

Sporting News, September 20, 1993.

Sports Illustrated, September 17, 1990; July 15, 1991; September 16, 1991; June 15, 1992; July 13, 1992; June 14, 1993; July 12, 1993; September 20, 1993.

Tennis, September 1993; October 1993.

USA Today, May 6, 1993.

World Tennis, November 1990.

ARANTXA SANCHEZ VICARIO

Collins, Bud, and Zander Hollander, eds. *Bud Collins' Modern Encyclopedia of Tennis.* 2nd ed. Detroit: Visible Ink Press, 1994.

Sports Illustrated, June 19, 1989; July 17, 1989; May 14, 1990; July 22, 1992.

Time, June 26, 1989.

RYNE SANDBERG

Boys' Life, June 1993.

Lundgren, Hal. *Ryne Sandberg: The Triple Threat.* Chicago: Children's Press, 1986.

New York Times, November 14, 1984; October 5, 1989.

Sport, June 1991; June 1993.

Sports Illustrated, March 18, 1991; March 16, 1992; July 27, 1992.

BARRY SANDERS

Chicago Tribune, November 3, 1991.

Detroit Free Press, December 17, 1989.

Gutman, Bill. *Barry Sanders: Football's Rushing Champ.* Brookfield, Conn.: Millbrook Press, 1993.

Kavanagh, Jack. *Rocket Running Back.* Minneapolis: Lerner Publications Co., 1994.

Knapp, Ron. *Sports Great Barry Sanders.* Hillside, N.J.: Enslow Publishers, 1993.

Philadelphia Daily News, August 28, 1991.

Reiser, Howard. *Lion With a Quiet Roar*. Chicago: Children's Press, 1993.

Sporting News, October 24, 1988; December 19, 1988; April 24, 1989; November 20, 1989; January 15, 1990.

Sports Illustrated, December 12, 1988; April 10, 1989; September 10, 1990.

DEION SANDERS

Esquire, June 1992.

Sports Illustrated, June 12, 1989; November 13, 1989; April 27, 1992; August 24, 1992.

Thornley, Stew. *Deion Sanders: Prime Time Player*. Minneapolis: Lerner Publications Co., 1993.

MONICA SELES

Collins, Bud, and Zander Hollander, eds. *Bud Collins' Modern Encyclopedia of Tennis*. 2nd ed. Detroit: Visible Ink Press, 1994.

New York Times, May 27, 1991.

Sports Illustrated, June 19, 1988; August 22, 1988; June 18, 1990; May 27, 1991; July 15, 1991; September 16, 1991; June 15, 1992; July 13, 1992; November 30, 1992; June 14, 1993; September 20, 1993.

Tennis, March 1994.

World Tennis, June 1989; March 1990.

EMMITT SMITH

Sport, August 1993.

Sporting News, September 20, 1993.

Sports Illustrated, November 16, 1987; November 27, 1989; October 21, 1991; September 7, 1992; September 27, 1993.

Sports Illustrated for Kids, September 1993.

LYN ST. JAMES

Sports Illustrated, May 3, 1993.

St. James, Lyn. *Lyn St. James' Car Owner's Manual for Women*. New York: Penguin Books, 1984.

FRANK THOMAS

Sports, April 1992.

Sporting News, September 20, 1993; October 11, 1993; October 18, 1993.

Sports Illustrated, September 16, 1991; September 13, 1993.

Sports Illustrated for Kids, July 1993.

ISIAH THOMAS

Boston Globe, November 1, 1981; April 26, 1985; June 7, 1987.

Chicago Tribune, February 8, 1987.

Hollander, Zander, ed. *Complete Handbook of Pro Basketball: 1991*. New York: Signet, 1991.

Jet, January 31, 1994.

Knapp, Ron. *Sports Great Isiah Thomas*. Hillside, N.J.: Enslow Publishers, 1992.

Los Angeles Times, February 10, 1986; June 7, 1988; June 11, 1988; June 20, 1988.

Myers, Gene, ed. *Bad Boys*. Detroit: *Detroit Free Press*, 1989.

New York Times, January 9, 1994.

Sport, June 1992.

Sports Illustrated, April 6, 1981; January 19, 1987; May 18, 1987; June 20, 1988; June 27, 1988; June 4, 1990; June 11, 1990; June 25, 1990; March 18, 1991; September 30, 1991; January 17, 1994.

Thomas, Isiah, and Matt Dobek. *Bad Boys: An Inside Look at the Detroit Pistons' 1988—89 Championship Season*. Grand Rapids, Mich.: Masters Press, 1989.

THURMAN THOMAS

Houston Post, October 11, 1987; August 5, 1988; August 29, 1989; January 19, 1992.

Newsday, August 4, 1991; January 21, 1992.

St. Paul Pioneer Press, December 15, 1989; January 24, 1992.

Sports Illustrated, January 28, 1991; February 3, 1992; February 1, 1993.

Washington Post, October 10, 1991.

Wichita Eagle-Beacon, August 20, 1987; October 11, 1987.

ALBERTO TOMBA

Chicago Tribune, February 7, 1992.

Detroit Free Press, February 24, 1994.

Los Angeles Times, February 3, 1992; February 19, 1992.

New York Times, December 23, 1990.

The Olympic Factbook: A Spectator's Guide to the Winter Games. Detroit: Visible Ink Press, 1994.

Philadelphia Inquirer, January 14, 1988; February 26, 1988; February 28, 1988; February 6, 1992.

Skiing, September 1988; February 1991; January 1992; February 1993.

Sporting News, February 14, 1994.

Sports Illustrated, January 23, 1988; March 7, 1988; February 3, 1992; March 2, 1992.

Time, March 7, 1988; March 2, 1992.

USA Today, February 28, 1994; March 1, 1994.

Washington Post, February 26, 1988.

REGGIE WHITE

Hill, Terry. *Reggie White: Minister of Defense*. Brentwood, Tenn.: Wolgemuth and Hyatt, 1991.

Philadelphia Daily News, June 7, 1991; April 7, 1993; April 8, 1993.

Sports Illustrated, September 3, 1986; November 27, 1989; March 15, 1993; May 3, 1993; September 20, 1993.

DAVE WINFIELD

Sport, December 1975.

Sports Illustrated, July 9, 1979; January 5, 1981; September 10, 1984; April 11, 1988; May 30, 1988; June 29, 1992; November 2, 1992; December 28, 1992; September 27, 1993.

Winfield, Dave. *Winfield: A Player's Life.* 1st ed. New York: Norton, 1988.

KATARINA WITT

Chicago Tribune, February 17, 1988; February 21, 1988.

Christian Science Monitor, February 4, 1988.

Coffey, Wayne R. *Katarina Witt.* 1st ed. Woodbridge, Conn.: Blackbirch Press, 1992.

Current Biography, 1988 Yearbook.

Maclean's, February 1988; January 14, 1991.

Newsweek, November 29, 1993.

The Olympic Factbook: A Spectator's Guide to the Winter Games. Detroit: Visible Ink Press, 1994.

Sports Illustrated, March 18, 1985; January 20, 1986; March 23, 1987; March 7, 1988.

USA Today, February 10, 1994.

KRISTI YAMAGUCHI

Chicago Tribune, February 15, 1991; February 7, 1992.

Detroit Free Press, February 14, 1991; February 22, 1992.

Los Angeles Times, February 15, 1991; January 26, 1992.

Miami Herald, February 19, 1992.

Newsday, February 2, 1992; February 22, 1992.

The Olympic Factbook: A Spectator's Guide to the Winter Games. Detroit: Visible Ink Press, 1994.

St. Paul Pioneer Press, February 22, 1992.

San Jose Mercury News, February 4, 1990; April 28, 1990; February 10, 1991; February 2, 1992; February 9, 1992.

Sports Illustrated, February 20, 1989; March 25, 1991; January 20, 1992; March 2, 1992.

USA Today, February 6, 1990; January 28, 1992.

STEVE YOUNG

Sport, August 1993.

Sporting News, January 11, 1993.

Sports Illustrated, September 30, 1991; November 23, 1992; May 31, 1993.

Sports Illustrated for Kids, November 1993.

Street and Smith's Pro Football, June 1993.

SPORT

BASEBALL

Baseball Encylopedia: The Complete and Official Record of Major League Baseball. 11th ed. New York: Macmillian Publishing Co., 1993.

Hollander, Zander, ed. *Complete Handbook of Baseball.* New York: Signet, annual.

James, Bill. *The Bill James Historical Baseball Abstract.* New York: Villard Books, 1988.

LaBlanc, Michael L., ed. *Professional Sports Team Histories: Baseball.* Detroit: Gale Research, Inc., 1994.

Neft, Donald S., and Richard M. Cohen, eds. *The Sports Encyclopedia: Baseball.* 14th ed. New York: St. Martin's Press, 1994.

The Series: An Illustrated History of Baseball's Postseason Showcase, 1903—93. St. Louis: *Sporting News* Publishing Co., 1993.

Thorn, John, and Pete Palmer, eds. *Total Baseball: The Ultimate Encyclopedia of Baseball.* 3rd ed. New York: HarperCollins Publishers, 1993.

BASKETBALL

Carter, Craig, and Alex Sachare, eds. *The Sporting News Official NBA Guide.* St. Louis: *The Sporting News* Publishing Co., annual.

Hollander, Zander, ed. *Complete Handbook of Pro Basketball.* New York: Signet, annual.

Hollander, Zander, and Alex Sachare, eds. *The Official NBA Basketball Encyclopedia.* New York: Villard Books, 1989.

LaBlanc, Michael L., ed. *Professional Sports Team Histories: Basketball.* Detroit: Gale Research, Inc., 1994.

Savage, Jim, ed. *The Encyclopedia of the NCAA Basketball Tournament: The Complete Independent Guide to College Basketball's Championship Event.* New York: Dell Publishing, 1990.

FOOTBALL

Dienhart, Tom, and Joe Hoppel, eds. *The Sporting News Complete Super Bowl Book.* St. Louis: *The Sporting News* Publishing Co., annual.

Hollander, Zander, ed. *Complete Handbook of Pro Football.* New York: Signet, annual.

LaBlanc, Michael L., ed. *Professional Sports Team Histories: Football.* Detroit: Gale Research, Inc., 1994.

Neft, David S., Richard M. Cohen, and Rick Korch, eds. *The Sports Encyclopedia: Football.* 11th ed. New York: St. Martin's Press, 1993.

Shimabukuro, Mark, ed. *The Sporting News Pro Football Register.* St. Louis: *The Sporting News* Publishing Co., annual.

GOLF

Golf Magazine's Encyclopedia of Golf: The Complete Reference. 2nd ed. New York: HarperCollins Publishers, 1993.

HOCKEY

Hollander, Zander, ed. *The Complete Encyclopedia of Hockey.* 4th ed. Detroit: Visible Ink Press, 1993.

Hollander, Zander, ed. *Complete Handbook of Hockey.* New York: Signet, annual.

LaBlanc, Michael L., ed. *Professional Sports Team Histories: Hockey.* Detroit: Gale Research, Inc., 1994.

The National Hockey League Official Guide and Record Book, 1992—93. Chicago: Triumph Books, 1992.

OLYMPIC

The Olympics Factbook: A Spectator's Guide to the Winter Games. Detroit: Visible Ink Press, 1994.

The Olympics Factbook: A Spectator's Guide to the Winter and Summer Games. Detroit: Visible Ink Press, 1992.

SOCCER

LaBlanc, Michael L., and Richard Henshaw, eds. *The World Encyclopedia of Soccer.* Detroit: Visible Ink Press, 1994.

TENNIS

Collins, Bud, and Zander Hollander, eds. *Bud Collins' Modern Encyclopedia of Tennis.* 2nd ed. Detroit: Visible Ink Press, 1994.

Index

A

Aaron, Hank 567
Abbott, Jim 1-7
Abdul-Jabbar, Kareem 55, 241, 424, 426, 430
Acquired Immune Deficiency Syndrome (See AIDS)
Admiral, The (See Robinson, David)
AFC Championship game
    Elway, John 124, 125
    Kelly, Jim 272
    Marino, Dan 371-373
    Montana, Joe 402
    Thomas, Thurman 545, 546
Agassi, Andre 8-14, 93, 94, 103, 104, 106, 476, 478, 479, 508
AIDS 36, 244, 245
Aikman, Troy 15-22, 518
Ali, Muhammad 164, 165, 209
All-Star game, Baseball

Alomar, Roberto 26, 28
Alomar, Sandy, Jr. 26
Dykstra, Lenny 118
Fielder, Cecil 151, 153
Gonzalez, Juan 172
Griffey, Ken, Jr. 195
Jackson, Bo 228
Maddux, Greg 348
Puckett, Kirby 443
Ripken, Cal, Jr. 458
Sandberg, Ryne 493
Winfield, Dave 564
All-Star game, NBA
    Drexler, Clyde 112
    Patrick Ewing 137
    Johnson, Earvin "Magic" 245
    Johnson, Larry 252
    Jordan, Michael 256, 257
    Malone, Karl 357
    O'Neal, Shaquille 431
    Olajuwon, Hakeem 424
    Pippen, Scottie 436

Robinson, David 465
Thomas, Isiah 537
All-Star game, NHL
    Hull, Brett 214, 216
    Lemieux, Mario 319, 320
    Messier, Mark 377
Alomar, Roberto 23-29, 472
Alomar, Sandy, Jr. 24
Alomar, Sandy, Sr. 23
Alpine skiing 391
Alworth, Lance 450
American Football Conference
    (See AFC)
American League Championship
    Series
    Alomar, Roberto 27, 28
    Clemens, Roger 99, 100,
      101
    Jackson, Bo 230
    Puckett, Kirby 443, 444
    Ripken, Cal, Jr. 456
    Ryan, Nolan 470
    Thomas, Frank 532
    Winfield, Dave 567
Anderson, Sparky 151
Andretti, Mario 159, 160
Apartheid 34
Arizona State University
    Bonds, Barry 79
"Arnie's Army" 340
Arthur Ashe Foundation for the
    Defeat of AIDS 36
Ashe, Arthur 30-36, 479, 512
Ashford, Evelyn 131, 200
Athletes for Abstinence 499
Atlanta Braves 28, 80, 81, 120,
    444, 468, 567
    Maddux, Greg 349
    Sanders, Deion 503
Atlanta Falcons
    Sanders, Deion 502
Auburn University
    Barkley, Charles 45
    Jackson, Bo 225
    Thomas, Frank 529
Australian Open
    Ashe, Arthur 34
    Courier, Jim 106, 107
    Graf, Steffi 178-181

Navratilova, Martina 413-
    416
Sampras, Pete 479
Sanchez Vicario, Arantxa
    485, 486
Seles, Monica 509, 510,
    512
Avery, Steve 350
Azinger, Paul 144

B

Baiul, Oksana 37-42
Baltimore Orioles 468, 470
    Ripken, Cal, Jr. 454
Banks, Ernie 82, 491
Barkley, Charles 43-49, 260,
    357, 358, 424, 438, 465
Barraso, Tom 321
Baseball All-Star game (See All-
    Star game, Baseball)
Baseball no-hitters
    Abbott, Jim 6
    Ryan, Nolan 24, 469-472
Baseball records
    Ripken, Cal, Jr. 457, 458
    Ryan, Nolan 469, 470-473
    Sandberg, Ryne 491-493
Baylor, Elgin 259
Beamon, Bob 329
Becker, Boris 10, 179, 478, 479
Belmont Stakes
    Krone, Julie 278
    Shoemaker, Willie 279
Bench, Johnny 171, 192
Berra, Yogi 82
Big Hurt, The (See Thomas,
    Frank)
Bird, Larry 50-57, 240, 242,
    245, 251, 258, 423, 538
Birdie 142
Blair, Bonnie 58-64, 131
Blanda, George 268
Blyleven, Bert 473
Boggs, Wade 444
Bogie 142
**Bogues, Tyrone "Muggsy" 65-
71**
Boitano, Brian 72-77, 572
Bollettieri, Nick 9, 104, 508

Bonaly, Surya 39
Bonds, Barry 78-82, 120, 472
Bonds, Bobby 78, 472
Borg, Bjorn 479
Boston Bruins 187
Boston Celtics 46, 242, 423, 538
    Bird, Larry 52
Boston Red Sox 82, 118
    Clemens, Roger 98
Bowe, Riddick 83-88, 209, 210
Bowman, Scotty 322
Boxing scoring 87
Bradley University
    Puckett, Kirby 442
Bradshaw, Terry 401
Brigham Young University 583
    Young, Steve 582
British Open
    Faldo, Nick 143-146
Bronze medals, Summer Olympics
    Griffith Joyner, Florence
        202
    Holyfield, Evander 207
    Joyner-Kersee, Jackie 267
    Miller, Shannon 384
    Robinson, David 464
    Sanchez Vicario, Arantxa
        485
Bronze medals, Winter Olympics
    Blair, Bonnie 62
Brown, Dale 427-429
Brown, Jim 451, 520
Brown, Larry 464
Buckner, Bill 100
Budge, Don 178
Buffalo Bills 20, 21, 125, 373,
    402, 519, 520
    Kelly, Jim 271
    Thomas, Thurman 544
Button, Dick 74

C

Calder Trophy
    Lemieux, Mario 319
Calgary Flames
    Hull, Brett 214
California Angels 99
    Abbott, Jim 4
    Ryan, Nolan 469

Winfield, Dave 566
Campbell, Earl 520, 543
Canadian Football League 406
Canseco, Jose 173, 532
Capriati, Jennifer 180, 510
Carew, Rod 116, 444
Carlton, Steve 101, 473
CART Indy Car World Series
    championship
        Fittipaldi, Emerson 159
Carter, Joe 27, 29
Cartwright, Bill 423
Cauthen, Steve 276
Central Arkansas University 434
    Pippen, Scottie 434
Cepeda, Orlando 532
Challenger Division 6
Chamberlain, Wilt 55, 259, 424,
    426
Championship Auto Racing
    Teams 156
Chang, Michael 89-95, 475, 482
Charlotte Hornets
    Bogues, Tyrone "Muggsy"
        69
    Johnson, Larry 251
Chicago Bears 399
Chicago Bulls 48, 113, 139, 244,
    329, 540
    Jordan, Michael 255
    Pippen, Scottie 436
Chicago Cubs
    Maddux, Greg 347
    Sandberg, Ryne 488
Chicago White Sox 28, 456
    Jackson, Bo 229
    Jordan, Michael 260
    Thomas, Frank 530
Cincinnati Bengals 272, 398,
    400, 449
Cincinnati Reds 80
    Sanders, Deion 506
Cincinnati Stingers
    Messier, Mark 376
Clark, Will 348
Clay, Cassius 165
Clemens, Roger 96-102, 172,
    351, 443
Clemente, Roberto 170
Cleveland Browns 124, 125

Clinton, Bill 202, 393
Clinton, Hillary Rodham 393
Cobb, Ty 171, 195, 492
Coffey, Paul 321, 378
College World Series
    Clemens, Roger 98
    Sanders, Deion 502
    Winfield, Dave 563
Collins, Bud 181, 418
Collins, Phil 486
Conn Smythe Trophy
    Gretzky, Wayne 186, 187
    Lemieux, Mario 321, 322
    Messier, Mark 377
Connors, Jimmy 9, 30, 34, 36,
    479
Courier, Jim 12, 90, **103-108,**
    478, 479, 508
Court, Margaret 178, 412, 416-
    418, 510
Craig, Roger 401
Crawford, Sam 171
Crescent Moon Foundation 409
Cy Young Award
    Clemens, Roger 99-101
    Maddux, Greg 349, 351

D

Dallas Cowboys 273, 274, 329,
    398, 451, 463, 547, 585, 586
    Aikman, Troy 18
    Smith, Emmitt 517
Daly, Chuck 538
Dan Marino Foundation 374
Dantley, Adrian 356, 539
Daulton, Darren 119
Davis Cup 106, 107
    Agassi, Andre 11
    Ashe, Arthur 33-35
    Chang, Michael 94
    Sampras, Pete 478
Dawson, Len 402
Denver Broncos 273, 401, 449,
    546
    Elway, John 123
Detroit Lions 498
    Sanders, Barry 498
Detroit Pistons 56, 113, 243, 244,
    257, 258, 436

    Thomas, Isiah 537
Detroit Tigers 2, 443
    Fielder, Cecil 151
Dickerson, Eric 543
Dimaggio, Joe 82, 171
Dionne, Marcel 188
Dorsett, Tony 370
Douglas, James "Buster" 209
Douglas, Michael 243
Dream, The (See Olajuwon,
    Hakeem)
Dream Team
    Barkley, Charles 47
    Bird, Larry 56
    Drexler, Clyde 113
    Ewing, Patrick 139
    Johnson, Earvin "Magic"
        245
    Jordan, Michael 259
    Malone, Karl 358
    Pippen, Scottie 438
    Robinson, David 465
Dream Team II
    Thomas, Isiah 540
Drexler, Clyde 109-114, 422,
    540
Duke University 250
Dykstra, Lenny 115-120

E

Eagle 142
Eastern Conference finals
    Barkley, Charles 46
    Bird, Larry 53, 56
    Ewing, Patrick 139
    Jordan, Michael 257-260
    Pippen, Scottie 436,
        437
    Thomas, Isiah 538, 540
Eckersley, Dennis 567
Edberg, Stefan 93, 94, 106, 478,
    479
Edmonton Eskimos
    Moon, Warren 406
Edmonton Oilers
    Gretzky, Wayne 184
    Messier, Mark 376
Elway, John 121-126, 270
Erving, Julius 46

Esposito, Phil 188
European Figure Skating Championships
    Baiul, Oksana 39, 41
    Witt, Katarina 571-573
Evans, Janet 127-132
Evert, Chris 177, 178, 412-415, 417, 418, 481, 508
Ewing, Patrick 133-140, 260, 422, 430, 466

F

Faldo, Nick 141-147
Federation Cup
    Navratilova, Martina 416
    Sanchez Vicario, Arantxa 485, 486
Fellowship of Christian Athletes 558
Female Athlete of the Year
    Joyner-Kersee, Jackie 266
Fernandez, Mary Joe 179, 180
Fernandez, Tony 27
Fielder, Cecil 148-153
Fisk, Carlton 172
Fittipaldi, Emerson 154-161
Fleming, Peggy 575
Florida State University
    Sanders, Deion 501
Floyd, Raymond 145
Foreman, George 162-168, 209
Formula One 155
Formula One driving championship
    Fittipaldi, Emerson 155
Foster, George 152
Fouts, Dan 371
Foxx, Jimmie 82, 152, 195, 531
Franco, Julio 170
Frank Thomas Charitable Foundation 532
Frazier, Joe 164
French Open
    Agassi, Andre 11, 104, 106
    Chang, Michael 92, 94
    Courier, Jim 104, 106, 107
    Graf, Steffi 177-180
    Navratilova, Martina 413, 415

Sanchez Vicario, Arantxa 482, 484-486
Seles, Monica 508-510
Futch, Eddie 86

G

Garrison, Zina 179, 181
Garvey, Steve 490
Gaston, Cito 27
Gehrig, Lou 458, 531
Georgetown University 139, 255, 422
    Ewing, Patrick 134
Gervin, George 259
Glavine, Tom 349-351
Glide, The (See Drexler, Clyde)
Gold Glove Award
    Alomar, Roberto 27
    Bonds, Barry 80, 82
    Bonds, Bobby 82
    Clemente, Roberto 170
    Griffey, Ken, Jr. 195
    Maddux, Greg 348
    Puckett, Kirby 443
    Ripken, Cal, Jr. 458
    Sandberg, Ryne 489, 491-493
    Winfield, Dave 565
Gold medals, Summer Olympics
    Ali, Muhammad 165
    Evans, Janet 129, 131
    Foreman, George 163
    Graf, Steffi 176, 178
    Griffith Joyner, Florence 201, 202
    Johnson, Earvin "Magic 245
    Jordan, Michael 255
    Joyner-Kersee, Jackie 266, 267
    Lewis, Carl 328-330
    Sanchez Vicario, Arantxa 482
Gold medals, Winter Olympics
    Blair, Bonnie 62, 63
    Boitano, Brian 75
    Button, Dick 74
    Jansen, Dan 236
    Moe, Tommy 393

Tomba, Alberto 551, 554
Witt, Katarina 571, 572
Golden Gloves
Holyfield, Evander 207
Golf scoring 142
Gonzalez, Juan 169-174,
195
Goodwill Games
Evan, Janet 129, 131
Joyner-Kersee, Jackie 266
Graf, Steffi 93, **175-182,** 415,
417, 482, 484, 485, 508-512
Grand Slam [tennis]
Graf, Steffi 177
Laver, Rod 476
Navratilova, Martina 416
Grant, Horace 257
Gray, Pete 5
Great One, The (See Gretzky,
Wayne)
Green Bay Packers
White, Reggie 561
Greenberg, Hank 152, 532
Gretzky, Wayne 183-190, 215,
216, 317, 318, 320-322, 332,
335, 336, 365, 375, 377, 378
Grey Cup
Moon, Warren 407
Griffey, Ken, Jr. 191-196, 472
Griffey, Ken, Sr. 191, 192, 194,
195
Griffith Joyner, Florence 197-
203, 266
Guthrie, Janet 526
Gwynn, Tony 444, 491

H

Hall of Fame, LPGA
Lopez, Nancy 343
Hamill, Dorothy 575, 576, 579
Hanshin Tigers
Fielder, Cecil 150
A Hard Road to Glory 35
Harding, Tonya 41
Hart Memorial Trophy
Gretzky, Wayne 185, 320
Hull, Brett 215
Lemieux, Mario 323
Messier, Mark 378, 380

Heavyweight championship
Bowe, Riddick 87
Foreman, George 164, 167,
168
Holyfield, Evander 209,
210
Heiden, Eric 60
Heisman Trophy
Detmer, Ty 583
Jackson, Bo 226
Rozier, Mike 582
Sanders, Barry 497
Staubach, Roger 463
Testaverde, Vinny 583
Torretta, Gino 583
Walker, Herschel 122
Ware, Andre 517
Henderson, Rickey 152
Henie, Sonja 40, 572, 573
Hill, Graham 159
Hodgkin's Disease 322
Holmes, Larry 209
Holyfield, Evander 87, 88, 167,
204-211
Hornsby, Rogers 491
Houston Astros 117
Ryan, Nolan 470
Houston Gamblers
Kelly, Jim 271
Houston Oilers
Moon, Warren 407
Houston Rockets 53, 55, 242
Olajuwon, Hakeem 358,
422
Howe, Gordie 184, 187, 188, 216
Hull, Bobby 188, 212, 216
Hull, Brett 212-217
Hutson, Don 450

I

Indiana State University 240
Bird, Larry 52
Indiana University
Bird, Larry 51
Thomas, Isiah 536
Indianapolis 500 526
Fittipaldi, Emerson 156,
157, 159, 160
St. James, Lyn 525, 526

Indianapolis Racers
    Gretzky, Wayne 184
    Messier, Mark 376
Induráin, Miguel 218-222
Irvin, Michael 518

J

Jackson, Bo 223-230, 503, 506,
    533, 564
Jackson, Michael 243, 574
Jackson, Reggie 442, 455, 532
Jansen, Dan 231-237
Jansen, Jane 231, 232
Jesse Owens Award
    Griffith Joyner, Florence
      201
    Joyner-Kersee, Jackie 266
Joe, Montana 402
Johnson, Bill 393
Johnson, Earvin "Magic" 53,
    55, 56, 111, **238-246,** 258, 356,
    365, 423, 437, 464, 537, 539
Johnson, Jimmy 16, 517
Johnson, Larry 69, **247-252**
Johnson, Walter 470
Jones, Jerry 18, 519
Jordan, Michael 45, 47, 48, 55,
    113, 135, 138, 245, 249,
    252,**253-261,** 357, 422, 423,
    431, 433, 436, 438, 540
Joyner, Al 200, 263-265
Joyner-Kersee, Jackie 200,
    262-267
Jurgenson, Sonny 373
Justice, Dave 505

K

Kaline, Al 195
Kansas City Chiefs 547
    Montana, Joe 402
Kansas City Royals
    Fielder, Cecil 149
    Jackson, Bo 226
Karolyi, Bela 384
Kelly, Jim 268-274, 367, 401,
    545, 583, 585
Kentucky Derby
    Shoemaker, Willie 279

Kerrigan, Nancy 39
Kersee, Bob 198, 200, 264-266
Killebrew, Harmon 151
Killy, Jean-Claude 552
Kiner, Ralph 152
King, Billie Jean 416, 417
Knight, Bobby 45, 536
Knight, Ray 341, 342
Kosar, Bernie 21
Koufax, Sandy 100, 101, 351, 473
Krone, Julie 275-280
Kruk, John 119
Krzyzewski, Mike 250

L

Ladies' Professional Golf Associ-
    ation (See LPGA)
Lady Byng Trophy
    Gretzky, Wayne 185
    Hull, Brett 215
Laimbeer, Bill 436, 539
Landry, Tom 18
Largent, Steve 450
Laver, Rod 178, 475, 476
Lee, Spike 261
Lemieux, Mario 187, **317-324,**
    332
LeMond, Greg 219, 220
Lendl, Ivan 92, 178, 476, 479,
    482
Levy, Marv 272, 544
Lewis, Carl 325-331
Lindros, Eric 332-337
Liston, Sonny 165
Lopez, Nancy 338-345
Los Angeles Dodgers 118, 565
Los Angeles Express
    Young, Steve 582
Los Angeles Kings
    Gretzky, Wayne 187
Los Angeles Lakers 54, 55, 113,
    240, 258, 356, 423, 437, 539
    Johnson, Earvin "Magic"
      240
Los Angeles Raiders 545
    Jackson, Bo 227
Los Angeles Rams 401
Louisiana State University 428,
    536

O'Neal, Shaquille 427
Louisiana Tech
    Malone, Karl 354
Louisville Cardinals 111, 135,
    422
LPGA Championship
    Lopez, Nancy 340, 342,
      343
Lucas, John 465
Lyn St. James' Car Owner's
    Manual 524

M

Maddux, Greg 100, **346-352,**
    492
Madonna 42, 574
Mailman, The (See Malone, Karl)
Malone, Karl 49, 259, **353-359,**
    430
Malone, Moses 46, 55, 241, 421
Mandela, Nelson 34
Mansell, Nigel 159, 160
Mantle, Mickey 82, 121, 152,
    195, 532
Maradona, Diego 360-366
Marino, Dan 268, 270, **367-374**
Maris, Roger 82, 152
Masters
    Faldo, Nick 144, 145
Masterton Trophy
    Lemieux, Mario 323
Mathews, Eddie 171, 195
Mattingly, Don 196, 444, 566
Maynard, Don 450
Mays, Willie 78, 81, 121, 152,
    171, 567
McCarver, Tim 504
McEnroe, John 12, 103, 476,
    478, 479
McGriff, Fred 27, 150, 350
McGwire, Mark 171
McHale, Kevin 53
McLain, Denny 100, 351, 532
McMahon, Jim 583
Mears, Rick 157, 159, 160
Memphis Showboats
    White, Reggie 557
Messier, Mark 375-380
Metric skating 59

Miami Dolphins 399, 547
    Marino, Dan 370
Michael Jordan Foundation 258
Michigan State University 240
    Johnson, Earvin "Magic"
      240
Mikita, Stan 188
Miller, Shannon 381-387
Minnesota North Stars 321
Minnesota Twins 27
    Puckett, Kirby 442
    Winfield, Dave 567
Minnesota Vikings
    Moon, Warren 410
Mississippi Valley State
    Rice, Jerry 447
Mize, Johnny 152
Moe, Tommy 388-394
Montana, Joe 20, 125, 268, 371,
    395-403, 410, 449-451, 583-
    586
Montreal Canadiens 188, 214
Moody, Helen Wills 418
Moon, Warren 404-410
Morgan, Joe 82, 192
Morris, Jack 444
Most Valuable Player, American
    League Championship Series
      Alomar, Roberto 28
Most Valuable Player, Baseball
    Bonds, Barry 80, 82
    Clemens, Roger 99
    Clemente, Roberto 170
    Ripken, Cal, Jr. 456, 458
    Sandberg, Ryne 490
    Thomas, Frank 532
Most Valuable Player, Baseball
    All-Star game
      Griffey, Ken, Jr. 195
      Jackson, Bo 228
      Ripken, Cal, Jr. 458
Most Valuable Player, College
    World Series
      Winfield, Dave 563
Most Valuable Player, NBA
    Barkley, Charles 48
    Bird, Larry 54, 55
    Johnson, Earvin "Magic"
      242-244
    Jordan, Michael 257, 259

Olajuwon, Hakeem 424
Most Valuable Player, NBA All-
Star game
Bird, Larry 53
Johnson, Earvin "Magic"
245
Jordan, Michael 257
Malone, Karl 357
Pippen, Scottie 438
Thomas, Isiah 537, 538
Most Valuable Player, NBA Finals
Bird, Larry 54, 55
Johnson, Earvin "Magic"
55, 241, 242
Jordan, Michael 258-260
Thomas, Isiah 540
Most Valuable Player, NCAA
Basketball Tournament 136
Johnson, Earvin "Magic"
240
Olajuwon, Hakeem 422
Thomas, Isiah 536
Most Valuable Player, NFL
Rice, Jerry 449
Smith, Emmitt 519
Thomas, Thurman 546
Young, Steve 585
Most Valuable Player, NHL
Gretzky, Wayne 185
Hull, Brett 215
Lemieux, Mario 320, 323
Messier, Mark 378, 380
Most Valuable Player, NHL All-
Star game
Hull, Brett 216
Lemieux, Mario 319, 320
Most Valuable Player, NHL play-
offs
Gretzky, Wayne 186, 187
Lemieux, Mario 321, 322
Messier, Mark 377
Most Valuable Player, Pro Bowl
White, Reggie 559
Most Valuable Player, Super
Bowl
Aikman, Troy 20
Montana, Joe 398, 399,
401
Rice, Jerry 449
Smith, Emmitt 520

Most Valuable Player, United
States Football League
Kelly, Jim 271
Most Valuable Player, World Cup
Maradona, Diego 363
Mourning, Alonzo 70, 139, 431
Murphy, Dale 82
Musial, Stan 567

N

Namath, Joe 268, 270, 367, 395
National AIDS Commission 244
National Basketball Association
(See NBA)
National Collegiate Athletic
Association (See NCAA)
National Footbal Conference
(See NFL)
National Hockey League (See
NHL)
National Invitational Tournament
Bird, Larry 52
National Junior Pentathlon Cham-
pionship
Joyner-Kersee, Jackie 264
National Junior Tennis League
35
National League Championship
Series
Bonds, Barry 80
Dykstra, Lenny 117, 118,
120
Maddux, Greg 348, 350
Ryan, Nolan 468, 471
Sandberg, Ryne 490, 491
Sanders, Deion 504, 505
Navratilova, Martina 176-179,
411-418, 508, 510, 511
NBA All-Star game (See All-
Star game, NBA)
NBA finals
Barkley, Charles 48
Bird, Larry 53-55
Drexler, Clyde 113
Johnson, Earvin "Magic"
54, 55, 241, 242-244
Jordan, Michael 258-260
Olajuwon, Hakeem 55, 423
Pippen, Scottie 437, 438

Thomas, Isiah 538, 539
NBA records
    Johnson, Earvin "Magic"
      242
    Jordan, Michael 256, 259,
      260
    Thomas, Isiah 538, 539
NCAA Basketball Tournament
    Barkley, Charles 45
    Bird, Larry 52
    Drexler, Clyde 110, 111
    Ewing, Patrick 135, 136
    Johnson, Earvin "Magic"
      52, 240
    Johnson, Larry 250
    Jordan, Michael 255
    Malone, Karl 355
    O'Neal, Shaquille 429
    Olajuwon, Hakeem 421,
      422
    Robinson, David 462
    Thomas, Isiah 536
Neon Deion (See Deion Sanders)
New England Patriots 372
New York Giants 124, 273, 401,
    450, 546
New York Islanders 185, 377
New York Knicks 259, 260
    Ewing, Patrick 137
New York Mets 99, 471
    Dykstra, Lenny 117
    Ryan, Nolan 468
New York Rangers
    Messier, Mark 378
New York Yankees 29
    Abbott, Jim 6
    Elway, John 122
    Sanders, Deion 502
    Winfield, Dave 565
Newhouser, Hal 82
NFC Championship game
    Aikman, Troy 20, 21
    Montana, Joe 398-401
    Rice, Jerry 450, 451
    Sanders, Barry 498
    Smith, Emmitt 518, 520
    Young, Steve 585, 586
NFL Man of the Year
    Moon, Warren 410
NFL Offensive Player of the Year

Moon, Warren 408
NFL records
    Marino, Dan 371-373
    Montana, Joe 401
    Moon, Warren 409
    Rice, Jerry 448, 450, 451
    White, Reggie 559
NHL All-Star game (See All-Star
    game, NHL)
NHL records
    Gretzky, Wayne 185-189
    Lemieux, Mario 321
Nicholson, Jack 243
Nick Faldo Charity Fund 147
Nicklaus, Jack 142, 145
Nike 10, 49, 107, 228, 258, 261,
    439, 466, 473, 499, 506
Noll, Chuck 542
Norman, Greg 145
North American Soccer League
    362
North Carolina State University
    111, 422
Nunno, Steve 382, 384
NutraSweet World Professional
    Figure Skating Championships
      Boitano, Brian 75

O

Oakland Athletics 27, 100, 567
Oakley, Charles 137
Oates, Adam 216
Oklahoma State University 496
    Sander, Barry 496
    Thomas, Thurman 543
Olajuwon, Hakeem 45, 110,
    135, 255, **419-425**, 430, 466
Olympics (See Summer
    Olympics, Winter Olympics)
O'Neal, Shaquille 426-432
Orlando Magic
    O'Neal, Shaquille 430
Ott, Mel 195
Owens, Jesse 198, 326, 329

P

Pack-style speedskating 59
Palmeiro, Rafael 170

Palmer, Arnold 340
Palmer, Jim 100, 101, 173, 351
Pan-American Games
    Abbott, Jim 3
    Jordan, Michael 255
    Robinson, David 464
Par 142
Parish, Robert 53, 423
Paterno, Joe 270
Payton, Walter 494, 521
Pele 361, 362
Pendleton, Terry 80
Penn State University 270
Perez, Tony 192
Perry, Gaylord 351
Petrenko, Viktor 38
PGA Championship
Philadelphia Eagles
    White, Reggie 558
Philadelphia Flyers 186
    Lindros, Eric 336
Philadelphia Phillies 28, 118,
  351, 456, 471, 505
    Sandberg, Ryne 488
    Faldo, Nick 144, 146
Philadelphia 76ers 53, 241
    Barkley, Charles 45
Phoenix Suns 113, 260, 438
    Barkley, Charles 48
Pinella, Lou 195
Pippen, Scottie 257, 260, **433-439**
Pitino, Rick 138
Pittsburgh Penguins
    Lemieux, Mario 318
Pittsburgh Pirates 504
    Bonds, Barry 79
Pittsburgh Steelers 371
Player of the Year, LPGA
    Lopez, Nancy 340-343
Portland Trail Blazers 244, 259,
  358, 438, 540
    Drexler, Clyde 111
Powell, Mike 329
Preakness Stakes
    Shoemaker, Willie 279
President's Council on Physical
  Fitness and Sports
    Griffith Joyner, Florence
    202
Price, Nick 146

Prime Time (See Deion Sanders)
Pro Bowl
    Aikman, Troy 20
    Elway, John 126
Jackson, Bo 228
    Marino, Dan 370
    Rice, Jerry 448
    Sanders, Barry 498
    Sanders, Deion 503, 505,
     506
    Smith, Emmitt 517
    Thomas, Thurman 546
    White, Reggie 559
    Young, Steve 585
Professional Golfers' Association
  (See PGA)
Puckett, Kirby 440-445

Q

Quebec Nordiques 335

R

Reebok 91, 174, 431, 532
Reeves, Dan 123, 125
Retton, Mary Lou 384, 385
Rice, Jerry 400, 446-452
Riley, Pat 138, 241, 243
Ripken, Cal, Jr. 153,
  453-459
Ripken, Cal, Sr. 453, 456
Robinson, David 430, **460-466,**
  499
Robinson, Frank 195, 457, 532
Robinson, Jackie 32
Rocket Man 96
Rod Carew on Hitting 116
Rodriguez, Ivan 169
Rookie of the Year, Baseball
    Alomar, Sandy, Jr. 26
    Ripken, Cal, Jr. 455
Rookie of the Year, LPGA
    Lopez, Nancy 340
Rookie of the Year, NBA
    Bird, Larry 53
    Ewing, Patrick 137
    Johnson, Larry 251
    Jordan, Michael 256
    O'Neal, Shaquille 431

Robinson, David 464
Rookie of the Year, NFL
   Marino, Dan 370
   Sanders, Barry 498
   Smith, Emmitt 517
   White, Reggie 558
Rookie of the Year, NHL
   Lemieux, Mario 319
Rose, Pete 192
Round Mound of Rebound (See
  Barkley, Charles)
Rudolph, Wilma 202
Russell, Bill 55, 424, 426
Ruth, Babe 100, 152, 153, 531
Ryan, Buddy 559, 560
Ryan Express (See Ryan, Nolan)
Ryan, Nolan 2, 24, 97, 116, 345,
  467-473
Ryder Cup
   Faldo, Nick 142, 144

S

Sabatini, Gabriella 178-180
Safe Passage Foundation 35
Sampras, Pete 11, 90, 107, **474-
479**
Sampson, Ralph 111, 422, 423
San Antonio Spurs
   Robinson, David 463
San Diego Padres 490
   Alomar, Roberto 24
   Winfield, Dave 564
San Francisco 49ers 20, 21, 125,
  371, 518, 520
   Montana, Joe 397
   Rice, Jerry 448
   Young, Steve 583
San Francisco Giants 79, 348,
  350, 491
   Bonds, Barry 81
Sanchez Vicario, Arantxa 93,
179, **480-486,** 511
Sandberg, Ryne 348, **487-493**
Sanders, Barry 466, **494-499,**
545
Sanders, Deion 500-506
Santiago, Benito 25
Schmidt, Mike 82, 532
Seattle Mariners

Griffey, Ken, Jr. 193
Seattle Supersonics 48
Seaver, Tom 101
Seles, Monica 9, 179-181, 417,
  482, 484, 485, **507-513**
Shaq (See Shaquille O'Neal)
Shaq Attack 431
Shaq Diesel 431
Shoemaker, Willie 279
Shriver, Pam 414-416
Shula, Don 370, 371
Siefert, George 400, 449
Sierra, Ruben 170
Silver medals, Summer Olympics
   Evans, Janet 131
   Graf, Steffi 180
   Griffith Joyner, Florence
     199, 201
   Joyner-Kersee, Jackie 265
   Miller, Shannon 384
   Sanchez Vicario, Arantxa
     485
Silver medals, Winter Olympics
   Lindros, Eric 336
   Moe, Tommy 394
   Tomba, Alberto 554
Smith, Bruce 560
Smith, Dean 254, 255
Smith, Emmitt 20, 498, **514-
521,** 545, 547
Smoltz, John 350
Spinks, Leon 165
Spitz, Mark 60
Sportsman of the Year
   Ashe, Arthur 36
Springsteen, Bruce 486
St. James, Lyn 522-526
St. Louis Blues
   Hull, Brett 214
St. Louis Cardinals 443
Stanford University 130
   Elway, John 122
Stanley Cup finals
   Gretzky, Wayne 185-188
   Hull, Brett 214
   Lemieux, Mario 321, 322
   Messier, Mark 377, 378
Staubach, Roger 401, 463, 582
Steinbrenner, George 565
Stevens, Kevin 321

Stewart, Jackie 155
Stewart, Payne 146
Stich, Michael 106
Stockton, John 356
Strange, Curtis 144
Streisand, Barbara 13
Sullivan Award
  Abbott, Jim 4
  Griffith Joyner, Florence
    201
  Joyner-Kersee, Jackie
    266
  Lewis, Carl 327
Summer Olympics
  Abbott, Jim 4
  Ali, Muhammad 165
  Barkley, Charles 48
  Bird, Larry 56
  Bowe, Riddick 85
  Drexler, Clyde 113
  Evans, Janet 129, 131
  Ewing, Patrick 136, 139
  Foreman, George 163
  Graf, Steffi 176, 178, 180,
    482
  Griffith Joyner, Florence
    199, 201
  Holyfield, Evander 207
  Johnson, Earvin "Magic"
    245
  Jordan, Michael 255, 259
  Joyner-Kersee, Jackie 265,
    266, 267
  Lewis, Carl 328-330
  Malone, Karl 358
  Miller, Shannon 383
  Pippen, Scottie 438
  Robinson, David 464, 465
  Rudolph, Wilma 202
  Sanchez Vicario, Arantxa
    485
  Spitz, Mark 60
Super Bowl
  Aikman, Troy 20, 21
  Elway, John 124, 125
  Kelly, Jim 273, 274
  Marino, Dan 371
  Montana, Joe 125, 398-401
  Rice, Jerry 449
  Smith, Emmitt 519, 520

Staubach, Roger 463
  Thomas, Thurman 546,
    547
  Young, Steve 584
Swift, Bill 351
Switzer, Barry 16

T

Tampa Bay Buccaneers
  Young, Steve 583
Tarkenton, Fran 371
Tennis records
  King, Billie Jean 417
  Navratilova, Martina 416-
    418
Tennis surfaces 107
Texas Rangers
  Gonzalez, Juan 170
  Ryan, Nolan 472
Thomas, Debbie 571, 572
Thomas, Frank 527-533
Thomas, Isiah 243, 244, **534-
  541**
Thomas, Mary 536
Thomas, Thurman 496, **542-
  548**
Thompson, John 135, 136, 464
Thurman Thomas Foundation
  548
Tomba, Alberto 549-555
Toronto Blue Jays 120, 230, 444,
  505, 532
  Alomar, Roberto 27
  Fielder, Cecil 149
  Winfield, Dave 566
Tour de France 221
  Induráin, Miguel 219-221
Trevino, Lee 144
Trottier, Bryan 188, 377
Tyson, Mike 167, 208, 209

U

U.S. Figure Skating Champi-
  onships
  Boitano, Brian 73, 74, 76
  Kerrigan, Nancy 41
  Yamaguchi, Kristi 578,
    579

U.S. Gymnastic Championships
  Miller, Shannon 383
U.S. Junior Davis Cup Team
  Ashe, Arthur 33
U.S. Naval Academy
  Robinson, David 461
U.S. Open (Golf)
  Faldo, Nick 144, 145
U.S. Open (Tennis)
  Agassi, Andre 11
  Ashe, Arthur 34
  Chang, Michael 90, 94
  Courier, Jim 106
  Graf, Steffi 176-179, 181
  Navratilova, Martina 414-
    416
  Sampras, Pete 476, 478,
    479
  Sanchez Vicario, Arantxa
    485, 486
  Seles, Monica 510, 511
U.S. Women's Open
  Lopez, Nancy 339
UCLA (See University of Cali-
  fornia, Los Angeles)
Unitas, Johnny 268, 367
United States Football League
  271, 557, 582, 585
University of California, Los
  Angeles 33, 198, 264
  Aikman, Troy 18
University of Florida 516
  Smith, Emmitt 516
University of Houston 135, 327
  Drexler, Clyde 110
  Olajuwon, Hakeem 421
University of Kentucky 135, 138
University of Miami 583
  Kelly, Jim 270
University of Michigan
  Abbott, Jim 3
University of Minnesota
  Winfield, Dave 563
University of Minnesota-Duluth
  Hull, Brett 214
University of Nevada-Las Vegas
  Fielder, Cecil 149
  Johnson, Larry 249
University of North Carolina
  110, 135, 421, 536

Jordan, Michael 254
University of Notre Dame
  Montana, Joe 396
University of Oklahoma
  Aikman, Troy 15
University of Pennsylvania 240
University of Pittsburgh
  Marino, Dan 368
University of Tennessee
  White, Reggie 557
University of Texas 98, 131
  Clemens, Roger 98
University of Tulsa 339
University of Virginia 422
University of Washington
  Moon, Warren 405
Unser, Al, Jr. 157
Unser, Al, Sr. 157
Utah Jazz
  Malone, Karl 356

V

Van Buren, Steve 520
Vare Trophy
  Lopez, Nancy 340-342
Vilas, Guillermo 479
Villanova Wildcats 136

W

Wake Forest University
  Bogues, Tyrone "Muggsy"
    67
Walker, Herschel 19, 122, 585
Walsh, Bill 397, 399, 400, 448,
  449, 583
Walton, Bill 423, 430
Warfield, Paul 450
Washington Bullets
  Bogues, Tyrone "Muggsy"
    68
Washington Redskins 125, 273,
  398, 498, 546
Webb, Spud 71
West, Jerry 259
Western Conference finals
  Barkley, Charles 48
  Drexler, Clyde 113

Johnson, Earvin "Magic"
242, 244
Malone, Karl 356, 358
Olajuwon, Hakeem 423
White, Reggie 556-561, 585
Wilander, Matts 479
Wilkens, Dominique 259
Williams, Ted 195, 531
Wills, Maury 472
Wilma Rudolph Foundation 202
Wilson, Hack 152
Wimbledon
Agassi, Andre 12, 13
Ashe, Arthur 34
Chang, Michael 90
Courier, Jim 107
Graf, Steffi 177-180
Navratilova, Martina 413-417
Sampras, Pete 477
Seles, Monica 510, 511
Winfield, Dave 27, **562-568**
Winfield Foundation 565, 568
Winfield: A Player's Life 566
Winter Olympics 572
Baiul, Oksana 41
Blair, Bonnie 60-63
Boitano, Brian 74, 76
Bonaly, Surya 41
Button, Dick 74
Heiden, Eric 60
Jansen, Dan 232, 234, 235
Johnson, Bill 393
Kerrigan, Nancy 41
Lindros, Eric 336
Moe, Tommy 391, 392
Tomba, Alberto 551, 553, 554
Witt, Katarina 552, 571, 572, 574, 575
Yamaguchi, Kristi 579
Witt, Katarina 75, **569-574**
Women's Sports Foundation 417, 525
World Basketball Championships
Bogues, Tyrone "Muggsy" 68
World Cup (skiing)
Moe, Tommy 391
World Cup (soccer) 362, 364

Maradona, Diego 361, 362
World Figure Skating Championships
Baiul, Oksana 39
Boitano, Brian 73, 75
Witt, Katarina 571, 572
Yamaguchi, Kristi 579
World Gymnastics Championships
Miller, Shannon 382, 385
World Hockey Association 184, 216, 376
World records, speed skating
Blair, Bonnie 61
Jansen, Dan 234, 235, 236
Rothenberger, Christina 61
World records, swimming
Evans, Janet 129
World records, track and field
Griffith Joyner, Florence 200, 201
Joyner-Kersee, Jackie 266
Lewis, Carl 329
World Series
Alomar, Roberto 28
Clemens, Roger 99
Dykstra, Lenny 117, 120
Puckett, Kirby 443, 444
Ripken, Cal, Jr. 456
Ryan, Nolan 468
Sanders, Deion 505
Winfield, Dave 565, 567
World Track and Field Championships
Griffith Joyner, Florence 200
Joyner-Kersee, Jackie 265
World University Games
Bird, Larry 52
Worthy, James 135

Y

Yamaguchi, Kristi 575-580
Yastremski, Carl 567
Young, Brigham 581
Young, Steve 399, 401, 402, 450, 451, **581-586**
Yount, Robin 195

Z

Zmeskal, Kim 383, 384
Zmievskaya, Galina 38